Tonga

Other Places Travel Guides
Tonga

Kate Asleson
Steve Hunsicker, Jason Schneider, Shawn Quast

Published by
OTHER PLACES PUBLISHING

First edition
Published July 2011

Tonga
Other Places Travel Guide
Written by: Kate Aselson, Steve Hunsicker, Jason Schneider, Shawn Quast
Edited by: Megan McCrea
Cover designed by: Carla Zetina-Yglesias
Published by:
Other Places Publishing
www.otherplacespublishing.com

Cover photograph courtesy of Kate Aselson
Back cover photographs: Whales courtesy of Brian Heagney, and
boy courtesy of Steve Hunsicker
All interior photographs courtesy of Kate Asleson, Steve Hunsicker, and Shawn Quast

All text, illustrations and artwork copyright
© 2011 Other Places Publishing

ISBN 978-0-9822619-4-1

The Authors

Kate Asleson *(Lead Writer, Ha'apai)*

Kate grew up in Minnesota. From a young age, she developed a love of travel thanks to long road trips with her family. She went on to study abroad in Australia, backpack across Europe, study tropical biology in Central America, explore the *hutongs* of Beijing, and travel New Zealand in a packed camper van. From 2008 to 2010, Kate served as a Peace Corps Volunteer on a six mile-long island in the remote island group of Ha'apai in Tonga. She worked with local government offices, a computer lab, the youth congress, and the Tourism Bureau. During this time, Kate immersed herself in Tongan culture, learned to cook from scratch, and made lifelong friends. Kate now works in marketing, but she still takes every chance she gets to travel.

Steve Hunsicker *(Contributing Writer, Vava'u)*

Steve is currently the South Florida Recruiter for Peace Corps.   He served as a Business Development Peace Corps Volunteer in Tonga from 2007 to 2009. As a Peace Corps Volunteer in Tonga, Steve helped the islanders start and expand businesses, he created websites for local businesses, he tutored students on business topics at the University of the South Pacific, and he produced several videos, including one video for the Peace Corps itself. That video helped to explain Tonga to incoming volunteers.

Steve is the author of *Steve's Adventure with the Peace Corps*, a book detailing his experiences as a volunteer in Tonga. The book, a chronological account of his adventures, begins from the day he first decided to apply to Peace Corps until the day he finished his service. It is available in both printed and electronic versions from Amazon.com and other online book retailers. Steve currently lives in West Palm Beach, where he enjoys volunteering with the United Way, along with speaking with people who share an interest in Peace Corps service.

Jason Schneider *(Contributing Writer, 'Eua)*

Having traveled extensively for both work and school, Jason finally decided, after a number of years staying put in a small town in the Midwest, that it was time to go for a while. He ended up living in 'Eua from 2007 to 2009, serving as a Peace Corps Volunteer. While there, Jason split his time between assisting the tourism industry to build their infrastructure, organizing youth development programs, and occasionally teaching in the neighboring kindergarten. Not to mention exploring the area enough to help write this guidebook.

Jason currently lives in Marquette, Michigan, where he works as a city commissioner and manages an online retail business.

Shawn Quast (*Contributing Writer, Tongatapu*)

Shawn was born and raised in the Midwest, spending most of his time around the Great Lakes, in Minnesota, Wisconsin, and Chicago. Sick of wearing a suit to work every day and eager to satisfy a deep-seated hunger for travel, adventure, and altruism, Shawn joined the Peace Corps. He was posted in the remote South Pacific island nation of Tonga. It was there that he traded his suit and leather shoes for a skirt and flip-flops.

While in Tonga, Shawn spent two months living with a local family in the village of Leimatua in Vava'u, learning the Tongan language and culture, before moving to Nuku'alofa to spend the next two years working as a Business Development Volunteer. While he spent the majority of his time working with local fishermen to develop their business skills, he also assisted with a variety of other activities, from helping a local resort with marketing to teaching tennis at a nearby high school. After finishing Peace Corps, he spent a year traveling Australia, and now lives just outside Yosemite National Park in California.

Megan McCrea *(Editor)*

As a longtime writer, traveler, and devotee of perfection, Megan McCrea was thrilled to receive the opportunity to edit this guidebook. As a girl, she grew up in the sha-

---

About this Book

The team of writers for this guidebook lived in each of the main island groups throughout Tonga, so they can give readers real insider information, as well as cultural insights which travelers simply won't find anywhere else. All of the writers have not only lived as locals, but also traveled as tourists within Tonga, and each writer has worked with the local tourism industry on their own island. Along with providing traditional guidebook sections – such as where to stay and what to see – this book also contains personal stories, as well as traditional Tongan customs and myths which have been passed down orally for generations. These anecdotes are scattered throughout the book.

This guide also delves deeper into Tonga's culture and way of life than any other guidebooks do, thus making readers not just tourists, but real cultural travelers. This book will give readers a glimpse into the indescribable beauty of Tonga, enticing them to go explore it firsthand themselves. The book is divided into the sections listed in the table of contents; however, it is not meant to be read linearly. The reader should feel free to skip around between sections based upon their individual travel itinerary.

Instead of using a ranking system or giving recommendations, we have chosen to include only places which we recommend in this guidebook, with the exception of those instances on remote islands, upon which there are only a couple of options in any given category. We hope that readers will enjoy the guide!

dow of the Rocky Mountains (Denver, Colorado); then got schooled in the shadow of old tobacco factories (Durham, North Carolina); and finally served as a Peace Corps Volunteer in the shadow of giant coconut palms (Kosrae, Micronesia & Ngeremlengui, Palau). So I guess you could say that she's a bit of a wanderer. Megan contributed to Other Places Publishing's guide to her country of service, Micronesia. Megan now lives in Berkeley, California, where she works as an editorial assistant for Poetry Flash.

Acknowledgments

Thank you to all of the local Tongans who shared their culture with us, and who made us feel like a true part of their families and communities each and every day. Thank you to all of our fellow Tonga Peace Corps volunteers for all of your advice and comments on the book, for your support while we served together, and for all of the incredible times we had together in Tonga. Thank you to the Tonga-based Peace Corps staff for your guidance and support. Finally, thank you to the publisher, for giving us the opportunity to put off-the-beaten path destinations, such as Tonga, on the map.

- The Writers

Thank you to my husband for following me the world over and for all of these incredible adventures, may they never end. Thank you to my wonderful family for your support, prayers, and many, many care packages. Thank you to our Tongan family, Sailosi and Ana: your generosity taught us what it really is to love your neighbor. Thank you, Site, Suve, Masi, Sefita, Pa'ane, and Mele. Suve, I would like to dedicate this writing to you; you packed in a lifetime of love, energy, and laughter into your eight short years here. You will always be remembered. Thank you Teisa, Lolo, Ilaise, Tevita, and all my other coworkers and students. Thank you to all our Peace Corps and expatriate friends in Ha'apai; you became our family. Thank you Phil Curtis, Alicia Green, Sarah Bond, Grant Kouri, Sabine Frank, and Brian Heagerny, for all of your assistance with researching, writing, editing, and taking photographs for this book. Last but not least, thank you to my fellow writers. I could not have done this without you.

- Kate Asleson

I would like to thank all the members of Tonga Peace Corps Group 71, 72, 73 and 74 with whom I served and for their input into the book. I would also like to thank the staff of the Tongan Development Bank especially Fuku Kupu, Leta Havea Kami,

Kolokesa Paunga, 'Oholei Tu'i and Folau Vaea. A special thank you as well to Al Coldrick at Dolphin Pacific Diving, Sheri Roberts at the Ark Gallery and Puke 'Esau with Peace Corps. A special thanks to Sarah LaRosa for her essay "This Provincial Life" and to Saskia Nauenberg for her last minute help with the final version of the book.

Most importantly, I would like to acknowledge the work of all Peace Corps Volunteers, past, present and future for their commitment to making the world a better place.

- *Steve Hunsicker*

Since I have been intensely editing, I extend sincere apologies to anyone whom I may have forgotten. First of all, thank you, Christopher Beale, for giving me the opportunity to edit this book: it has been amazing. All my deepest gratitude to Joyce Jenkins: thanks for the constant encouragement, and for your confidence in my abilities. Thank you, Chris C. and Ted O.: I couldn't have done this without you. Intense short-distance love to my many Berkeley families: the 3038sters; the *Flash*-ers; the Nomads; the Megan-McCrea-Bay-area-homeslices; and, finally, to the Eme-ryville brunch crowd—for supporting the arts through generous tipping. Finally, long-distance sunshine rays: to my loving friends and family in Colorado, North Carolina, NYC, Paris, et all (over); to mwet nukewa ne Kosrae ac Palau ac Peace Corps, for my own amazing Peace Corps experience; and to all of my English teachers past, for drilling me on all of those grammar rules for which I once thought that I would never have any use. Haha. *Malo aupito*, everyone.

- *Megan McCrea*

Quick Reference

Official name: Kingdom of Tonga

Capital: Nuku'alofa

Regions: Tongatapu, Ha'apai, and Vava'u

Population: 122,580

Neighboring countries: Samoa, Fiji

Government: Monarchy (changed to democracy in fall 2010)

Language: Tongan, English (English is the second official language)

Religion: Christianity

GDP (2009 estimate): $551.7 million

GDP per capita (2009 estimate): $4,600

Unemployment rate: 36%

Life expectancy at birth: 71.03 years

Median age of Tongans: 21 years

Infant mortality rate: 11.28 (deaths per 1,000 live births)

Adult literacy rate: 98.9% (includes Tongan and/or English)

Electricity: 240V (the same type used in Australia and New Zealand)

Measurement: Metric

Calling code: +676

Internet: Tongan websites are .to

Time: GMT + 13

*Tonga does not operate on Daylight Savings Time.

Driving: Left-hand side of the road

Typical business hours: 8:30 am – 12:30 pm, 1:30 pm – 4 pm

All prices are listed in the local Tongan *pa'anga* currency TOP, unless otherwise noted. Rates listed in the book are current at time of publication, but are subject to change.

Exchange rate at time of publication

1 TOP	= 0.56 USD
	= 0.39 Euro
	= 0.53 AUD
	= 0.69 NZD

Most businesses accept only local currency, and there may be an extra charge of approximately 5% for using a credit card at those businesses which do accept cards.

National Holidays (2011 dates):

New Year's Day, January 1

Good Friday, April 22

Anzac Day, Easter Monday, April 25

Crown Prince's birthday, May 4

Emancipation Day, June 4

Official Birthday of the King of Tonga, August 1

Constitution Day, November 4

Tupou I Day (The First King's Day), December 4

Christmas Day, December 25

Boxing Day, December 26

Contents

Getting Started 13

Introduction, History, Recent Events, Government & Politics, Economy, Culture, Food, Drinks, Dance, Sports, Music, Handicrafts, Holidays, Festivals & Events, Natural Environment

Basics 62

Getting There, Visa Information, Getting Around, Money & Costs, Communications, Tourist Information, Accommodations, Local Business Hours, Water, Eating, Cultural Considerations, Activities, Health & Safety, Giving Back

Tongatapu 93

Introduction, Nuku'alofa, Western Side, Eastern & Southern Side, Interior & Northern Side, Nearby Islands

'Eua 122

Introduction, Sights & Activities, Hikes, Shopping, Eating, Nightlife, Accommodation

Ha'apai 139

Introduction, Lifuka & Foa Islands, Lifuka Sights, Foa Sights, Shopping, Eating, Nightlife, Accommodation, Uoleva, Outer Islands

Vava'u 182

Introduction, Activities, Shopping, Eating, Nightlife & Entertainment, Accommodation

Niua Islands 209

Introduction, Niuafo'ou, Niuatoputapu

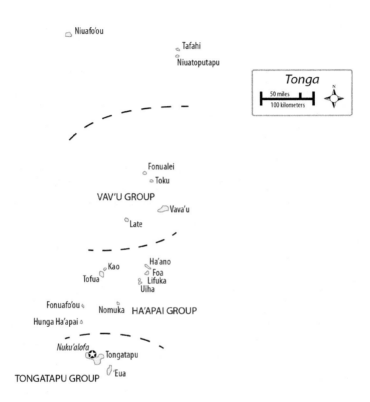

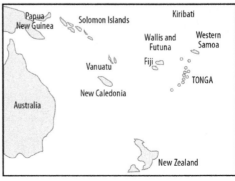

Getting Started

Introduction

Time begins and then stands still in the Kingdom of Tonga, a South Pacific island archipelago of one hundred seventy-six coral and volcanic islands scattered over a 270,000 square-mile stretch of ocean. Only fifty-two of these islands are inhabited. Tonga lies just west of the International Dateline, which curves around the island nation, making it the first country on earth to greet each new day. As the only country in the South Pacific which has never been colonized, Tonga is a proud nation with a long-standing culture.

Commonly known as the "Friendly Islands," a nickname conferred upon the nation by the famous Captain Cook, Tongans seem to be always smiling, laughing, singing, and dancing. The islands are not only home to some of the friendliest people on earth, Tonga boasts gorgeous, deserted sandy beaches and incredible reefs bursting with exotic marine life—providing world-class snorkeling and diving. Each island group in Tonga has unique attractions, from hiking in rainforests, to swimming with humpback whales, to enjoying eclectic international cuisine, to simply relaxing on pristine sandy beaches. And there is no need to worry about being overrun by tourists as Tonga has remained relatively off the radar to most.

Since Tonga is divided into several different island groups, travelers may have to choose which island group to visit depending on the length of their stay. Those spending one week or less in Tonga would do best to limit their travels to one island group. In two weeks, it is possible to spend time in several of the island groups. Those who choose to spend three weeks or longer in Tonga will be able to see even more of this fascinating country.

TONGATAPU

Most visitors will spend a night or two on the main island of Tongatapu on a layover between international flights. This offers plenty of time to explore the capital city, Nuku'alofa, as well as to explore the island's historical sights, resorts, beaches, rock formations, caves, and plantations that dot the island. A couple days is also enough time to enjoy the restaurants and shopping which the city offers, the best in all of Tonga.

Surfers should consider spending extra time in Tongatapu, as it boasts the world-renowned Ha'atafu Surfing Beach, as well as a number of resorts on the western end of the island. The rest of the islands of Tonga do not have good surfing spots.

'EUA

'Eua is paradise on earth for hikers and rock climbers. Though the island is located a stone's throw from the main island of Tongatapu—thirty minutes away by ferry, several minutes away by plane—'Eua often goes by the nickname of the "Forgotten Island." 'Eua acquired this name because, despite its proximity to Tongatapu, the island sees very few tourists. Those who do visit, however, describe 'Eua as an experience not to be missed. The island is covered in dense tropical rainforest, with paths winding through the trees, as well as rocky cliffs and caves, ripe for climbing and exploration. Traditional villages are strung, like pearls, along the main road. While there are a few guesthouses, 'Eua contains little in terms of tourism infrastructure.

HA'APAI

Ha'apai is for beach lovers. While the island group is composed of many small coral islands, the main islands of Lifuka, Foa, and Uoleva are by far the most popular to visit. These islands are surrounded by white sandy deserted beaches and fringed by gorgeous coral reefs. The waters surrounding Ha'apai teem with humpback whales in the winter, and colorful fish year-round. With several dive shops on Ha'apai, it is easy to get out and explore the reefs and aqua waters surrounding the islands. The main town, Pangai, is a sleepy hamlet: there's not much in the way of nightlife there. However, Pangai offers a wonderful opportunity to become immersed in village culture. Bicycles are also available for rent and provide a great way to explore the islands of Lifuka and Foa.

VAVA'U

Vava'u, the most scenic island group in all of Tonga, caters specifically to tourism. Vava'u's lush green hills, set neatly against turquoise-blue waters, mesmerize all those who set foot there. In addition, Vava'u offers one of the most protected harbors in the South Pacific, the Port of Refuge, which attracts many yachts. Vava'u is surrounded by many small islands, all of which can be easily accessed from the main island. What's more, the reefs and waters surrounding Vava'u offer excellent deep-sea fishing, snorkeling, diving, and whale-watching, and there are numerous dive operators and whale-watching companies from which to choose. While the main city, Neiafu, provides the cosmopolitan pleasures of restaurant dining and nightlife, it is also quite easy to escape the city and explore the rural villages which lie further out upon the island. There are only a couple of beaches on the main island, but many small surrounding islands abound, simply awaiting exploration.

NIUAS

The Niua Islands, Niuatoputapu and Niuafoʻou, are the most isolated, offering the most authentic cultural experiences. Niuatoputapu boasts views of Tafahi Volcano, and Niuafoʻou offers a beautiful crater lake. Both islands feature amazing secluded beaches. These islands are much more difficult to reach than the others and, thus, it requires much more time to visit them.

History

Tonga, which translates to mean "south," is one of the oldest settlements in the South Pacific. As the only country in this region which has never been colonized, Tonga has a rich and fascinating history. Since Tongan history was not written or recorded until the nineteenth century, most current knowledge of the country's early history is based upon stories which were passed down through generations as myths and legends through Tonga's traditional oral culture. Archeologists have also excavated numerous sights, contributing more insights into Tonga's early history, based upon the artifacts that they have found there.

THE LAPITA PEOPLE: TONGA'S ORIGINAL INHABITANTS

One thing that is known for certain is that the first known inhabitants of the Pacific Island region were the Lapita people. Anthropologists hypothesize that the Lapita originated in Southeast Asia and traveled eastward through Melanesia, before finally reaching Polynesia. In the scientific community, debate persists about when exactly the first villages in Tonga were actually settled. Based on carbon dating of ancient Lapita pottery shards from Tongatapu and Lifuka, it would seem that the earliest peoples arrived around either 3000 BC or 1300 BC.

> **Pieces of History**
> Some pieces of Lapita pottery are on permanent display at the Tonga National Museum, on the south side of Nuku'alofa.

Many believe that the Lapita people were the very first inhabitants of Polynesia. That is, given the fact that Polynesia was settled from west to east, it can be concluded that Tonga was one of the first Lapita settlements in Polynesia. Evidence supports this theory as Lapita pottery shards dating to 2900 BC were found in Nukuleka village in a 2007 excavation. This indicates that the site, just east of Nuku'alofa, Tongatapu, is in fact the very first settlement in all of Polynesia. These findings challenge neighboring Samoa's claim as the "Cradle of Polynesia."

With its large lagoon, Tongatapu could very well have served as the starting point for the eastern expansion of the Lapita people. Another important discovery in the Lapita pottery was the fact that the intricate designs on the pottery closely resembled designs later found in *tapa* cloth (pg 52) and tattoos in Tonga. This shows that the Lapita people who first came to Tonga could have adapted their culture and become the Polynesians who set out to inhabit the rest of the islands.

These early people were great sea navigators, sailing in certain directions intentionally, in order to discover and settle some of the more remote islands of the Pacific. Traveling through Polynesia in simple dugout canoes with sails, the ancient Tongans fought fiercely, conquering many of the neighboring island nations of the South Pacific, including Fiji, Samoa, and many others.

It's a Man-Eat-Man World Out There

Although cannibalism was a harsh reality of early Tongan history, it is infrequently discussed today. Furthermore, the exact motives behind the cannibalism lie shrouded in a veil of mystery. Some think that cannibalism in Tonga arose because of wars, and the warriors' desire to consume the spirits of their enemies. Others argue that cannibalism evolved simply due to a widespread lack of meat on the small islands. Either way, cannibalism has not existed in Tonga since the early European explorations, when several missionaries ended their island adventure in the pot. Some artifacts remain to attest to the country's cannibalistic past, including war clubs which the Tongans used to beat their opponents before devouring them.

ANCIENT TONGAN RELIGION

Before Westerners arrived in Tonga, the Tongans practiced their own ancient Polynesian religion. However, since the Tongans had no written language at the time and all of their ancient religious artifacts have since been destroyed, our contemporary knowledge of their ancient religion is limited. All the knowledge of their religion which remains today has been passed down either through Tongan stories and myths or through the written accounts of early European explorers.

In early times, the Tongans worshipped a number of gods. They believed that many of the gods lived in Pulotu, a spirit world located to the far northwest of Tonga. Some of these gods were thought to be eternal and original, while other secondary gods were actually the spirits of deceased chiefs. The chiefs and nobles of high-ranking classes were thought to have eternal spirits, in contrast to the commoners,

The Creation of Tonga and Other Business

According to the Tongan creation myth, the god Tangaloa formed the islands of Tonga. One day, long ago, Tangaloa realized that he had grown tired of seeing only sea, sky, and nothing else. Therefore, to combat this boredom, Tangaloa threw down some wood chips from the carving he was making. These wood chips formed the islands of 'Eua and 'Ata. Later on, when the god Maui was out fishing, his hook got caught on the bottom of the sea, so he fished the land up to the surface. This formed the rest of the Tongan islands, including the main island, Tongatapu.

Some people think that Tonga's earliest inhabitants made their way to the South Pacific from South America, while others contend that these early settlers came from southern Asia. Early European explorers to the region developed theories of a "sunken continent" or "Southern continent" to explain the existence of these small isolated populations in the Pacific. Whatever the explanation behind where Tongans came from, it was certainly a mystery which gave birth to many theories; new developments continue to this day.

who did not have a chance of eternal life. The Tongans also believed in Tangaloa, a group of sky gods, and Maui, a group of underworld gods.

The Tongans believed that their gods communicated with them through the movements of animals and living creatures. They built sacred houses or temples for the gods, and so they often represented the gods through animal items such as whale teeth, carved animals, and human figures. Different earthly situations called for intervention from different gods. For example, during an earthquake, the Tongans would run outside crying loudly and beating the ground with sticks. While, to an untrained outsider, this behavior might seem bizarre, to the Tongans, it was perfectly rational. They believed that Maui, the underworld god, held the world upon his shoulders, and so, if there was an earthquake, that meant that Maui had fallen asleep and needed to be woken up. Interestingly, this custom lasted even into the twentieth century, when people would still run outside banging pots and pans during earthquakes. Furthermore, different Tongan families and regions worshipped different gods, many of whom were not even known to other Tongans. They would call upon these gods in prayer to cure sicknesses and in a festival, *inasi*, which was thought to provide plentiful harvests.

WESTERN CONTACT

The first Western contact occurred in 1616, when Dutch explorers Willem Schoouten and Jacob Le Maire landed in the northernmost islands of Tonga, Niuatoputapu and Niuafo'ou. While there, Le Maire compiled a list of approximately thirty Tongan words, thus giving Tongan the distinction of being

> **The Lost World?**
> Tonga was neither accurately charted nor placed on maps until the late 1800s.

the earliest recorded South Seas language. No other Europeans voyaged to Tonga until 1643, when Abel Tasman "discovered" 'Eua and Tongatapu, which he named Middleburch and Amsterdam, respectively. (He would then continue his voyage, "discovering" Tasmania and New Zealand as well.) The native Tongans, astonished at the sight of these foreign white creatures, traveling in upon the large wooden ships with sails, coined the term *papalangi*. The word, later shortened to *palangi*, is still used today to mean "white foreign person." *Papalangi* literally means "from the sky," suggesting that these foreign people sailed down from the skies with their big white sails. The term is not meant to be derogatory; it simply evolved into part of everyday Tongan language. After these first two visits from Europeans, there was a pronounced gap in time before any explorers would return to Tonga, thus leaving the Tongans again untouched by the outside world.

Tonga continued to remain isolated for a number of reasons, one of which may have been the difficulty in navigating the nation, particularly the Ha'apai island group, with its numerous islands and treacherously shallow reef systems. Furthermore, Tonga offered neither a great deal of farmable land nor valuable goods for trading, so the incentives for early European explorers to visit were not as strong as they may have been in other parts of the world.

It was not until the late 1700s that the first Europeans began to arrive, inhabit, and actually integrate into Tongan life. Escaped convicts and castaways from ships bound for the Australian prisons came to Tonga first, followed by Christian missionaries.

In their writings, the European explorers noted that the Tongans worked with extreme precision, excelling in agriculture—having neat gardens and farms with fences—and building well-planned roads. The earliest explorers reported that the native Tongans were very much naked; however, according to later accounts, the Tongans wore small loincloths and *tapa* mats. These explorers noted one particularly curious feature: many of the Tongans were missing part of their little fingers. No one knew why. Some theorized that this trait was related to grieving or showing respect. Others thought that perhaps the Tongans had cut off the ends of their fingers as a sacrifice to the gods. During this time period, Tongans skillfully played the nose flute. While this activity is no longer practiced today, many cultural matters—from diet to handicrafts—have remained essentially unchanged from Tonga's early days to the present.

FAMOUS HAPPENINGS

Renowned explorer Captain James Cook made several voyages to Tonga between 1773 and 1777. After a visit to some of the outer islands of Ha'apai, he dubbed the

Missionaries

The first missionaries, Wesleyans who traveled to Tonga from England, started their work in 1826. Under their guidance, a vast number of islanders converted to Christianity. The missionaries' work spread quickly through the islands; today, 99% of Tongans consider themselves Christians, and over one-third of these people are affiliated with the Wesleyan Church. Most importantly, the missionaries' work reached all the way up through the social ranks to the first king, George Tupou I, who united Tonga as a nation and incorporated Christian beliefs and traditions into the nation's government.

Along with the religious work that the missionaries completed, their influence can also be felt through some profound cultural changes which they ushered in during their time there. For instance, the missionaries are partially responsible for transcribing the Tongan language into writing, since they needed to do so in order to translate the Bible into Tongan. The missionaries also introduced and enforced a stricter dress code; this included sleeves which covered shoulders, and skirts or pants which fell below the knees. This dress code specified that men were not allowed to go shirtless in public, and that everyone had to wear full clothing when swimming. Both of these rules still apply today; in fact, it is written into law that men can be arrested for going shirtless in public, despite the fact that this practice is becoming more common in urban areas.

Visitors can even hear the effects of the missionaries in Tongan church services today. Before each verse of a hymn is sung, someone at the front of the church reads the next verse aloud to the congregation as a whole. This occurs because, when the missionaries first arrived in Tonga, the Tongan language did not yet exist in writing, so the church members needed to recite each verse before singing it, so everyone could follow the hymn.

country "The Friendly Islands," due to the incredible warmth and hospitality which he had received there. At the time, however, he was unaware that all of the native Tongans, in the midst of a giant feast, were in fact arguing about how best to kill and eat him and his crew. Before the Tongans could settle this dispute, Captain Cook and his crew took leave for their ship, escaping the fate of the famed missionaries who wound up in the pot. Despite the obvious irony of this tale, Tonga retains the name "The Friendly Islands" to this day.

In addition to coining Tonga's nickname, Captain Cook introduced some new plants to the islands and brought dogs to Tonga. However, he did not discover Vava'u, because the higher-ranking chiefs and nobles actually threw him off of the scent there. One day, Captain Cook heard the Tongans discussing a trip to Vava'u to exchange some goods. Intrigued, he asked to join the Tongans on the trip. The Tongans, however, told Cook that there was no safe harbor or bay there, thus delaying the Europeans from discovering one of the safest harbors in the entire South Pacific.

The famous mutiny on *The Bounty* occurred in the waters of the Ha'apai island group, between Lifuka and the Volcanic Islands of Kao and Tofua, in 1789. Some of *The Bounty*'s crew wanted to return to Tahiti, where they had met many beautiful women. Captain William Bligh, however, disagreed, wanting to push forward to Australia. As a result of the disagreement, the crew mutinied and pushed Bligh, along with about a dozen of his followers, off in a small boat. Bligh and the other castaways made land on the volcanic island of Tofua, in the Ha'apai island group. Eventually, they ran into some of the local Tongans who were farming on the island. At first, the locals appeared friendly, but then things turned ugly when some of the Tongans began to gather on the shores with rocks. As Bligh and his frightened crew were pulling away from shore, the Tongans stoned one sailor to death. They then buried the man next to the grave of one of their fiercest warriors, because they were scared that the sailor's spirit would come back to haunt them, and they hoped that the warrior could help to protect them from his spirit.

In 1806, the British private warship *Port au Prince* made land in the Ha'apai island group. The Brits' metal guns and cannons, along with many of the other supplies onboard, were extremely tempting to the Tongans. Therefore, while the ship sat at anchor just off of Lifuka, the Tongans laid siege to the ship, massacring nearly the entire crew, seizing many of the weapons, and burning the ship to ashes. A sixteen year-old clerk boy, William Mariner, was one of the very few to survive the attack. Chief Finau 'Ulukalala, of Ha'apai, took a great liking to William, and he adopted him as a son. He took the boy to many different island groups, including Vava'u and Tongatapu, on his various war campaigns to gain control of all of Tonga. Mariner ended up spending four years living with the natives in Tonga before he gained his freedom to return to England, where he later published his journal. Mariner's book, *An Account of the Natives of the Tonga Islands*, is one of the few written accounts of pre-Westernized Tonga. Reading the book, what is striking is the amazing number of similarities between Tonga of 1806 and Tonga of today. For instance, the Tongan diet has remained essentially unchanged over the last two hundred years.

UNIFICATION OF TONGA

Throughout much of the country's early history, each island group within Tonga was governed by its own chief and noble class, whose titles were hereditary. In larger areas, such as Tongatapu, each region and village had its own chief, who had absolute power over the people. There were complicated hierarchies and systems in place with different-ranking chiefs, nobles, and even kings. This baffled the European explorers. Captain Cook was introduced to the highest ranking chief from an island, only to then be introduced to a supposedly higher-ranking chief, and so on, and so on, and so on.

Around the late eighteenth century, Taufa'hau, the king of the Ha'apai island group, began his war campaigns to consolidate power over the islands of Tonga in order to unify them. Taufa'hau, already the leader of all of the Ha'apai Islands, soon overtook Vava'u. It took his armies many years to gain control of Tongatapu, with its many villages and chiefs; once this was done, however, Taufa'hau became the first king of a unified Tonga. At that time, he took the name George Tupou (the current king, Tupou V, descends from the same royal family). Tupou had a close advisor named Shirley Baker, a British man who had settled in Tonga in order to serve as a Wesleyan missionary. Baker had gained the king's trust in Ha'apai before the unification of Tonga, and he became a very important influence in the unification of Tonga and the formation of its political and legal system. While some claim that Baker was a puppeteer, ruling the country from behind King Tupou, there were in fact many ideas which King Tupou could only have enacted into law with Baker's help. That is, Baker brought valuable expertise and experience with Western constitutional governments. Their partnership, which lasted for over thirty years, laid the foundation for Tonga as a sovereign nation.

Together, Tupou and Baker wrote the first constitution, a document which was put into effect in 1875. Its passage marked an important first step on the path to keeping Tonga sovereign, unlike its neighbors, Fiji and Samoa. In these nations, European powers were already stepping in to colonize. With their new constitution, the Tongans were able to negotiate treaties of friendship with countries such as Germany and England, which thus granted Tonga recognition as an independent nation. In return, Tonga gave Germany and England access to its harbors and trading.

The constitution also outlined Tonga's government as a constitutional monarchy, with a hereditary succession in which power was passed down to King Tupou's heirs. The legislative assembly was composed of twenty chiefly title-holders, along with twenty elected representatives of the common people. One key tenet of the constitution dealt with land: King Tupou decided that he did not want Tongan land to be overtaken by outsiders and declared that no foreigners could ever own land in Tonga.

Interestingly, Tupou's idea of "Tonga for the Tongans" had its genesis in Australia. While on a visit to Sydney, King Tupou had seen beggars for the first time. He could not understand why these men were forced to beg for food, why they couldn't grow it themselves. Upon asking his hosts, he had learned that the beggars were too poor to own land. After this experience, he decided that every male Tongan should be allotted a plot of land once he reached adulthood; that way, no Tongan would ever be reduced to the humiliation of begging.

King Tupou enacted many other innovative laws, including some which ended the traditional obligations of the lower common class to provide food and free labor to chiefs and nobles. Finally, both the first government schools and the tax system were set up under King Tupou's reign. When Tupou died of pneumonia in 1893, the country mourned for six months. Because he had created the Kingdom of Tonga, he earned the title of "Grand Old Man of the Pacific."

While King Tupou's advisor, Shirley Baker, played a vital role in writing the constitution and securing Tonga's place as an independent nation, some Europeans in the Pacific disapproved of his involvement in Tongan affairs. In addition to the constitution forbidding non-Tongans from owning land, the government was levying heavy taxes upon foreigners. Due to the tensions created by these laws, Baker was eventually forced to leave Tonga and flee to New Zealand. After his retirement, Baker came back to Ha'apai, where he lies buried just north of Pangai, in the cemetery which bears his name.

ROYALTY: PAST & PRESENT

Tonga's royal family, also known as the House of Tupou, descends from King Tupou I, the first king of the united Tonga. However, prior to the unification of Tonga, there were three ancient dynasties: the *Tu'i Tonga*, the *Tu'i Ha'atakalaua*, and the *Tu'i Kanokupolu*. According to legend, the very first king of ancient Tonga, Aho'eitu, owed his parentage to a pretty girl on Tongatapu named 'Ilaheva, and a Tongan sun god named Tangaloa. While the current royal family is technically descended from the *Tu'i Kanokupolu* dynasty, due to intermarriage within the royal family, all three dynasties are now effectively intertwined.

Art Imitates Life

Interestingly enough, contemporary Tongan handicrafts tie back to these historical royal bloodlines. For instance, *tapa* mats often feature dyed patterns of a vine with leaves, symbolizing the intertwining and mingling of the royal bloodlines. Patterns also tend to feature sets of three matching objects, such as three dots. This symbolizes both the three ancient dynasties and the three main island groups of Tonga.

King Tupou I outlived the first two generations set to succeed him to the throne. Therefore, Prince George Taufa'ahau, Tupou's great-grandson, became Tupou II at the age of eighteen. Due to the unique and privileged place he enjoyed, both within his own family and within society at large, the boy was quite spoiled. He refused to marry the woman whom the high chiefs of Tonga suggested for him, choosing instead to marry an outsider. This decision created extreme tensions, almost igniting a civil war. Tupou II also regularly overspent government money. In fact, the government financial situation was so bleak that some ministers contemplated asking the

British to annex the country. However, Tupou II grew ill and died before this could happen, leaving his daughter to reign. While Tupou II was not a great king from a political viewpoint, he was nonetheless known as a gentle person and a good father. In addition, he did begin the movement to build *sima vai*, cement rainwater tanks, all over Tonga, in order to provide the Tongan people with clean drinking water.

When King Tupou II died in 1918, his daughter began her reign as Queen Salote, at the age of eighteen. During her forty-seven year reign, Queen Salote brought Tonga into the modern world. Unlike her father, Queen Salote chose to marry a high-ranking man from one of the other ancient dynasties; their children, therefore, shared the blood of all three ancient dynasties. One famous tale concerns Queen Salote's appearance at the coronation of Queen Elizabeth II in England. On the day of the coronation, it was pouring rain. However, instead of riding along the parade route in a covered carriage, as everyone else was, Queen Salote rode with her carriage top down, in order to show respect to the Queen. This was, simply, the Tongan way: a Tongan would never cover himself in the presence of a higher chief, no matter how cold or wet it was. In addition, by riding with the top down, Queen Salote was also sharing the discomforts of the crowd which had gathered to watch the coronation procession, who did not enjoy such ready protection from the elements.

In her concern for national unity and independence, Queen Salote resembled her great-great grandfather, King Tupou I. She was also a great poet, and she knew a great deal of local history, Tongan practices, and etiquette. Her door was always open to the common people, and her amazing generosity was well-known. Queen Salote used her power to advocate for education, health care, the arts, religion, and the welfare of women. During her near five decade reign, she shepherded the Kingdom of Tonga from a small, isolated island nation to an increasingly urbanized country, in close contact with the outside world. Tongans still refer to her as "Our Beloved Queen." She was a queen of the people.

King Taufa'hau, Tupou IV, followed Queen Salote to the throne, and he reigned until his death in 2006. Tupou IV enjoyed worldwide renown for his large stature; he stood six feet five inches tall and weighed 440 pounds. In his later years, his involvement in investment scandals, including one which involved the sale of Tongan passports, led to controversy, as well as public calls for increased government transparency and for a more democratic system of governance. In the 1980s, Tupou IV was involved with a Hong Kong businessman who sold Tongan passports and citizenship to foreigners, mainly to Asians who were wary of the impending handover of Hong Kong to China. Many countries refused to honor these mail-order passports, thus making it more difficult for Tongans themselves to travel abroad. By 1998, when the illegal sale of Tongan passports finally stopped, an estimated 7,000 had been sold. The 26 million US dollars netted from this scheme were deposited into a foreign bank. Later, the king's appointed American "court jester," with whom he had entrusted the money, invested it in a mysterious company in Nevada before it all simply disappeared.

The current King George Tupou V has reigned ever since his father's death, although he handed over his absolute power in November 2010, when Tonga's monarchy ended and its democracy began. Since King George Tupou V did not marry, his younger brother will be next in line for the crown. There is a rumor that he loved a woman and that she bore him a daughter, but they could not marry due to her lower societal status. Since his daughter was born out of wedlock, she cannot inherit the throne, and she is not recognized as royalty. The woman who had been chosen to marry King Tupou V due to her high social status later married his younger brother.

Royal Tortoise

Uniquely, Tonga may be the only country on earth which can lay claim to a royal tortoise. The tortoise, named *Tu'i Malila* (*tu'i* means king) came to the Tongan royal family as a gift from the famous Captain Cook in 1777. *Tu'i Malila* was passed down through the royal family as a pet, living on the royal palace grounds. The turtle lived until 1965, and it now sits preserved in a glass box at the Museum of the Tonga National Center in Tongatapu.

Recent Events

In the mid 1970s, an increasing number of Chinese immigrants began to settle in Tonga and by the 1990s, this number had risen drastically. By 2001, there were over one hundred-twenty Chinese-run businesses in Nuku'alofa, ranging from little roadside stands up to large convenience stores. Some of the Chinese immigrants came because they were leaving Hong Kong as it became part of China, while others came simply to work.

Before long, many Chinese businessmen owned and operated local stores in

Tupou V's Coronation: A Red Carpet Performance

The coronation of King George Tupou V was scheduled to occur in 2007, after a six-month mourning period for his father, King George Tupou IV. However, riots and protests exploded in the streets of Nuku'alofa in November 2006, causing King George Tupou V to postpone the coronation ceremony in order to focus on rebuilding and re-establishing order in Nuku'alofa. The coronation, which finally did occur on August 1, 2008, was an incredibly extravagant, lavish event, and celebrations continued throughout the entire month. In fact, the king had such a good time that he declared August 1, the coronation day, as his official birthday, even though it wasn't. Therefore, August 1 is now celebrated as an annual holiday for The King's Birthday.

For the coronation, over two hundred Tongan nobles and chiefs gathered at the royal palace in order to acknowledge King George Tupou V as rightful heir to the throne, in accordance with the traditional Tongan ritual of the royal *kava* ceremony. They presented the king with gifts from all over Tonga, including food, woven mats, *tapa*, and more than seventy cooked pigs. Once all of the gifts had been given, a formal European-style coronation ceremony was held at a church in Nuku'alofa. Once the ceremonty was completed, the king toured all of the island groups of Tonga. The local people rolled out the proverbial red carpet, decorating gateways across streets, preparing food, giving gifts, and performing songs and dances in honor of the king.

Tonga, some utilizing shrewd business skills, others benefitting from the cheap, plentiful goods and food that they could easily procure from China. Once they had effectively established themselves within the marketplace, the Chinese-owned stores began selling supplies to the local Tongan stores. The Chinese stores also tended to have longer business hours than the Tongan-owned shops, opening early and staying open late. Frustrated by this competitive business environment, as well as by the royal family's questionable dealings with Asia, some Tongans became resentful, abusive, and racist toward the Chinese.

In November 2006, riots broke out in the streets of Nuku'alofa. The legislative assembly was on the verge of closing for the year and, despite promises to move the government further toward democracy, little real change had occurred. Tongan rioters took to the streets in the afternoon, starting at Molisi Store, a store owned by the prime minister's family, then targeting government buildings, along with other enterprises owned by the prime minister and king, including ANZ Bank and Shoreline Group of Companies. First, the crowds overturned cars, they then moved to throwing rocks at buildings, breaking windows, and looting. A few hours later, fires had broken out in many buildings, and chaos reigned supreme. The rioters represented a broad cross-section of the Tongan population—male and female, young and old. Some people even believe that, amidst the general chaos, a number of the rioters seized the opportunity to target Chinese and Indian-run businesses. The government declared a state of emergency, and all entry to Nuku'alofa's business district was closed. By the end of the unrest, between sixty and eighty percent of the main business district had been burned to the ground. The Chinese embassy chartered a plane to evacuate Chinese nationals. Fortunately, with the help of the New Zealand and Australian police forces, order was restored within a few days.

Even today, the impact of this riot is still very much evident in the central district of Nuku'alofa. Flat cement slabs sit empty where buildings used to stand. Although some of the businesses have been rebuilt, recovery will take a long time. Just recently, beginning in 2009, there has been a great deal of renovation, with more large buildings being constructed. China bankrolled much of the construction work, and a great deal of this work was completed by Chinese workers.

Government & Politics

Ruled by the last and longest-standing Polynesian monarchy, Tonga was the only nation of the Pacific Islands never conquered or colonized. Some historians believe that this occurred because all three pillars of Polynesian culture—the king, the land, and the ethnic people of the land—have lasted throughout the nation's history.

Although traditionally in Tonga's constitutional monarchy, the king wielded near-absolute power, in recent years, the king has been guided by the prime minister. Specifically, the current king was guided by the Prime Minister Feleti Sevele, who ran the day-to-day government affairs. Traditionally, the prime minister is appointed by the king, and he serves for life. The last prime minister, Dr. Feleti Sevele, was the first person to hold this position who was neither a noble nor a member of the royalty. His predecessor was the current king's younger brother, who quit suddenly, following the unrest and riots of 2006, which called (violently) for less involvement in politics by the royal family.

Up until November 2010, the Legislative Assembly was comprised of sixteen members of cabinet, nine nobles (out of thirty-three noble titles in all of Tonga), and nine elected representatives of the people (out of a general population of 100,000). Recently, as the government has shifted further toward democracy, more seats have become available for commoners, in order to give them more of a voice in government. Most of these government offices and jobs are located in the capital, Nuku'alofa, and there are representatives from each island group.

Three days before his coronation ceremony in August 2008, Oxford-educated King Tupou V announced that he would relinquish most of his powers, and that he would rely upon the Prime Minister for guidance and the run of day-to-day affairs of state. He also announced that, in 2010, there would be a great deal of parliamentary reforms, along with elections, in order to move Tonga in the direction of becoming a more democratic society, as both the people of Tonga and the king himself wanted. In this new system, he explained that the common people would enjoy much more representation in the Legislative Assembly. Although the king would remain as a figurehead, he would not do much governance, much like the monarch in England.

Fielakepa, the spokesman for the Royal Palace, said, "the Sovereign of the only Polynesian kingdom is voluntarily surrendering his powers to meet the democratic aspirations of many of his people. The people favor a more representative, elected Parliament. The King agrees with them." Both New Zealand and Australia are helping Tonga make this governmental transition, holding seminars, giving advice, and helping with the election process.

November 25, 2010 was a historic day for Tongans. That day, the first governmental elections ever occurred. Eighty-nine percent of eligible voters turned out to cast their ballots. Voters dressed in their most formal Tongan attire, and the election

---

Culture of Corruption?

Corruption has long been an issue in Tonga. The royal family and the nobles have benefitted from many laws and businesses. For instance, the government sold Tongan passports to Iraqi, Afghani, and Chinese citizens in order to make money; as a result, it is now much more difficult for Tongans to travel overseas, because the validity of their passports often comes into question. Furthermore, the princess became a multi-millionaire on a satellite business scheme. There have also been reports of Parliament members tampering with documents that were being passed into law, and of the police raiding the Department of Finance computers. Another prime example of government corruption involves the sinking of the *Princess Ashika* ferry (see pg 145). Although an official report upon the incident was filed, the government has not released that document to the public, presumably because it is highly critical of the prime minister and other public servants. However, as Tonga moves into a new era of democracy, many hope for change and for decreased government corruption.

results were posted online and announced on local radio stations the very next day. While candidates did campaign using traditional Western methods, like posters and billboards, they focused the bulk of their energy on grassroots campaigns, meeting with local groups in the villages. There are now twenty-six new members of Parliament, nine of whom were elected by nobles from within the noble class (there are a total of thirty-three noble titles in Tonga), along with seventeen commoners elected by the people of Tonga (twelve of these seventeen representatives are affiliated with the new Democratic Party). These seventeen representatives serve to represent the general population of the islands, 100,000 people.

From within this new Parliament, the representatives elected a new prime minister, a noble representative, named Lord Tu'ivakano. He won by a narrow margin, garnering 14 of the 26 votes, after assembling support from the noble representatives and the remaining independent common representatives. He defeated the pro-democracy leader Akilisi Pohiva. The King has still held onto his veto power over new laws and decisions from Parliament, and he was informed of the results of Parliament's election of the new Prime Minister before that result was publicly announced. Shortly thereafter, he left the country unannounced, and so he was not present for the swearing-in of new cabinet members. With democracy beginning to take root, it is now an incredibly exciting time in Tongan history.

Economy

Tonga's economy is very complex, dependent on foreign aid, as well as remittances from Tongans living overseas. Tonga receives an average of TOP$200 million per year in remittances; thus, remittances far outweigh the local economy of agriculture and tourism. It has almost become a truism to say that Tonga's biggest export is people, and its biggest import is remittances. Tongans travel overseas to Western countries to work seasonal jobs and, at the end of the season, they return to Tonga and bring their earnings back with them. Those Tongans who do move overseas but who do not return home are expected to send most of their income back to their parents and relatives in Tonga. Many grants and awards are available to small countries in the South Pacific, like Tonga; the top donors are Australia, New Zealand, Japan, China, and the European Union.

After extracting remittances and foreign aid from the equation, Tonga's local economy depends most heavily upon agriculture. The other important industries are tourism, fishing, and construction. In the past, Tonga exported a lot of copra and bananas but these industries have declined over time. Other exports include squash, vanilla beans, fish, kava, and root crops. While most of the food that Tongans grow is for subsistence and not intended for export, some crops are shipped between island groups to sell in the markets. Some handicrafts, including *tapa* cloth made by women's groups, are also exported overseas.

Unemployment is a growing problem in Tonga, as there are not enough jobs to support the younger generation. Currently, the unemployment rate is estimated at about one-third of the population. Many of those jobs which do exist are located in the main cities at government offices, schools, and banks, with the Tongan government being the nation's single largest employer. Outside of the cities, agriculture remains the largest producer of jobs, with over one-third of the population relying upon agriculture for their income. On small outer islands, fishing plays a vital role in people's day-to-day subsistence. Usually, everyone in the village pitches in money for gas to operate the boats. Fishermen, in turn, share their catches with the entire population of the village. In these remote places, not everyone needs a job. Instead, most people fish or grow crops and then supplement this with the income that they receive from remittances from relatives living overseas.

Westernization

Looking to the future, Tonga faces the difficult challenge of balancing its traditional culture with trends toward globalization. For instance, there are clashes between Western business models and Tongan family obligations, Western styles of dress and traditional Tongan dress, Western materialism and Tongan communalism. While many older Tongans hold tenaciously to their traditional culture, some younger islanders find themselves increasingly drawn to Western ways. Tongans are very proud of their cultural heritage, so hopefully they will find an appropriate balance, one that allows them both to hold onto their cultural identity yet to still make the necessary adaptations to the inevitable changes wrought by and in the outside world.

In small villages, Tongans either rely on agriculture or open family-run stores in the front of their houses. This can be problematic, since Tongan culture, and the ensuing responsibilities to family, often strongly conflicts with Western ways of operating a business. For instance, if a family member owns a *falekoloa*, or store, it is expected that the family member will donate food and supplies from the store to church events, as well as family events, such as weddings and funerals. Due to these involuntary "donations," the family member may well lose money in the end. Such a culture can be a heavy burden to Tongans running businesses, since so much is ex-

To Aid or Not To Aid

Foreign aid is always a controversial subject. Although it comes from the best of intentions—to help the local economy and people—some people argue that developing countries can easily become too dependent on the foreign aid. Those who argue this viewpoint claim that, in countries which receive a great deal of foreign aid, the local people stop making an effort to improve their own situation. For instance, instead of holding local fundraisers or building their own new schools and gardens, the local people in these countries will just sit around expecting that money will be handed to them, or that foreigners will come in to complete projects for them. Opponents of foreign aid also argue that the money may be mismanaged or that it may go missing. In other cases foreign aid can create incredible outcomes that simply would not have been possible otherwise. Often, there simply needs to be a healthy balance between foreign aid and local involvement. Some governments and NGOs have recognized this common problem, and, thus, require a certain percentage of the total cost of any given project to be raised locally.

pected of them, but other job opportunities are quite limited. Even if young Tongans do obtain a better education than their parents did, there are few jobs available which utilize these newly-learned skills. In order to overcome these challenges, those Tongans who can afford it tend to move overseas to New Zealand, Australia, or the United States, where there are more job opportunities. These Tongans who move overseas are then expected to send money back home to their family in Tonga.

Culture

PEOPLE

The people of Tonga are proud Polynesians, and their culture is unique from those of other South Pacific nations. The Tongans stand out from other groups because of both their friendliness and their homogeneity. Due to the small population of each island cluster, everyone knows everyone on their island and they are, most likely, related as well. The population within the islands of Tonga hovers near one hundred thousand, while another one hundred thousand Tongans live overseas, mainly in Australia, New Zealand, and the United States. The majority of the population living in Tonga inhabits the main island, Tongatapu, specifically in the capital city, Nuku'alofa. Nuku'alofa offers the most job opportunities, with positions available in government offices, nonprofit organizations, and the hospitality industry. Nuku'alofa also houses the top schools in the nation and if given the opportunity, many Tongan children and young adults move there in order to further their education.

SOCIAL HIERARCHY AND FAMILY

Rank and hierarchy play a vital role in the Tongan way of life. Every occasion and interaction requires a show of respect, or *faka'apa'apa*. Rank determines the way in which Tongans interact, and even the speech they may use in order to address particular people. Rank also determines who goes first when giving speeches or taking communion at church. In meetings and community events, Tongans will always claim to agree with the highest-ranking person present and, often, they will not even voice their own opinions.

Beautifully Big

The Tongans are noted for their large size, in terms of both height and width. In fact, they hold the title for the largest people in the world. The former king, Tupou IV, who reigned until his death in 2006, set an impressive example, standing over six feet tall and weighing in at four hundred-forty pounds.

In the Tongan view, to be big is to be beautiful. Often, when they are describing someone, a Tongan will readily note that the person in question is "fat." This is not meant as an insult, and travelers should not be offended if a Tongan says that they are fat, or *sino lahi*, or *fati*. As a matter of fact, if they believe that someone is too skinny, the Tongans won't hesitate to force that person to eat. Tongans will often say, "*Kai ke mate*," which roughly translates to mean, "eat until you die."

Tongan society is structured along matriarchal lines, with women holding a higher social status than in most other Polynesian countries. The oldest sister in each family, or the *mehikitonga*, holds the highest status within her family. According to long-standing tradition, if the *mehikitonga* asks anything of her brothers or younger sisters, her siblings have no choice but to obey her orders. For instance, the

> At special events, the *mehikitonga* presides over the procession. For instance, at funerals, the *mehikitonga* divides up all the gifts, deciding which objects each family member will receive.

oldest sister might ask her siblings for sought-after items, such as a TV or a computer. More dramatically, when the oldest sister cannot bear a child, it is not uncommon for her to ask a younger sister for her baby. When this happens, the younger sister must give up the baby and allow the older sister raise it as her own.

Dangerous Liaisons?

Many taboos exist surrounding the relationship between brothers and sisters. For instance, brothers and sisters cannot go into each others' bedrooms. Sometimes, the boys will even stay in a separate sleeping house, apart from the main house, where the sisters stay. In addition, brothers and sisters cannot interact with each other in situations where profanity or sexual connotations exist. In practical terms, this means that brothers and sisters will not watch movies together, and they must be separated by gender when discussing sex education in school.

Despite women's relatively high status within Tongan society, men still outrank women. In accordance with this system, the husband's side of the family outranks the wife's side of the family. Therefore, for important events, such as funerals, weddings, and baptisms, the family will return to the husband's home village and church. In addition, upon asking a Tongan person where they are from, that Tongan will not respond by saying the name of the place where they currently live; they will instead answer by saying the name of the village from which their father hails. Due to the rules surrounding *mehikitonga*, the oldest sister from the husband's side of the family holds the highest status within the extended family.

Even today, women cannot own land in Tonga; only men can own land. If a husband dies, the man's widow can remain on the property until she marries again. Since King Tupou I's time, every boy has been allotted a plot of land when he came of age, in order that he could grow crops and provide for his family. In the past, each man would receive eight acres; today, that number has been reduced to four acres, since open space is rapidly diminishing in these small islands. Sometimes, the allotted land is located on a different island than the one on which the boy lives, or it is difficult to access. Girls are not allotted land.

Traditional Tongan gender roles dictate that the women remain at home, taking care of the children and doing household chores. On the other hand, the men provide for the family by doing more physical labor outside of the house, performing tasks like planting crops in the bush. Today, however, more women are working outside of the home, in professional settings such as banks, stores, schools, and government offices.

However, children are still raised according to more traditional gender roles, with the young girls assisting with cooking and cleaning, and young boys helping their fathers with planting and fishing. In fact, these gender role divisions are even reinforced by the schools. Therefore, many Tongan families hope to have both boys and girls, in order to ensure that they will have all of the help that they need with the different categories of domestic tasks. Tongan children will be often passed between families, to aunts or uncles. Due to this informal system of adoption within the extended family, neither orphanages nor adoption agencies exist in Tonga. Kids simply get passed around.

If a family has a lot of boys but no girls, that family may raise the youngest boy as a girl, encouraging him to help his mother with household chores. This boy is then called a *fakaleiti*, which translates to mean "like a lady." The family will dress the *fakaleiti* in girls' clothing and let his hair grow out long. This long-standing practice still continues to this day. Ironically, in Tonga, it is illegal to be gay.

In Tonga, there is a traditional, conservative pattern to dating. If a boy is interested in dating a girl, he will first go over to the girl's house to meet with her parents in order to obtain the father's permission for him to date the daughter. If the father says yes, the boy will then ask the girl to be the *tou'a* (pg 48) at a kava circle. Once the couple has arrived at the *kava* circle, the boy will sit to the girl's right-hand side, showing that he is her boyfriend. The couple will never go out in public together alone; they will always have friends with them. Couples also never hold hands or show affection in public. Although this is the traditional way of dating, today, more young couples have begun to sneak around and see each other on the sly. Tongans will often joke about how many *moa* they have.

Some More Moa?

Moa, meaning, literally, "chicken," is a Tongan slang word, commonly used to mean the person that someone is dating. Although it is most likely derived from the English slang word "chick," in this case, *moa* can be used to mean both "boyfriend" and "girlfriend."

Elderly Tongans hold a high social status and command a great deal of respect. For instance, when a younger Tongan addresses an older person, they are expected to use a more formal greeting. Traditionally, the oldest child in a family will take care of their elderly parents, making nursing homes nonexistent in Tonga. However, as more and more of the younger generation have begun to move overseas, and those who do remain are being influenced by Western culture, this trend is starting to change. Teachers and other professionals also enjoy a high level of respect. In Tonga, it is very rare for a student to disobey a teacher. If a student does disobey the teacher, they know that they will be immediately punished and, most likely, their parents will side with the teacher in any dispute.

Tongan society also possesses a class hierarchy. While the hierarchy may not be as strict as it once was, some class divisions certainly remain today. Traditionally, there were four classes: the commoners, the nobility, the talking chiefs, and the royalty. The common class comprised by far the largest section of the population, and it included everyone not born of royal or noble blood. The common class had to respect and obey the noble class. For example, if properties were permitted to be built upon royal or noble-owned land, the commoners living in those properties needed to pay respects by presenting gifts to that noble or royal family each year.

The talking chiefs, or *matapule*, were high-ranking people in each village who mediated interactions between the common people on one hand and the royalty and nobility on the other. The position of the talking chief was created in response to the fact that, traditionally, royalty and nobles spoke one version of the Tongan language, and the commoners spoke another. Thus, since the talking chiefs could speak both languages, they would act as translators between the parties, since it would be considered extremely rude to speak the common language to high-ranking Tongans.

Today, thirty-three noble families exist in Tonga, all of whom hold hereditary titles. The nobles still own most of the land in Tonga, and a certain number of seats in Parliament are reserved for them. The royalty descend from the Tupou lineage, dating back to the 1800s in the Ha'apai island group.

LANGUAGE

The Tongan "yes" is not the same as the Western "yes." That is, Tongans will say "yes" to nearly any question that anyone asks them regardless of what the answer may be. This is not meant to create confusion—Tongans simply do

> In Tongan, *io* (pronounced "yo") translates to yes.

not want to answer any question in a manner that will upset the person who asked the question. This practice does not mean that Tongans want to lie all the time or want to be deceitful; it is simply their culture.

Tongans will also tend to give the simplest, easiest answer to any given question, and they will not elaborate unless specifically asked to do so. So if a person asks "Is the market open?", "Is it safe to swim here?", "Can I wear this to town," they will get a *io*, yes, in response to each of these questions. With this in mind, it is best to format the question so that there is no simple yes/no answer (for example, instead of asking "Can I wear this to town," ask "What should I wear to town?")

Dr. Yes

The Tongan *io* has many different sounds. As a reply to a greeting in passing, Tongans will say a short staccato *io* ("yo"). However, if a Tongan uses the expression to agree in conversation, they will exaggerate and elongate the *io* to a more excited incarnation ("ee-yo, ee-yo"). In church, the men occasionally interject in agreement with the sermon, using a long, low-sounding *io* ("yooooo").

Because they live in such small communities, Tongans tend to avoid confrontation and arguments whenever possible. Instead of confronting someone directly with a complaint about them, a Tongan will tell mutual friends, coworkers, or neighbors about the problem which they have with that particular person. That way, the message will reach the person indirectly and no one will have to face an argument or an uncomfortable situation. Outward appearances are incredibly important in these small villages. If someone does something wrong, they will immediately apologize, and the person whom they wronged will immediately forgive them, even though perhaps neither party may really mean what they say. They will simply publicly reconcile in order to smooth out problems for appearances, so that they can both attend church or meetings together without awkward feelings or difficult situations.

In formal group situations, due to the traditional social hierarchy, Tongans often will not express their own opinions. Instead, everyone will wait for the highest-ranked person to state their ideas and then everyone will agree with that person (even if another answer is known to be better). This can become quite annoying to anyone who needs an honest, straightforward answer. One workaround is to ask the question in private, or ask them to write their opinion on a piece of paper.

Tongan village life affords precious little privacy. A common greeting is *Alu ki fe*? which literally translates to mean, "Where are you going?" Although, as a Westerner, it is not typical to hear this phrase used as an everyday greeting, in Tonga, this is completely normal. In fact, Tongans do not really want to know exactly where the other person is going; the phrase is simply a common greeting, the Tongan equivalent of "how are you?" Usually, it is acceptable to just answer with *i he*, or "over there", and point straight ahead. Some say that the Tongans obtain their information from the "coconut wireless," that is to say, by word of mouth. For instance, if there are tourists in a small village, everyone will know. If the ferry is late, the news will travel faster via the "coconut wireless" than by other, more official means.

BEHAVIORS

Certain behaviors and body language are specific to Tonga. Some may seem strange at first, so it's good to be prepared by knowing what these behaviors are and what they mean.

Perhaps the most important fact to note is that everything on Tonga—from store openings to meetings to taxi cabs—happens on "island time." Things do not occur on time there. While people may give an estimate of when a particular event will start or finish, these times are guesses at best. For Tongans, time is relative. It is typical to wait for long periods of time for events to occur; travelers should plan ahead for this, and they should not let it upset them.

Although Tongans carefully restrain their anger, they tend to wear other emotions on their sleeves. In fact, the islanders will even force certain emotions, when deemed necessary. Therefore, it is not unusual to see Tongans, of both genders, cry openly in public. This happens often at church services, feasts, funerals, weddings, and other social events. When Tongans give speeches they often cry, sometimes genuinely, sometimes not.

Tongans also laugh quite a lot. They laugh when they are happy, of course, but they also laugh when they are sad, angry, or even confused. The Tongans love making jokes, and their laughter is absolutely infectious.

Despite the fact that they restrain their anger toward other adults, Tongans will not hold back their emotions or actions when children are misbehaving. Parents will hit their children to punish bad behavior. Furthermore, adults and teachers will hit other people's children. Depending on the perceived severity of the offense committed, the child may be hit multiple times. While this will rarely occur in the presence of a foreigner or guest, it can be quite disturbing for a first-time visitor.

Tongan ideas about community and sharing also differ greatly from Western

Are You Afraid of the Light?

Interestingly, Tongans will do anything in order to avoid direct sunlight. For instance, they usually work in the bush around dawn and dusk, resting in the shade during the middle of the day. If Tongans have a picnic, or *kaitunu*, at the beach, they always spread the mats and food in the shade. They're also much more likely to swim in the rain or in the evenings than on a bright, sunny day. While most Tongans possess umbrellas, they are far more likely to use them on sunny days than on rainy ones.

An outsider will be most struck by the hats that the Tongans wear in order to escape the hot rays overhead. Tongans will use anything and everything which could possibly shade a head to do so. For example, it wouldn't be out of the ordinary to see a six foot-five, three hundred pound rugby player walking down the street sporting a 1940s-style, rose-rimmed, pink women's church hat. Nor would it be unusual to see a teenager with a t-shirt wrapped over his head, turban-style. You might see a middle-aged woman wearing a rectangular piece of cardboard as a brim around her head, with nothing in the middle except a hole just large enough for her scalp to push through the cardboard. Similarly, Tongans often alter cowboy-style hats by ripping off the tops in order to use the brims to shade themselves. Even those who have neither cardboard nor cowboy hats at their disposal will hold banana leaves, paper, or books over their heads in order to escape the glaring sun.

One day, I came across two Tongan men who were building a small *fale*, or building, at the north end of Foa Island in Ha'apai. At first, they enjoyed perfect work weather, chopping beams for the building under the protection of a cloudy, overcast sky. As the clouds started to disappear above them, the men looked east, into the wind. When they did so, they saw nothing but clear sky approaching. Afraid, they disappeared into the bush. Twenty minutes later, the men returned, wearing objects which looked suspiciously like inverted birds' nests on their heads—each man had woven a green, succulent-looking vine into a kind of helmet which would fit over his head and reach down to ear level.

As it turned out, their strange-looking headgear was the perfect answer to the change in weather. They had woven the vines tightly enough to shade their scalps, yet not so tight that they did not allow air into their heads. What's more, due to the large amount of water evaporating off of the hats, the hats cooled the men's heads remarkably well. The hats were a sort of Tongan swamp bag, and they emanated a pleasant, freshly-cut grass smell.

- Phil Curtis

ideas. Objects, food, and other items are viewed not as individual property, but as community property. For instance, Tongans will never eat food in front of others without offering the other people some of their food. (Tongans even have a word, *kai po*, for eating food in secret in order to avoid sharing food.) Another way in which the communal culture manifests itself is through borrowing or, as some might call it, stealing. That is, if a Tongan has a nice machete, and their neighbor asks to borrow it, the person will offer the machete to the neighbor, knowing very well that they may never see their machete ever again. The machete will simply continue getting "borrowed" around the community. If a Tongan asks to borrow an iPod or another valuable item, it's best just to say no. It's best to avoid the issue by simply keeping valuable objects hidden from public view. That way, no one will ask to "share" them.

When playing a card game, or any other type of game, Tongans often find it humorous to cheat. To Tongans, rules are made to be (playfully) broken. In fact, this is true in many contexts, outside of card games. Another interesting thing that Tongans will do when playing cards is that they slap each card down on the table very hard, as if it is the winning card. Everyone does this; it is simply a part of playing cards in Tonga.

> When playing games with Tongans, travelers should not let this cheating bother them; they should just play along.

BODY LANGUAGE

Body language varies widely among different cultures; each culture has its own nuances, and some movements are completely unique to a particular culture. Tonga is no different and it is vital to understand basic Tongan body language in order to better understand what Tongans are trying to communicate.

Without doubt, the eyebrow flick is central to Tongan communication. It occurs thousands of times daily, and travelers will observe it in every conversation that they have with a Tongan. If they don't understand what the flick means, they will be forced to ask the same question over and over, or else they will miss out on half of the conversation. Either situation can be very frustrating for both people involved. Quite simply, a quick lifting of the eyebrows means "yes." When Tongans do this, they are not flirting; they are merely saying "yes" nonverbally. For example, if someone asks, "Is the market open?", and the person whom they asked the question looks at them and raises their eyebrows, that means "yes." In fact, it is completely possible to have entire conversations in Tonga without saying a word. This is another reason to try to ask questions that demand a more detailed explanation: these complex questions will require more than an eyebrow flick in response.

> It is easy after spending a significant amount of time in Tonga to unintentionally pick up the eyebrow flick.

The Tongan greeting is also uniquely Tongan. When Tongans exchange a formal greeting, they will go in for a hug. However, instead of hugging each other, each Tongan will put their head next to the side of the other person's head and inhale deeply, essentially sniffing each other. This greeting, used on formal occasions, is more common with adults and the elderly. Those who feel comfortable with this greeting can do the same thing while greeting a Tongan. Those who do not feel comfortable with the Tongan greeting, on the other hand, can just hug the Tongan back while the Tongan sniffs them. Many Tongans will explain that they are not actually smelling anyone, this gesture is simply their custom. Either way, it is a good idea to keep this greeting in mind when attending a formal event or a church service, since it occurs frequently at these types of events.

Visitors in Tonga will most likely take photos of the island surroundings, as well as, perhaps, the local island people. Tongan kids, especially, love to have their picture taken. In particular, they love to have their picture taken with a digital camera, since a digital camera will allow them to see the photo instantly. When they have their picture taken, however, the kids tend to do something a little strange: they all throw up gang signs. They do this due to the influence of Western TV and movies that they have seen. This will happen everywhere, even in the smallest of villages. It is perfectly acceptable to ask the children to not make signs and they will understand that it might not be appropriate.

Finally, it is quite common to see physical contact between two Tongans of the same sex. Often, boys will hold each others' hands, and girls will play with each others' hair or hold hands. Even Tongan men will give each other massages at the *kava* circles. This same-sex contact is very common in Polynesian culture. Because it is considered inappropriate for men and women to have any physical contact in public, Tongans will have physical contact with their friends of the same sex in public. For a traveler, it is unlikely that a Tongan will initiate this kind of contact unless they are an acquaintance.

Do keep in mind that public displays of affection are not common in Tonga, so travelers are advised to respect the Tongan culture by refraining from kissing in public, or from showing a great deal of outward affection in any way. These types of behaviors make the Tongans extremely uncomfortable.

WORK ETHIC

Tonga differs greatly from Western cultures in terms of work ethic. In Tonga, jobs rarely define a person's identity, except perhaps for ministers, or for others who hold high-status positions. Tongans instead define themselves by their families and by their religious affiliations. This means that if there is a funeral, or an important church event, or a school concert, Tongans will be absent from work in order to attend these important events. It is expected that this will occur. And when Tongans take vacations from work, they will often miss a month or more at a time. When Tongans are at work, they will spend much of their time socializing, or sometimes even taking a quick nap.

DRESS

Traditionally, women in Tonga cover their shoulders and thighs, and they refrain from wearing anything too revealing. Women usually wear a skirt, along with either a t-shirt or a button-down shirt, depending upon the activity or occasion. For formal occasions, women wear either a long skirt with a button-down shirt, or a dress. For casual wear around the house, women typically wear a *lava lava*, a wrap-around piece of fabric which becomes a skirt. In the larger towns and urban areas, women are starting to wear jeans, pants, long capris pants, and tank tops. For water activities or swimming, however, Tongan women never wear swimsuits. Instead, they swim or wade in whatever clothes they happen to be wearing at the time that they go to the beach. In order to avoid staring and unwanted attention, it is best to dress as the local women do. While at resort areas, or out on the water with tourist operators, it is acceptable to wear swimsuits, shorts, and tank tops.

Given the hot, humid weather of Tonga, hairstyles are born of practicality. Typically, women will wear their hair up in a bun. Schoolgirls almost always wear their hair in braids. Tongan women keep their hair very long, and they rarely cut it. Traditionally, a Tongan woman only cuts her hair when a close relative dies, in order to show respect.

Men traditionally wear a button-down shirt with a *tupenu*, that is, a skirt which ties together at the hips. Men will wear this outfit both for work and around town. On less formal occasions, for instance, around the house, men may wear shorts, pants, t-shirts, or *lava lavas*. Due to the conservative social norms ushered in by the missionaries, it is actually illegal for men over the age of sixteen to be shirtless in public; this law, however, is not strictly enforced in larger towns. In tourist resort areas, the law is overlooked entirely. Those who happen to be in public around Tongans would be wise to avoid going shirtless in order to be culturally sensitive. For swimming, Tongan men do not wear Western swim trunks; like Tongan women, they swim in whatever clothes they have on at the time they go to the beach.

Children wear school uniforms, and each kind of school has its own color. Students at government primary schools wear red and white; students at government secondary schools wear maroon. Wesleyan school students wear blue, Church of Tonga school students wear orange, and Mormon school students wear green. This color system does not vary at all within the Kingdom. When they are at home, children wear the same kinds of casual clothes that men and women do. Often, small children below school-age go naked or half-naked.

> Travelers who decide to buy a *tupenu* skirt in order to blend in with the locals should know that many colors specifically represent certain schools. Buy a black or neutral-colored *tupenu* in order to avoid looking like school-boys.

Unfortunately, very few Polynesian nations have retained their original dress for wear in everyday life. As one of the few places where traditional garments are still worn today, Tonga proves the exception to the rule. By combining Western dress with their own traditional dress, the Tongans have succeeded in keeping their history and culture alive. The Tongans share a fierce pride in their heritage, and they show this pride in their dress.

For work, church, and other, more formal occasions, women will wear a *kiekie*. A *kiekie* is a belt which sits around the waist, with long strands hanging down to knee level. It is usually made from pandanus leaves, which have been woven, braided, or tied together in unique patterns. These days, women sometimes use more modern materials to make their *kiekie*, using materials like plastic bags, recycling these foreign materials into traditional island art. For the most formal occasions, women wear a *ta'ovala*, or a woven mat made of pandanus leaves. The mat's age determines its relative value, and a larger mat indicates higher status. That is, the older the mat, the more formal and precious it is. Do not be fooled by old, tattered mats since these *ta'ovala* actually exceed all of the other mats in terms of value and respect.

Men wear a *ta'ovala* over their *tupenu* skirt for work, church, and other formal occasions. They tie the *ta'ovala* around their waists with a *kafa* rope. In the hot, humid climate of Tonga, the *ta'ovala* can be very heavy to wear. For these types of occasions, children wear a mini *ta'ovala* or *kiekie*.

RELIGION

Today, Tonga is a completely Christian nation. In fact, the practice of any other religion is completely forbidden there. However, this was not always the case. Missionaries spread Christianity throughout the Kingdom in the nineteenth century. At that point in time, King Tupou I became so enamored of the Church that he mandated Christianity as the "official national religion" of Tonga. He then illegalized the practice of other faiths. Nonetheless, the Tongans have kept some of their traditional beliefs, mixing them into the Christian church in Tonga. For instance, their evil Polynesian demons became synonymous with the Devil.

Religion is central to everyday life in Tonga, and Christian churches act as social and community-centered organizations. Several different Christian sects exist in Tonga: the Wesleyan Church, the Mormon Church, the Church of Tonga, the Free Church of Tonga, and a few scattered new churches. Recently, Scientology has begun to establish itself in Tonga. Many Tongans, however, do not identify Scientology as a religion, because Scientologists present themselves to the Tongan people as educa-

---

Devil's Advocates

Tongans are very serious about *teivolo,* the Devil. People who fear nothing else in the world, who will willingly hunt and swim with sharks, who live in a place which could literally be swept away by a large wave, are absolutely terrified of the Devil. At nighttime, they avoid the bush at all costs, because that's where the Devil lives. People never live alone, for if they do, the Devil will inevitably come possess them. In fact, the Devil bears responsibitility for every bad thing which happens in Tonga, and he spends his days plotting every single Tongan's personal destruction.

Needless to say, Tongans constantly asked me, with shock and awe, "Why are you living alone? Why are you walking to the store alone? Why are you leaving my house alone at night? Why are you dressing up for Halloween? Aren't you afraid of the Devil!?" In response, I fluctuate between nervous laughter and bold assertions such as, "*Palangi* are not afraid of the Devil."

- Alicia Green

tors. A few Bahai centers are also scattered throughout the islands. On the other hand, some Tongans joke that they belong to the church of *hangatonu sisu*, which translates to "straight to God," so they can avoid attending church service.

In Tonga, the church bells toll early every morning of the week besides Saturday. On Sundays, the air vibrates thickly with ringing church bells and beating wooden drums. Smoke from the *umu*, or underground ovens, fills the air, as every family prepares the day's meal in their backyards. Even in the main cities, businesses can operate on Sundays only if they possess a special license. In smaller towns, only bakeries can remain open. Those who venture out for a Sunday walk will be greeted with the sound of church choirs singing a cappella. In order to appreciate the music firsthand, travelers can ask their guesthouse to direct them to a local church, where they can experience both the beautiful singing—and a fiery sermon in Tongan—firsthand.

Because church occupies such an important space in the fabric of Tongans' lives, it deserves a special outfit. Those who attend services at the Church of Tonga may notice that many of the women will be wearing big "Easter-looking" hats. In a Mormon church service, Tongans will be dressed in more Western-style dress clothing, including ties. Depending upon the church, service lengths vary, but they usually last approximately one hour. However, some church services can stretch to as long as two or three hours. The church conference is the biggest event of the year; it involves a week-long gathering for feasts. These feasts sometimes occur as often as three times each day.

Tongans donate a great deal of money to the church. They view church donations as an obligation, in that these donations are very much expected. Churches will often publicly announce the amount of money that each family donated during that day's offering. Families prefer to take out loans in order to give a big donation, rather than face the embarrassment of not donating enough money to the church.

Due to their strong religious beliefs, Tongans tend to be extremely socially conservative. For example, public displays of affection between people of the opposite sex simply do not happen in Tonga. Furthermore, Tongans dress conservatively, and the islanders bring religion into the workplace, meetings, and schools. In fact, every meeting begins with a prayer, as does every school day.

Tongans also believe in superstitions, talking often about the Devil, or *teivolo*. This belief comes directly from the Tongans' traditional beliefs in gods and spirits. For instance, Tongans will not go to cemeteries at night for fear of spirits and the *teivolo*. Furthermore, they believe that if a person swims or does other forbidden activities on a Sunday, a shark will come and attack that person, or the person will fall ill. Those who ask Tongan children what items they might pack to bring to an uninhabited island will hear answers like, "a frying pan to hit the *teivolo*," "a machete to kill the *teivolo*," or anything else they can think of in order to protect themselves against the *teivolo*. That's right. Going to a deserted island, the children would be more scared of the *teivolo* than of the lack of adequate food and water there.

Tongan Kids

When it comes to games and play time, Tongan kids are incredibly creative. Since they don't have "conventional toys" like video games, Barbie dolls, or toy cars, the children will improvise games using the materials that they have at hand: sticks, rocks, sand, leaves, string, pieces of garbage, and other random objects they may find inside or outside of their houses. Many times, they can be seen playing with very large, sharp machetes. The rule "don't run with scissors" simply doesn't apply there.

As a Peace Corps Volunteer living in Tonga, I am constantly surprised to see Tongan kids digging through any of the garbage that we don't happen to burn right away. The kids are absolutely amazed at the perfectly good objects we discard: old containers which can be used to play in the sand, curious wrappers with bits of food still left in them which can be eaten. One day, as I stood there watching the children digging through our trash, I realized that, maybe, it is true, the old cliché that "one man's trash is another man's treasure." Once, we had thrown away a Pepcid AC mini-container; later that day, we saw the kids using it as a little coin purse.

Tongan children also love videotapes. If they get their hands on an old VHS tape, they will pull out the long lengths of tape and string them through the entire yard: in the trees, along laundry lines, along the fences…everywhere! Whenever I see one of the neighborhood kids carrying a length of videotape, I run out of the house like a madwoman, snatch the VHS tape away, and hurl it into a well-hidden garbage pile behind a fence, where the kids can't find it. (I have already had to disentangle far too many videotapes from around our backyard.) None of the Tongans seem to mind this behavior, though, as if, perhaps, they regard the VHS strings as a beautiful decoration.

When they are not already occupied by digging through the trash or decorating the neighborhood with VHS streamers, Tongan kids invent many funny, original games. For example, three of the boys from our neighborhood will roll a bicycle wheel back and forth, and wherever the wheel rolls, the nearest person has to hit it with a large hunk of metal as hard as he possibly can. That is the object of the game, beating the wheel with chunks of old metal. Often, when they're playing games like this, the children shout "weee-naaa, weee-naaa"—winner.

Tongan kids are also very adept at creating toys from their own surroundings. The neighbor boys make whistles and spinning wheels from leaves; spinning tops from bottle caps; kites from paper; and, most uniquely, noisemakers, which they make by combining a bike wheel spoke, a string, a nail, and a match. In order to make the noisemaker, the kids place the nail and the match inside of the tip of the bike wheel spoke, then tie the entire apparatus to a string. When they pound this object on pavement, it makes an incredibly loud noise, like a gunshot.

Tongan tykes, like kids everywhere, love to climb trees. However, unlike American kids, they do not have little tree forts or ladders, no. The Tongan kids climb barefoot up the huge trees until they reach the very top, or out onto the branches until they reach the very end. Once they reach the treetop or the end of the branch, they dangle down and then drop ten feet down onto the sand. All Tongan boys also know how to climb coconut trees. They do so by wrapping their arms and legs around the trunks and shimmying up the trunk. Once they reach the top of the tree, they will grab hold of the trunk with their feet, reach out to grab the coconuts, and throw them down to the ground.

- Kate Asleson

A Typical School Day in Tonga

One morning, I was teaching English to a class three (third grade). Suddenly, two or three of the boys looked out the window, conferred among themselves in rapid-fire Tongan, and ran out the door. Since the boys' regular teacher was sitting in the back of the classroom, naturally, I looked to her for support. She simply stood up, walked over to the window, and yelled after them, pointing first at one part of the schoolyard, then another, then another. Before long, the boys returned and settled quickly back to work. No one else made any comments.

Fifteen minutes later, the same exact thing happened again. From my position in front of the class, I could see two of the boys pick up long sticks from the porch before running out onto the grass. This time, their teacher didn't even look up from her work. Not wanting to distract the other students from the task at hand, I stayed where I was. A few minutes later, the boys were back.

When this happened again a third time, curiosity got the better of me. I walked over to the teacher, a look of exasperation splashed across my face. The teacher just pointed out the window and laughed. Outside, I could see my students chasing two pigs across the schoolyard toward a hole in the school fence. Apparently, the pigs had broken through earlier that morning, and the principal had given strict instructions for the students to chase the pigs out of the yard before they had a chance to root up the field. There seemed to be rotating shifts of kids going outside to run the critters off of school property.

Now, this particular school lies next to the airport. On another morning, I noticed a visibly increased level of excitement among the kids when I arrived for work. The class five teacher, with whom I'd be working with that day, explained that the first arrival of a plane from the new airline—which used much larger planes than the usual "puddle-jumpers" to which we had grown accustomed—was due to land within the hour. All of the kids and, apparently, many of the teachers, could hardly wait to see the amazing machine. We all started class with our ears primed for the sound of jet engines.

It didn't take long. They say that some people can pick up the mid-range hum of an aircraft sooner than others and, sure enough, before long, one or two of the kids leaned over and whispered to their neighbor. Soon, a general buzz overtook the room. By that point, all pretense of work had been completely abandoned, as we could all hear the plane in its approach. Suddenly, however, as the plane neared the tarmac at the end of the runway, the engine sound was suddenly diminished by the intervening trees. Finally, though, we were not disappointed: the plane shook the windows of our classroom as it roared by, wing flaps up, high and proud.

Everyone in the classroom looked at me. *What could I say?* The door burst open; everyone exploded out. Trailing slightly behind the mad rush, I could see a general classroom exodus, as kids and teachers streamed from buildings, across the yard, over the school fence. Soon, we all had our noses pressed to the chain-link barrier that surrounded the arrival surface, as we watched the new plane roll to a stop.

Sure enough, this plane was huge compared to the normal craft that usually landed here. (It could seat fifty passengers!) It had a much longer, higher set of stairs leading to the plane door. But, above all, it was loud. The kids were speechless. The teachers were speechless. I was speechless. Frozen in time, everyone simply stood stock still, mesmerized.

A few minutes later, the teachers had retired to the shade of a tree, and the kids were bouncing against the chain-link. The moment over, it was time to go back to class.

- Phil Curtis

EDUCATION

In Tonga, there are government schools and church-run schools. Primary school (elementary school) consists of classes one through six, and secondary school (high school) consists of forms one through six. Only students who plan to attend university finish form six as preparation for college. Since government schools receive better funding, they tend to have the better teachers. However, parents will sometimes place their children in church-run schools due to their strong connection to their church and to that particular community. The schools in Nuku'alofa enjoy wide renown as the best in all of Tonga. Both Tongatapu and Vava'u possess an all-English speaking school within their island group.

At the end of primary school, in class six, every student must take a three day-long test in all of the major subjects: English, Tongan, math, and science. This test score determines which secondary school that student can attend, which, in turn, basically determines the student's job options and, thus, the course of their life. In order to be accepted to attend a government-run school, the students must get a high score. Church-run secondary schools will take students with lower test scores. Tonga High School, in Nuku'alofa, stands highest of all Tongan schools in terms of prestige. Since no secondary schools exist on small outer islands, students hailing from those islands must move to the capital cities in their island groups in order to continue their education beyond primary school. Most of these students will stay with relatives; some outer islands even maintain a home on the main island in which their students can live while attending school there. Mothers from these outer islands will take turns traveling to the main island to take care of the students from their island. Most students will return to their home islands on weekends or holidays, depending upon the distance.

Students do not use textbooks in school; rather, they learn by copying and reciting from the blackboard. From an early age, Tongan students are taught to copy precisely into their notebooks, using rulers and certain pen colors. Some schools may have small libraries of books; most of these books, however, are infrequently used. Corporal punishment is used often in Tongan schools, although it is now against the law. Teachers will hit students for misbehaving and, sometimes, for giving an incorrect answer to a question.

English is taught in schools throughout Tonga. For Tongans, knowledge of English is invaluable. English is the language of business and tourism on the islands and, for Tongans who wish to go live overseas, knowledge of English opens doors to employment in Anglophone countries. Some people worry that this focus on English has caused a neglect of Tongan language reading and writing skills. Compounding this issue, there are not many books available in Tongan in the first place. In response to this concern, the Ministry of Education just altered certain components of the primary school education. Effective as of 2009, students will not start learning English until class three. That way, they can focus on Tongan first before learning to read and write in English. The idea is to strike a balance between the cultural need for Tongans to hold onto their own language and culture and the practical need for the students to learn English in order to be competitive in an increasingly global world. It is very important for Tongans to be able to keep their own language, but it is also important for them to learn English. Furthermore, proficient English skills are absolutely essential for those students wish to continue their education to the university level, either at home or overseas.

There are branches of the University of the South Pacific (USP) in Tongatapu, Ha'apai, and Vava'u. A few other tertiary schools exist in Nuku'alofa and Neiafu; they offer vocational education in trades like carpentry, cooking, and agriculture.

The Tongans use education in order to preserve their traditional Tongan heritage in other ways as well. Students learn traditional dances, songs, and handicrafts in school. Students also practice dances which have been passed down for generations, and they learn how to make small handicrafts from local materials.

Food

Because Tonga is an island nation, the food selection there is limited to crops, livestock, fish that can be harvested locally, as well as those foods which can be imported.

> Seasons play a major role in food availability.

SEAFOOD

Since Tonga is completely surrounded by sea, seafood is rarely in short supply there, and it's always delicious. In fact, Tongans will eat just about anything that comes from the ocean. They will walk around on the reefs at low tide and gather all of the shells and creatures they can find, eating them raw, right out of the sea. (Sashimi doesn't get much fresher than that!) Women and children often gather fish and shells along the shores or in the shallows. Typically, only men will go fishing in the more traditional sense, traveling out to sea on boats and casting long lines; throwing nets from shore to catch schools of fish, or heading out to the reefs to spear fish. The warm Tongan waters play host to blue-finned tuna, wahoo, grouper, parrot fish, eel, shark, surgeon fish, unicorn fish, sea cucumber, sea urchin, octopus, sea turtle, lobster, and many more. As with crops, the availability of any given type of fresh seafood will depend upon the weather and the time of year. During the colder winter months, Tongans do not fish as often. They also do not fish during stormy or rainy weather. So while it may be possible to find fresh seafood any time in Nuku'alofa, seafood availability may be more limited in the smaller islands, towns, and villages.

CROPS

Tongans grow a variety of root crops, the most common being yam, sweet potato, taro, and tapioca. They favor these crops because they are both easy to grow and huge. The giant taro, for example, can grow up to three feet long, so it will feed a family for a long time. Due to the law which grants every Tongan male land when he reaches adulthood, most Tongans have land and grow crops for subsistence. Increasingly, Tongans have begun to grow corn on their land as well.

Since it is much more difficult to grow vegetables in Tonga, vegetables are not traditionally part of the Tongan diet. However, the Ministry of Agriculture does plant vegetables, and occasionally locals might plant vegetables to sell in the market. The vegetables grown in Tonga include tomatoes, green onions, green peppers, white radish, green beans, snap peas, and broccoli. Since vegetables can only grow during the cool winter season, while it may be possible to find them in Nuku'alofa year-round, vegetables will, most likely, be unavailable on the smaller islands during the summer.

The Tongans do grow a few crops for export, including pumpkins and vanilla beans. In fact, locally-grown raw vanilla beans are available for purchase at both the tourist stores and the international airport.

FRUIT

Tropical fruits of all kinds thrive in Tonga. Most of these fruits abound in the hot summer season while others, like bananas and papaya, are available year-round. Many different types of bananas exist in Tonga, including the large, dense plantain; the small, sweet *pata*; and the regular bananas commonly found in Western supermarkets. During the summer, locally-grown pineapple, mango, guava, passion fruit, and Indian apples also flourish.

But, above all, there are coconuts. Young green coconuts offer sweet coconut water for drinking, while more mature, brown coconuts burst with delicious coconut meat. In order to procure the coconuts, Tongan boys will climb high in the coconut trees to hack them down. Once they have the coconuts on the ground, they crack them open with machetes. Coconuts can be found in the trees or on the ground, and they are also available for purchase at the market.

While anyone can take a coconut from any tree without asking, this same rule does not apply to other kinds of tree fruit, such as papaya or bananas, because these fruits are planted and grown specifically to harvest. Fresh fruit is always available for sale in the market.

LIVESTOCK

In Tonga, pigs are highly-prized and extremely expensive. Tongans will use the smaller pigs for church feasts or special meals, cooking them on a spit over an open fire. Large adult pigs, on the other hand, are saved for very special occasions, such as weddings and funerals. Larger pigs are cooked in the *umu*, or underground oven.

Tongans will often keep pigs and chickens at their homes as livestock. These animals roam freely around the property and it isn't unusual to see large black or brown pigs and small spotted piglets wandering around the island. The pigs know their owner's voice, and they will respond to calls of "*ma, ma, ma*," which means, in Pig, "feeding time."

Chickens usually run free, and they are caught for special meals. In addition, some groups have established chicken hatcheries in order to gather eggs. Should the opportunity arise, try a taste of Tongan chicken. The Tongan chickens are very lean and sweet-tasting because their diet consists mainly of coconut, and they are often prepared in boiling coconut water.

Horses and cows live in the bush plots, tied to trees. They are very valuable, and their meat is only used for funerals and weddings.

> According to the letter of the law, Tongans are supposed to keep pigs in pens because, if they do not, the pigs can make their way out of the towns and harm other people's crops in the bush. If pigs are found in bush plots, they are often shot.

IMPORTED FOODS

Canned meat is both a favorite import and a staple of the Tongan diet. While Palm is the most popular brand, a few others exist as well. Canned meats come in many sizes, as well as several varieties, including meat and beef. Many Tongans like it so much that they will eat the meat right out of the can without preparing it at all. Others will dip bread into the meat as a snack. Initially, when they were first imported, canned foods were a status symbol, a sign of prestige, since having them showed that the buyer could afford to buy food instead of growing it. Canned food is also highly

Chasing Bacon

At times, my house is completely surrounded by pigs. It feels like the island version of a Dr. Seuss book: big ones, little ones, fat ones, skinny ones, earless ones, and colored ones.

Some nights, I awaken to the sound of rushing water. At first, I think to myself, *is it raining?* Then I realize: *it's not rain, it's the pigs.* The pigs have broken into the water tank outside, where my drinking water is stored. In fact, the pigs have even discovered how to turn on the nozzle to the tank. Yes, we have smart pigs in Tonga. As I rush outside to turn off the water, I encounter a couple of pigs who are enjoying the water by taking a cool bath.

The water tank is only the beginning. I will often find the pigs uprooting the grass in our yard in order to make large mud pits. Normally, I would not mind this but most of the time the pigs make these pits right in front of my door. The pigs must have a penchant for water, because they have also, rather notoriously, gotten into the city water pipes. (Luckily, water from these pipes is generally used only for showering and doing dishes, not for drinking.) A few times, the pigs have bitten completely through the pipes, causing them to burst. One time, I had to call the city water works to come out and stop the ten-foot stream of water gushing through the air outside my window.

It is impossible to grow any type of vegetable in our yard because, once the plants sprout above ground, the pigs have their way with them, grinding them to a pulp or worse. Given my rising frustration due to the giant mud pits, plumbing mishaps, and vegetable carcasses, I occasionally throw rocks at the pigs, ostensibly to keep them away from the water tank or chase them off from the water pipes. After I had begun fighting back, some of the pigs began to recognize me and, whenever they saw me coming down the gravel road or out of the house, they would run the other way as fast as they possibly could. In fact, one pig could actually spot me from a distance and, when he did, he would immediately run away, emitting an ear-piercing scream as he went.

- Brett Asleson

prized because there are not many sources of meat on the islands.

Tongans also love to eat *sipi*, or mutton. *Sipi* is not the best quality meat, the lamb chops. In fact, it is actually the very fatty, on-the-bone mutton. Tongans will cut it up for soup, or use it in the local *lu* dish. Alternatively, *sipi* may simply be boiled and eaten.

Other popular imports include cans of soda, ice cream, popsicles, candy, hot dogs, crackers, and instant Chinese noodles. Often, the Tongans will eat Ramen straight out of the package without adding any water at all.

BAKED GOODS

Bakeries exist in each island group, though they differ substantially from each other. In Nuku'alofa, a wide variety of baked goods are available, including desserts, white and whole-grain bread, cakes, even meat pies! In the more isolated island groups, bakeries carry only white bread.

Keke, or donut holes, are a beloved lunch and snack food. Often, Tongans will spread butter on top of the *keke* as frosting.

You Can *Take It With You*

Don't be surprised to see Tongan kids, or even adults, pour soda into a whole loaf of bread, or fill a loaf of bread with ice cream, and then eat it. Tongans love anything sweet, and cold ice cream is a special treat. In the hot, humid island climate, ice cream melts incredibly fast; therefore, in order to help insulate it a bit longer on the boat or car ride home, Tongans will store the ice cream in a loaf of bread. Think of it as a real ice cream sandwich. On the other hand, pouring soda into a loaf of bread doesn't appear to serve any practical purpose, but Tongans love eating it regardless.

FOOD PREPARATIONS

Tongans do not use many spices in their cooking. Instead, they prefer to use a lot of coconut milk, or to simply eat their food plain. In terms of cooking methods, Tongans usually prefer frying and boiling. And instead of using a conventional indoor oven, Tongans use the outdoor underground *umu*, or else they cook over an open fire. The *umu* is made by digging a hole in the ground, making a wood fire inside the hole, and then placing rocks inside. Then, once the fire burns out, the ashes are removed, so only hot rocks remain. Meat is then placed over the rocks and covered with banana leaves to cook for several hours. On Sundays, the *umu*s virtually erupt smoke, as every family prepares their large Sunday meal.

LOCAL RECIPES

Coconut milk

Ingredients: Brown coconut, water

Directions: Open a mature brown coconut with a machete; cut in half. Scrape out all of the white coconut meat in pieces. Shred these pieces with a grater. Rip off some of the coconut husk from inside of the shell. Place a handful of the shredded coconut meat, gathered from inside of the coconut, inside of the husk. Pour some water over the top of this mixture, and wring the water out of the husk, from the coconut meat into a bowl. Continue this process until all of the coconut meat has been wrung dry into the bowl. (It is also possible to use a dishcloth to wring out the milk in lieu of the coconut husks.) In the end, there will be a bowl full of coconut milk, which can be used for cooking.

Lu Moa

Ingredients: Chicken, cubed (canned beef or fish can also be substituted); coconut milk; diced onion; diced tomato, and taro leaf (any leafy green vegetable, such as spinach or cabbage, can be substituted)

Directions: Make either tin foil or a large banana leaf into a cup shape. Line this cup with a large taro leaf, or with another green leafy vegetable, such as spinach leaves. Place raw cubed meat, a handful of diced onion, and a handful of diced tomatoes inside of the leaf. Smother this mixture in coconut milk, and cover the top with more leaves. Close the banana leaf or tin foil so that it is sealed up tight in a ball shape. The *lu moa* is traditionally baked for at least one hour in the underground *umu* ovens. However, it can also be baked for about one hour in a conventional oven at medium heat (around 350°F).

Ota Ika

Ingredients: Raw fish; coconut milk; chopped onions; lime or lemon juice; vegetables (lettuce, tomato); local red (hot) pepper

Directions: Cut the raw fish into cubes. Place these cubes in a bowl, and marinate the mixture with lemon or lime juice. Let sit for a few minutes. Add chopped onions, vegetables, coconut milk, small hot peppers, and salt, to taste.

FEASTS

There is nothing quite like a Tongan feast. Everyone who has the opportunity to attend a *kaipolo*, or local feast, should do so—they will be rewarded with an incredibly unique cultural experience. It is never a good idea, however, to simply show up at a feast uninvited, because many Tongan feasts are church-related. For the feast, long tables or ground mats are erected, along with a head table. Usually, families divide up the food preparation duties. If an overseas visitor is invited to a feast, they might be asked to sit at the head table as a guest of honor. The head table is reserved for the most important people, and those seated at the head table get to eat the best food. Once all of the guests have arrived, everyone waits until after a prayer has been said, and the most important person in attendance has started eating. Once this happens, everyone can begin eating.

Lobster, sweet-and-sour chicken, yam, taro, whole fish, hot dogs, and more will be served either on plates wrapped in cellophane or in plastic to-go containers. All of the plates or containers are then stacked up on top of each other, until the table beneath has, for all practical purposes, disappeared. At many feasts, there are no individual plates; each guest simply starts eating whatever is in front of them. There will usually be small pigs laid out and Tongans just stick a finger into the pig to grab some meat to eat.

During the feast, there will be many long speeches and prayers. Once the speeches are finished, everyone is free to leave whenever they like. At church and school fundraiser feasts, there will usually be Tongan dance performances. Guests may also be given food to take home with them.

Drinks

Alcohol, usually imported from Australia and New Zealand, is available in all of the main cities of Tonga. In the past, there was a locally-produced beer, *Ikale*. The brewery, however, closed in 2009, and Heineken will take over distribution instead. There is another Tongan beer, *Mata Maka*, but it is produced in New Zealand. A few locally-produced drinks still exist, including the local liquors made on Tongatapu and Vava'u, and a special wine made in 2008 to celebrate the coronation of King Tupou V.

Locals also brew their own alcohol, called *hopi*. I would not suggest consuming this drink, as both its alcohol content and ingredients are never certain.

It is generally wise to be wary of drinking alcohol with Tongans; many of the islanders do not know their limits, and they will continue drinking until they can't stand. They can often become angry, physical, and out-of-control. Some Tongans, who have lived overseas or who have come into contact with more Western influence, may be better able to control themselves around alcohol. Anyone who finds themselves in a situation which makes them uncomfortable may wish to quietly slip out.

Otai is a local, non-alcoholic Tongan drink made from fresh fruits. *Otai* is delicious; it contains chunks of fruit mixed with water and sugar. Those who do try this drink should be careful, because it is usually made using untreated rainwater, so it can make people sick.

Tongan tea may taste a little different from the standard Earl Grey. If a Tongan makes tea, it will be very sweet. If the Tongan has run out of tea, they may offer their guests "tea," but instead give them hot water with sugar added, until the water turns brown.

KAVA

Kava is a narcotic drink made from pepper roots. Traditionally, *kava* holds an important cultural position within Tongan society, as a social drink consumed only by men. In fact, *kava*-drinking is an ancient tradition, reaching far back in Tongan history. The *kava* plant grows all over Tonga. Before the roots can be harvested and dried, the plants must grow for over three years. Then, once the roots have been dried in the sun, they are crushed into a fine powder. This powder, which is later mixed with water, becomes the *kava* drink. When consumed, *kava* produces a numbing sensation in the lips and mouth; it also makes the drinker sleepy. Interestingly, unlike alcohol, the more often a person drinks *kava*, the sooner that person will become intoxicated from it, while the less often a person drinks *kava*, the more *kava* that person will need to drink in order to feel its effects.

Men love to gather in *kava* circles, usually in the evenings; these circles often last well into the night. *Kava* circles typically meet on weekends, although they can meet throughout the week as well. Sometimes, the men will gather in a traditional woven hut, which is used as a *kava* circle at night and as a weaving hut during the day for the women. Other times, the *kava* circle may meet in a town hall or a house. Some *kava* circles raise money for education, water supplies, or other causes, with each man donating a certain amount of money in order to join the circle. Other *kava* circles are church-oriented, with *kava* circles happening on Saturday night as a Bible study, and on Sunday morning before the church service.

The only girl allowed to be present at a kava circle is the *tou'a*; she dishes out the *kava* drinks to the men in coconut shells from a large wooden kava bowl. The *tou'a* has to be a single, unmarried girl. During the *kava* drinking, many of the men will give the girl a hard time, harassing her and making jokes. The girl can then give the men who are harassing her more *kava* in order to make them quiet down. The man sitting directly to the right of the *tou'a* is said to be her boyfriend. At some of the larger *kava* circles, there will be live music, with some men playing guitars and singing. Some of the best music in Tonga can be enjoyed at these gatherings. The men may also play cards at *kava* circles, or watch rugby on satellite TV.

Travelers who choose to attend a *kava* circle may find that they are the only foreigner there. The Tongans, however, will be happy to have them. When joining a *kalapu*, or casual *kava* circle, a donation is expected. Cash donations usually range from TOP$5 – $10, or a small bag of *kava* is also welcomed. These donations will likely go to a specific cause. A *kalapu* might raise money to bring water to the village,

The Origin of *Kava*

A local legend explains the origins of *kava*. A long time ago, the *Tu'i Tonga*, the King of Tonga, embarked on an expedition with some fishermen. The men soon grew hungry and thirsty, so they landed on a small island, 'Eueiki, to search for food and coconuts. Only three people lived on the island: an old couple with an only daughter named Kava. While his men searched for food, the King himself rested under the shade of a large *kape* plant. This plant turned out to be the only food on the island, as it was a time of famine. The old couple came to harvest this food for the King but, to their horror, they found him resting peacefully under that very plant. Not wanting to disturb the King, the couple went home and, with no other food available, they agreed that they must sacrifice their own daughter as an offering to the King. When the King found out what had happened, he was incredibly sad and moved. He ordered that the girl be buried. Later, two plants grew out of her burial mound: one at the head and one at the feet. The king ordered these plants to be harvested immediately; he found that one had a bitter taste and produced a numbing sensation, while the other was sweet. He named the bitter tasting one *kava* after the girl on the island, the other *to*, which we know today as sugar cane. Since then, *kava* has been an important part of Tongan culture and rituals.

to provide educational scholarships, or to help sponsor church activities. It is important to bear in mind that, like *otai*, *kava* is made using untreated rainwater, so it can make people sick. Anyone who attends a *faikava*, or formal *kava* ceremony at a church, should be aware that there is an order to the way in which the people are seated. Therefore, it's best to either sit toward the back of the circle or to ask someone where to sit. Women who wish to attend a *kava* circle can observe, but they should not drink *kava*, because they might offend the Tongans present. A female who attends the *kava* circle might also be asked to be the *tou'a* (pg 48). Not any woman can serve as *tou'a*, though: only unmarried women can be *tou'a*. Anyone who decides to accept the position of *tou'a* will probably get a lot of harassment. That said, all of the comments will be in Tongan, so anyone who does not know Tongan will not know what is being said.

Dance

Tongan dance has been passed from generation to generation, and it has changed very little in hundreds of years. Many Tongan dances are performed to accompany ancient songs depicting history, legends, and traditional Tongan gods. The female dancers move slowly and gracefully, while the male dancers move quickly and energetically, often accompanied by shouting or singing as they dance.

The *kailao* dance traditionally begins with pulsating drum echoes and a ringing, rhythmic high pitch, as a small boy beats a corrugated metal sheet. (If these instruments are not available, the dancers perform to recorded music, or to whatever resources are available.) Once the music has begun, a group of boys stomp in unison to the beat, as the coconut shell pieces tied to their ankles make noise every time they take a step. The boys wear green palm leaves around their waists, fresh flower *leis* on their necks, and coconut oil on their bodies. They also wield fake wooden swords, swinging and throwing them in the air in unison. This dance, the *kailao*, pays homage to the warriors of ancient Tonga.

More traditional songs feature guitars, along with people singing in Tongan. In one of these dances, the *tau'olunga*, a single young girl stands in one place, bends her knees slightly, and waves her arms gracefully, depicting the words of the song through movement. She wears the traditional Tongan *tapa* mat wrapped around her body, a white cowry shell necklace, and a single, long decorative piece sticking out of her hair. The girl is lathered in coconut oil and, as she dances, people from the audience approach her and stick Tongan money bills to her body or inside the top of her *tapa* mat. During the dance, some of the male dancers stomp around behind the young girl, and older women will get up and dance as well. In so doing, they are showing support for her dancing.

Usually, the dance is done by one girl, but sometimes, a small group of girls performs the motions together. The *tau'olunga* is performed only by young virgin girls. Legend has it that if the girl performing the dance is not a virgin, the money will not stick to her oiled-up body. Therefore, when girls perform this dance, they make sure to use a lot of coconut oil. These dances are often used as a fundraiser in Tonga. After the dance, the money raised will be used for the school or church sponsoring the dance performance.

The *lakalaka*, widely considered Tonga's national dance, is performed by a group of dancers standing in a row, doing simultaneous arm and hand motions. In 2003, UNESCO declared this dance an "Intangible Cultural Heritage of Humanity." The *lakalaka* can sometimes be done with hundreds of people at the same time, with the men and women on separate sides. The *lakalaka* is reserved for special occasions, such as the coronation of the king.

The *ma'ulu'ulu*, another group dance, is performed by both sexes together. For this dance, everyone lines up in rows, with the front row sitting cross-legged, the following row sitting on a bench, the third row standing behind them, and so on and so on, depending on the size of the group. This dance involves both hand and arm movements, along with some clapping and singing. In another dance, the *soke*, male and female performers bang sticks together to a drumbeat.

Tongan kids learn these traditional dances in school. Today, the younger generations are also learning Western-style dancing from the movies that they see or from the foreigners that they meet. In fact, a hip-hop competition occurs annually in Nuku'alofa. At feasts or celebrations, there is traditional Tongan dancing; in between staged dances, however, the DJ sometimes plays Western music, and the Tongans dance to that as well. Other times, Tongan DJs mix the music from popular Western songs with traditional Tongan singing. Tongans also love the songs from the movie *Grease*. It's fascinating to see this mix between modern and traditional music and dancing in Tonga.

Sports

Tongans love to play rugby, netball, and volleyball. The Tongans' large size and impressive strength play an important role in determining the sports that they prefer to play. Boys play rugby and volleyball, while girls play netball. Young Tongan boys excel in rugby and are often recruited to play on teams in New Zealand or Australia. Others are drafted to play American football in the NFL in the United States. Tongan girls play netball, a sport which is similar to basketball, but without the dribbling. Tongans learn to play sports early in primary and secondary school.

> **Gone Huntin'**
> In ancient times, chiefs and royalty enjoyed pigeon hunting. In order to do this, they stood on tops of mounds built high out of the earth.

During the school year, one week is usually devoted to schools competing against one another in sports, as the parents cheer for them or laugh at them. Soccer is also growing in popularity; it is also the only sport which boys and girls can play together. During sports week, the students also compete in short and long-distance races, the tug-of-war, and relay races.

Tonga has a national rugby team, called *'Ikale Tahi*, which competes in the international league. *'Ikale Tahi* start each match with a war dance, called the *sipi tau*, or *kailao*. The most interesting match to watch is the *'Ikale Tahi* against the All Blacks team from New Zealand. Before the match, both teams face each other and perform their war dances. Rugby first came to the South Pacific in the early twentieth century, brought by the sailors and missionaries.

Music

Tongans love to sing. In church, they sing traditional hymns. Usually, the church choir sits in the middle rows of the church. They then stand up and face the front of the church when performing. Tongans sing mostly a cappella and, usually, very loudly. To hear this music, attend a Sunday service or walk around outside between the churches.

There are also traditional Tongan songs which accompany the traditional dances. Sometimes these songs are sung a cappella; other times, they are accompanied by guitar or drums. Traditional Tongan songs have a soft, Polynesian sound and usually depict a story or a piece of history. Tongans often perform these songs at festivals and dances, or even at small *kava* club gatherings, where men bring guitars and sing together.

Tongans also love brass marching bands, a musical style imported from Europe. Every high school has its own marching band, and many of the Wesleyan churches have brass bands as well.

On the other hand, recently, Tongan youth have increasingly been drawn to Western rap and pop music. They hear it in movies, download it from the Internet, or get it from relatives overseas. An "American Idol"-type competition was recently conducted on the main island, Tongatapu. Often, Western songs will get remixed into traditional Tongan songs or even with Christmas music, creating a very interesting combination. Of course, like all Tongan music, these songs are blasted at the loudest possible volume.

Handicrafts

Tongan handicrafts are another unique aspect of Tonga's cultural heritage. Each item is handmade from local materials, and items are seldom mass-produced or imported from other countries. When a person purchases a handicraft in Tonga, they can rest assured that someone spent time creating each unique piece of art. Some common handicrafts available for purchase include bone-carved pendant necklaces; shell necklaces and earrings; coconut shell necklaces and earrings; woven or beaded bracelets; wood carvings of whales, turtles, and Tongan *fales*; and other carvings. Tongan craftspeople also make coconut shell *kava* cups; woven baskets; woven or *tapa* purses; woven mats; *tapa* mats; and *tapa* postcards.

Given the incredible amount of work put into each item, the prices for the handicrafts are incredibly low. While bartering is not expected in the markets, if a buyer purchases multiple items, the seller will often give that person a discount. Jewelry prices start as low as TOP$5; wood carvings start at TOP$10. Woven mats and *tapa* cloth are generally much more expensive, though it is possible to buy smaller pieces of *tapa* with intricate patterns and designs for about TOP$10.

In Tonga, *tapa* and woven mats are extremely important. They are the most treasured possessions in every household and are used for many important occasions, including funerals and weddings. A Tongan is not considered wealthy unless they have *tapa*.

Tapa mats are made by hand, using local materials; therefore, no two pieces are exactly alike. The *tapa* material is made from the bark of mulberry trees. Before the bark can be used, however, the trees must be allowed to grow for at least a couple of years. At that time, the bark is torn off of the tree,

> The sound of women beating on bark with mallets forms the background soundscape of the island.

and the outer bark is separated from the inner layer, leaving only the soft inner bark. This inner bark is dried in the sun, then soaked in water. Once this process is complete, the women gather around to beat the bark with wooden mallets. When enough bark has been beaten to complete the project at hand, it is all smoothed flat and tied together with arrowroot. For some occasions, the mats can reach lengths of over one hundred meters.

Once the mats themselves are completed, the women paint traditional designs on them, using natural dyes boiled from sap. Since *tapa*-making is usually done by groups of women, the mats typically either have no particular owner, or else mat ownership rotates amongst all of the women within a given mat-making group. Other times, the women might make a large *tapa* mat and then divide it into smaller pieces. The women will keep the *tapa* for special occasions or gifts, or else they will sell it in the market. Making *tapa* mats is difficult, time-consuming work.

Like the *tapa* mats, woven mats are also very valuable in Tonga. Tongans give

Harmful Souvenirs and Customs

Avoid buying handicrafts and souvenirs made from turtle shell and whale bone while traveling through Tonga. Not only are these items illegal because the animals are endangered, they may be confiscated upon entering another country. Some Tongan vendors continue to sell turtle shell jewelry and items carved from whale bone despite this, so it's best to inquire about the origin of souvenirs and handicrafts before purchase. Purchasing such items will only encourage further detriment to these species.

Those who buy wood carvings can also run into difficulties with customs in New Zealand and Australia, because Tonga has no fumigation facilities for wood carvings. Travelers can still bring wood carvings into these countries, if they pay independently for fumigation. Other countries, such as the United States, do not have any problem with these wood carvings woven mats as gifts at weddings, funerals, and other occasions. These mats are made from pandanus leaves, which are cut, dried in the sun, and soaked in the ocean in order to bleach them bright white. Like *tapa* mats, woven mats are handmade using local materials. Women will gather in groups to make these mats. They also use pandanus leaves to weave baskets, fans, purses, trays, and more. Tongans will use the mats as floor coverings, or they will wear them around the waist as *ta'ovalas*.

Holidays, Festivals & Events

Tongans love any reason to celebrate or to have a feast. Many of these festivities are big community events with the biggest events being weddings, funerals, and church-related events. While some of the national holidays may not be too extravagant, they still serve as a viable reason to take the day off from work and have a *kaitunu*, or picnic, on the beach.

Tongans typically get married on Thursdays in a legal courthouse ceremony. The couple is not officially considered married, however, until the following Sunday, when they attend church together and host a big formal celebration. That day, the couple wears flowers and their finest woven mats; they will also cover themselves with coconut oil. After the church service ends, there is a big feast and celebration. At the *kava* ceremony, both the bride and groom drink *kava*. This is the only time in Tongan society when it is acceptable for a woman to drink *kava* and sit in the place of honor.

Today, however, this traditional structure of marriage is changing. That is, some younger couples are holding more Western-style weddings, or even eloping. A Tongan slang word, *faka-suva*, which translates, literally, to mean "in the Fijian way," is used to describe couples who break from traditional Tongan cultural norms by living together before getting married.

> After the wedding, it is not unusual for the wife to move to live with the husband's family.

Putu, or funerals, are another major community event. Following a death in Tonga, everything proceeds according to a traditional, highly ritualized process, which involves an extended period of mourning. No funeral homes exist in Tonga. Instead, the family of the deceased simply displays the body in a room with mats and *tapa* inside their home. The family also erects large tents in the yard and builds a large *umu*. They then fill the *umu* with the best and most expensive meat: large pigs, horses, and cows. Because a funeral requires the bereaved family to feed the entire community, funerals end up being quite expensive for the family.

Once the house has been prepared and the body has been laid out, the extended family and the community comes to the house in order to view the body, bringing gifts, such as *tapa* and mats. Once the family receives the gifts, the oldest female of the family divides them among all of the family members. Everyone gathers together and the group sings hymns, often throughout the night. On the following morning, a church service is held. After the service, everyone follows in procession to the graveyard for the burial. Because everyone feels an expectation to show their emotion publicly, there will be a great deal of crying and weeping at the graveside. Everyone wears black, and the closer that the relatives are to the deceased, the larger the mats they wear. Close relatives may wear black in mourning for a period that might extend from six months all the way up to one year. The closest relatives, along with those who were lower-ranking than the deceased, also cut their hair as a sign of respect and grief.

In addition to weddings and funerals, several other Tongan ceremonies revolve around the church. First of all, the annual church conferences happen between May and June; the church organizations rotate this event to a different island group each year. The church conference involves a weeklong celebration of church services, dancing, donations, and numerous daily feasts.

The *Faka Me*, or White Children's Sunday, happens each May. On this day, all of the children dress in white, wearing their best *ta'ovala* mats and decorating themselves with flowers. *Faka Me* honors and celebrates children with a big feast

> The heilala is the national flower of Tonga.

that is held after the service. The annual Roll Call also marks an important event in the calendar. On that day, all of the women—dressed in white with big, wide hats—attending the church service announce deaths and births in their families. The Roll Call of the Church of Tonga happens every September.

Finally, the Heilala Festival happens every July on the island of Tongatapu. During this festival, there are feasts, celebrations, and beauty contests. There is a "Miss Heilala" contest organized by the Tonga Visitors Bureau, along with a "Miss Galaxy" contest, which is actually a beauty contest for the *fakaleiti*, or boys dressed as girls (pg 30). The "Miss Galaxy" contest is a fun and very popular event not to be missed.

Natural Environment

Incredibly isolated from other land masses, Tonga has a unique environment. In addition to their secluded sandy beaches, the Tongan Islands boast a mix of majestic volcanoes, lush rainforests, natural blowholes, dramatic cliffs, and beautiful lagoons. Best of all, it is easy to enjoy Tonga's amazing natural beauty, without suffering the negative side effects of mass tourism.

GEOGRAPHY

Sitting directly on the Pacific Ring of Fire, Tonga possesses several volcanoes, some active, some dormant. The volcanoes cause a large number of earthquakes, although many of these disturbances are either so deep or so small that they are not felt on the surface of the islands. The Tonga Trench lies just east of the Tongan Islands; it is the second deepest trench on earth.

Tonga's nearest neighboring countries are Fiji to the west, New Zealand to the southeast, and Samoa to the north, just across the International Dateline.

Interestingly, the land in the island nation of Tonga is actually spread across seven hundred thousand square kilometers of ocean, that is, a region of ocean about the same size as Texas. However, once all of Tonga's land masses are put together, their combined square mileage would only be about the size of Dallas. Even that small land area may be shrinking due to global warming. Tonga's shorelines also change after major storms or earthquakes. The nation of Tonga itself is composed of five distinct island groups, each of which possesses different land characteristics.

The main island, Tongatapu, contains about one-third of the land area of Tonga; it is also home to about two-thirds of the nation's population. Due to the fact that the land is very flat, sometimes almost below sea level, a great deal of flooding occurs on Tongatapu during the rainy season. In terms of vertical footage, Tongatapu seems to sit almost at a slant, with part of the island lying very low, with higher cliffs on the southern shore, where there are natural blowholes. At these blowholes, water sprays up through the rocky ledges. On the northern shore of the island, near the capital, Nuku'alofa, sits a large lagoon. Sandy beaches cover the eastern side of the island. Since most of the land on Tongatapu has been cleared for either farming of for villages and resorts, there are no natural forests remaining on Tongatapu.

The island of 'Eua has very unique geography and vegetation. Much older than the rest of the Tongan Islands, 'Eua is thought to have risen from the ocean forty million years ago, making it arguably the oldest island in all of the South Pacific. It is, without doubt, the highest coral island in the world, and it possesses the largest tropical rainforest in Tonga. It also features dramatic cliffs, scores of hiking trails, and craggy caves overlooking the ocean. Because it lies farther south, 'Eua usually enjoys cooler temperatures than the rest of the Tongan Islands.

Ha'apai consists of over sixty-two islands scattered over a thirteen thousand square kilometer area of ocean. These are low-lying coral islands, most of which are very small in size. Sandy beaches ring most of the islands of Ha'apai, and some rocky formations dot the coastlines. Ha'apai is notorious for its extensive reef systems, which made it nearly impossible to navigate these islands in early times before they were mapped out. The Volcanic Islands, Kao and Tofua, are the largest islands in the group and boast extensive tracts of forest. The rest of the islands, though, are so small that they are easy to circumnavigate on foot.

There is also an island referred to as "Jack-in-the-box Island," or *fonuafo'ou*, meaning "new land." Jack-in-the-box Island is unusual in that, in the past, it has been submerged in the water as a shoal. However, it periodically appears as an island for

> A new island was formed on the south side of Ha'apai, as a result of a volcanic explosion in 2009.

short periods of time, before disappearing once again into the surrounding sea. Jack-in-the-box Island has been hidden underwater for approximately the last one hundred years.

Vava'u is a beautiful island group, possessing terrain that is at once lush, green, and hilly. The Vava'u island group consists of approximately forty islands. Vava'u's main island guards one of the largest and most protected natural harbors in the

South Pacific. The main island also possesses a couple of beaches, though there are more sandy beaches on the smaller outer islands. Coral reefs pervade the entire group.

Because they are the farthest north and the closest to Samoa, the two Niua Islands are grouped together. However, the islands differ substantially from each other, and they lie quite far—about one hundred kilometers, or sixty miles—apart. Niuatoputapu, to the northeast, has hilly terrain and white sandy beaches, along with a view of nearby Tafahi Island. Niuafoʻou, to the northwest, is a doughnut-shaped volcanic island with steep rocky cliffs, no beaches, and a large interior lake. Its lava fields attest to the numerous volcanic eruptions which have created and shaped the island.

CLIMATE

Tonga's climate is tropical. The Tongan winter lasts from May through late October or early November. Due to the cooler temperatures (averaging 22°C/71°F), combined with the relative lack of humidity, the winter season is the best time to visit Tonga. Since it is such a good time to visit, the Tongan winter is also the country's tourist season. The summer season, which is also, coincidentally, the rainy season, lasts from December through April.

> Although tropical storms and cyclones do occur in Tonga, there is never any thunder there. Visitors will never hear booming thunder crashes or see ligtning bolts, althought they may see lightning travel among the clouds.

Summer temperatures climb to about 27°C/80°F; there is also very high humidity and a lot of rain. Rainstorms can last up to one week during the summer, and cyclones can also hit during this time of year. On average, Tonga experiences about one cyclone per season. In very heavy rains, moderate flooding can occur in lower-lying areas, such as Nukuʻalofa.

Temperatures also vary greatly between the different island groups. ʻEua is the coolest region with the most rainfall, while Vavaʻu and the Niua Islands are the hottest. On the smaller islands, winds and breezes tend to keep everything a little cooler.

VEGETATION

Niu, or coconut trees, stand tall and iconic, emblematic both of the South Pacific and of Tonga in particular. Coconut palm trees grow naturally in Tonga, in abundance. The trees can grow up to thirty meters, or one hundred feet, tall.

Tongans use almost every part of the trees. They feed the coconuts to their livestock: pigs and chickens live on the coconut meat. Tongan boys scurry up the coconut trees to procure green coconuts for drinking, or brown coconuts for the meat needed to make coconut milk for cooking. Palm leaves can be used for thatching, the trunks for wooden building materials. The coconut husks and shells serve as excellent firewood.

Anyone can freely take coconuts from the trees. To open a green coconut for drinking, use a machete to hack open the part of the coconut directly opposite the roots. After that, cut a small square hole out of which to drink. In order to open a brown coconut for the meat, use a machete to hack the coconut open length-wise, or crack it open on a rock. Beware, however: it is never advisable to sit under a coconut tree for shade, especially on windy days, as coconuts often fall out of the tree and onto the ground in strong winds.

Several varieties of pandanus palm trees and bushes grow throughout Tonga. Pandanus palm trees have long, green leaves, which usually grow in bush-like formations. Their long root systems spike out into forks at the bottom of the tree. Pandanus trees are vital to the Tongans, because they use the pandanus leaves to make mats. To do this, they cut the leaves into narrow strands, tie them together, weigh them down, and bleach them in the ocean shallows. Once these strands have spent an adequate amount of time in the salt water to be sufficiently bleached, they are hung out to dry in curled bunches. Once they dry, they are ready to be woven into mats. The mulberry tree is also very important to Tongans. They strip its bark from the tree and pound it into a pulp; they use that pulp to make *tapa* mats. The Tongans also cultivate *kava* plants, which they sell for use in making the *kava* drink. It takes years for the *kava* plants to mature to a point where they can be harvested and sold.

> Tongans grow vanilla. Like *kava* plants, vanilla beans take years to mature.

Because they provide a great deal of shade from the hot, hot sun, giant banyan trees are often planted around public gathering areas such as wharves, schools, and common squares. These trees possess extensive root systems, and vines dangle from their highest branches, stretching to reach for the ground far below them. The relationship between the vines and the banyan tree itself is pretty fascinating. At first, the vines simply grow on the host trees. Eventually, however, the vines completely overtake their host trees. Because these trees have very shallow root systems, they often topple during major storms.

Myriad colorful tropical flowers thrive throughout the Tongan Islands. They grow not only in trees, but also as plants and bushes, in every shape and color imaginable. Their sweet fragrances float through the air along the streets of every village. Tongans use these flowers to make *leis*, and, often, both men and women will place a flower behind their ear or in their hair. The common flower varieties found in Tonga include hibiscus; bird of paradise; allamanda; frangipani; and heilala, the national flower. Only the heilala, however, can boast its own festival, which occurs each July.

Fruit trees flourish in Tonga, from mango trees to banana trees to breadfruit trees to papaya trees. Banana and papaya trees bear fruit all year-long. The large breadfruit trees usually bear fruit twice a year. When the breadfruit are fully ripened, they are nearly the same size as a human head. Mango trees have the shortest season, bearing fruit for one to two months, beginning in November. Pineapple plantations also dot the isles of Tonga; the majority of pineapples grown in Tonga grow in Vava'u during the winter season. Other fruits found on the islands include lemon, small sour oranges, passion fruit, avocado, guava, and many varieties of banana. Any mangoes found in the bush are fair game for the taking. When any given fruit is in-season, it is generally available at a very low price, either at the local markets or on roadside stands.

LAND INHABITANTS

Tonga also houses many land creatures, including dogs, chickens, pigs, cats, cows, horses, goats, rats, and the famous flying fox. As a matter of fact, the flying fox is actually a large fruit bat that lives throughout Tonga. These large bats, or *peka*, usually emerge at dusk to feed on fruit. Since the *peka* are considered to be sacred, their meat is a delicacy which can only be eaten by the royal family. However, despite the fact that it is illegal, the locals sometimes hunt and eat the bats anyway.

A few reptiles also exist in Tonga. These include iguanas, which are fairly rare; and *moko*, or small geckos, which can often be seen inside of buildings emitting high-pitched squeaking noises. There are no snakes on land; only sea snakes live in Tonga.

While some creepy-crawly creatures live in Tonga, the good news is that none of the land creatures there are lethally poisonous. Common insects in Tonga include large flying cockroaches, ants, small millipedes, mosquitoes, a large biting centipede, and a few varieties of large, harmless spiders, or *hina*. It is important to watch out for mosquitoes and for biting centipedes. Although prevalent year-round, the "mosquito season" occurs during the hot, rainy season from November through April. While most mosquitoes are harmless, it is possible to contract dengue fever (pg 82) from a bite from one of the black-and-white mosquitoes. Mosquitoes are most active at dawn and dusk. Some safeguards against mosquito bites include repellent sprays, mosquito coils, mosquito nets, and protective clothes, which cover as much of the skin as possible.

The biting centipede, or *molokau*, is usually black or brown in color, and it can run very fast. Sometimes, the small baby *molokau* appears almost blue in color. Once fully grown, the adult *molokau* can reach a length of up to twelve inches and a thickness of up to one inch. The *molokau* emerge from their holes when it rains; while they are more common in the bush and in long grassy areas, they can also be found in buildings, on occasion. (For information on the *molokau*, see page 83.)

Tongan birds include sea-faring frigate birds; wader birds, like the Pacific golden plover and Pacific black duck; swiftlets; Pacific swallows; the Tongan whistler, or *hengehenga*; and the blue-crowned lorikeets, or *henga*. In 'Eua, bright, color-

> Due to the vast distance between Tonga and other, larger land masses, no seagulls live in Tonga.

ful parrots live in the rainforest. In Niuafo'ou, the rare, endangered Niuafo'ou megapode birds make their homes; these are the last surviving megapodes in Tonga. The megapodes are large, flightless birds. They lay their large eggs in the warm volcanic soil to incubate. The megapode teeters on the brink of extinction, due to overhunting by both humans and animals. While the megapode is said to be protected on Niuafo'ou, the locals still poach its eggs. Fortunately, both the island's remote location and its small population have helped save this rare bird. Furthermore, some of the megapode eggs have also been transferred to other uninhabited islands in an attempt to try to save the population.

MARINE LIFE

An abundant variety of marine life flourishes in the large reef systems surrounding Tonga. The water clarity, the brilliant colors, and the preserved, untouched reefs yield unbelievable snorkeling and diving experiences. (See page 75 for more information on diving and snorkeling.)

Some of the fish species swimming in the Tongan waters include trevally, parrot fish, yellow fin tuna, barracuda, moray eel, lion fish, clown fish, red snapper, puffer fish, flying fish, blue marlin, surgeon fish, stone fish, wahoo, and many, many others. Snorkelers and divers will observe a brilliant array of fish of all colors, sizes, and shapes. Often, these fish won't even blink at the presence of humans; in fact, they will often allow divers to get quite close to them. Humpback whales also swim the Tongan waters in the winter season, along with sting ray, manta ray, and spinner dolphins. Many varieties of shark also patrol the waters, including blacktip and whitetip reef sharks, gray reef sharks, hammerhead sharks, oceanic white tip sharks, and leopard sharks. While the sharks may look terrifying, the reef sharks are generally harmless.

Many sea turtle species, including the hawksbill, green, loggerhead, and leatherback turtles, also spend time in Tongan waters. All of these species are listed as endangered yet are still threatened by local fishing. Fortunately, some laws protect certain species, and Tongans may only hunt the male turtles during the turtle-hunting season.

The Tongan reefs also house giant clams which, like the megapode, face possible extinction. Beginning in the 1980s, community clam circle projects began, in which the giant clams were placed in shallow waters in circles in order to help them reproduce so that their population could increase. However, the giant clams are still hunted and harvested frequently.

Foreigners have also been harvesting and hunting marine life in Tonga, causing grave environmental concern. Fishermen often harvest and hunt large numbers of sea slugs, certain types of tropical fish, and even some sharks, which are used in Asian countries to make shark fin soup. In response, some protected marine areas have been established around some of the Tongan Islands, including the islands of Ha'afeva and O'ua, in Ha'apai.

The Tongan Islands host a wide variety of coral, including hard and soft corals. The coral appear in countless shapes, colors, and forms, including bright red sea fans, brain coral, and fan coral. Some stretches of Tongan sea even contain underwater caves and coral archways. Inside of the reefs, big bright blue starfish abound.

DANGERS

Though wildlife is—by its very nature—unpredictable, in general, few animals will attack human beings unless provoked. Nevertheless, it is prudent to beware of several aquatic animals in Tonga.

Nofu, or stonefish, are flat, brown fish which live on the ocean floor, usually in murky conditions. The best way to guard against a stonefish sting is to wear shoes or sandals while walking the ocean, and to shuffle along the ocean bottom. These precautions are well worth the trouble as stepping on a stonefish is always very painful, and sometimes lethal. Anyone who does step on a stonefish needs to seek immediate medical assistance. They should also allow Tongans to treat the wound with whatever local medicines they feel appropriate.

'Anga, or reef sharks, generally avoid people, although an encounter with one will definitely start the adrenaline pumping. Should a person become uncomfortable around a reef shark, they should slowly back away, always facing the shark. Larger sharks in deep water pose more of a threat although, more often, the sharks will steer clear of humans.

Other potential dangers in the ocean include sea snakes, moray eel, and lion fish. Although sea snakes have incredibly venomous bite, their jaws are too small to injure humans (unless they manage to attack a little finger). Moray eel will only bite if provoked. Thus, as a local saying warns, "stick your hand in a crack, and you won't get it back." Eel teeth face backward, back inside their own mouths. Therefore, although a person's immediate natural reaction to an eel bite would be to yank their hand back out of the eel's mouth, that would be a very bad, painful idea. If a person is bitten by an eel, they simply need to wait until the eel releases their hand in order to avoid further injury from the teeth. The good news is that, like sharks, eels will usually avoid humans. To avoid eel bites, divers simply should not stick their hands or fingers in cracks in the reef.

In addition, some varieties of jellyfish live in Tonga, and they can sting. It is also wise to avoid touching any coral in the water, because some coral can sting as well. In fact, scraping up against coral can sometimes actually cause an infection. The black spiny sea urchins in the reefs also have a venomous sting. And lion fish may be pretty, but keep your distance and don't touch them as they are poisonous. A good general rule for divers is to look, but not touch, when in the ocean.

ENVIRONMENTAL CONCERNS

Pollution

Upon arriving on Tonga, it is hard not to be struck by the excess of garbage lying around the island, including plastic bags, tin cans, glass, even old rusting vehicles! While all this litter might seem careless, there is, in fact, an explanation for this phenomenon. Modern packaging and manufactured goods were only introduced to Tonga very recently, historically-speaking. Before the Europeans came to Tonga, Tongans would throw their leftovers and waste on the ground, where it would either disintegrate naturally or be eaten by animals. The Tongans wrapped their food in leaves in order to cook it in the underground ovens, and they drank from coconut shells. Since everything was biodegradable, they grew accustomed to tossing their waste on the ground because most, if not all, of it would simply disappear.

Land pollution has also become prevalent in Tonga because there is very little space on these tiny islands for trash disposal, especially on the outer islands. In the small villages of Ha'apai and 'Eua, as well as on the outer islands of Vava'u, no trash collection service exists, because there is no landfill to which they can take the garbage. Tongans either burn their trash or dump it in the bush. Tin cans and glass, however, will neither burn nor disintegrate. Sometimes, Tongans will simply bury these items in the sand. Those who are more knowledgeable may crush the glass into small pieces, so that it may be reused in cement.

Any recycling operation, however, seems an impossible dream. There are no recycling centers in Tonga, and it is unlikely that they will build any, due to prohibitive shipping costs, difficult logistics, and the general lack of reimbursement available for such efforts. Landfills do exist on the main islands

> While there is no centralized recycling program, some private businesses do collect recycling and ship it overseas.

of Tongatapu and Vava'u, but they are filling up very quickly, so many people still opt to burn their trash regardless. Foreign-funded clean-up projects have occurred, but they have not proven to be sustainable in the long term. Some Tongans have become more perceptive to this growing problem and are beginning to do more in order to help clean up their villages and coastlines.

Coastal Erosion

Since the nation lies so close to sea level, Tongans can no longer ignore the problems of climate change and coastal erosion. While rising sea levels may present a potential future issue to other, larger countries, the issue is already a terrifying reality in Tonga. The low-lying Ha'apai Islands are the most at-risk. Houses which used to sit on long, flat beaches are now nearly in the ocean; the residents fight the encroaching water with sandbags and seawalls. While every cyclone and storm has always had the potential to alter Tonga's coastlines, now, more than ever, the coastlines are shrinking at very noticeable rate. Trees are being uprooted and surrounded by ocean. This problem is largely due to global climate change and the ensuing repercussions on ocean levels. Local Tongan communities have also exacerbated the problem by building land causeways through the ocean and cutting down trees along the coastline. Because there has been some work to raise awareness of this issue locally, groups have begun planting new trees along coastlines.

Basics

Getting There

Flights arrive into Fua'amotu Airport (TBU) in Nu-
ku'alofa, Tongatapu from Auckland, Sydney, and Fiji.
Three airlines serve Tonga: Air New Zealand, Pacific
Blue, and Air Pacific. Air New Zealand flies directly into
Tonga five days a week from Auckland; Pacific Blue, a

> Fua'amotu Airport
> lies about forty-five
> minues away from
> Nuku'alofa by car.

subsidiary of Virgin Airlines, flies to Tonga twice each week from Sydney and Auckland; and Air Pacific flies to Tonga three days a week from Brisbane, Sydney, and Los
Angeles, with a layover in Fiji. Air Pacific usually offers the cheapest fare, although
Air New Zealand does offer great deals a few times each year. Air New Zealand also
offers better in-flight service than its competitors.

Those who plan travel to other islands in Tonga besides Tongatapu should not
plan to return to Tongatapu on the same day as their departing international flight. It
is always prudent to allow at least one day of leeway, because local flights are subject
to change or cancellation without notice, and ferry schedules are often unpredictable

---

Packing List

- ✓ Sunscreen
- ✓ Mosquito repellent
- ✓ Beach towel
- ✓ Sunglasses, sun hat
- ✓ Flashlight
- ✓ Plug-in adaptors, the same as those used in Australia and New Zealand
- ✓ Medicines: Tylenol, Benadryl, Band-Aids, antibiotic ointment
- ✓ Hand sanitizer
- ✓ Books for reading
- ✓ Comfortable sandals
- ✓ Women's clothing for towns: long skirts (at least knee-length), or knee-length ca-
  pri pants, t-shirts which cover the shoulder
- ✓ Men's clothing for towns: knee-length shorts or pants, t-shirts; men can also buy
  a *tupenu*, or wraparound skirt, once they have arrived

and dependent upon weather.

Though the international and domestic airports are located right next to each other, the commute between the two requires a five minute cab ride. In order to take a taxi, local currency will be needed, including smaller bills to make change. Currency can be changed at the international airport; there is also an ATM there.

Upon leaving Tonga, every person must pay a departure tax of TOP$25. This tax, levied at the airport, is payable in local currency only.

Those headed to Tonga from the United States will need to fly in through Auckland, Sydney, or Fiji. Many flights to these cities depart from Los Angeles or from another West Coast city. The flight from Los Angeles to Auckland, New Zealand takes approximately thirteen hours; many major airlines make this flight. In fact, anyone planning a visit to Fiji, Australia, or New Zealand will find that Tonga can easily be added into their travel itinerary to the region.

European travelers have two options: they can fly either east, through the United States, or west, through Asia, in order to reach Tonga. Traveling through the United States will allow for a larger baggage allowance than will traveling through Asia. To find the lowest fares, it is generally best to book directly with the airlines, not through a travel website. *Airlines: www.airnewzealand.com, www.flypacificblue.com, www.airpacific.com*

Another way to travel to Tonga is by boat: either by cruise ship or by private yacht. Cruise ships make stops in both Nuku'alofa, Tongatapu; and Neiafu, Vava'u. Some cruise ships also pass by the Niua Islands to the far north. Usually, the ships will only make a quick stop in each location. In Nuku'alofa, workers are busily reconstructing Vuna Wharf in order to accommodate more cruise ships and tourism. This project is scheduled to be completed in 2012. Anyone who arrives by yacht must register at the local customs office in each island group.

When to Go

The tourist season in Tonga takes place during the Tongan winter, which lasts from May through October or November. During this season, the weather is not too hot, the rain less frequent, and the chance of cyclones and other storms smaller. Tonga's winter months also coincide with the time period when humpback whales migrate into Tonga from Antarctica. During Tonga's "off-season," from December to April, there is a higher risk of storms or rainy weather. However, there are also cheaper prices on accommodations and activities during the off-season. Check the latest information on forecasts, sunrise and sunset times, and tide information online, at http://www.met.gov.to/.

Visa Information

Everyone who arrives in Tonga receives a free thirty-day visitor's visa; the only document required in order to receive this visa is an onward ticket out of Tonga. The visitor's visa strictly prohibits employment in Tonga, due to Tonga's high unemployment rate. Those who plan to work in Tonga must apply for a working permit prior to arrival.

Most nationalities do not need to obtain a visa prior to arrival in Tonga. Those traveling to Tonga from Australia, Austria, Barbados, Belgium, Brazil, Brunei Darussalam, Bulgaria, Canada, Cook Islands, Cyprus, Czech Republic, Denmark, Dominica, Estonia, Federated States of Micronesia, Fiji, Finland, France, French Polynesia (New Caledonia, Tahiti, Wallis & Futuna), Germany, Greece, Hungary, Ireland, Italy, Japan, Kiribati, Latvia, Lithuania, Luxembourg, Malaysia, Malta, Marshall Islands, Monaco, Nauru, Netherlands, New Zealand, Niue, Norway, Palau, Papua New Guinea, Poland, Portugal, Republic of Korea, Romania, Russia, Samoa, Seychelles, Singapore, Solomon Islands, Slovakia, Slovenia, Spain, St Kitts & Nevis, St Lucia, St Vincent & the Grenadines, Sweden, Switzerland, The Bahamas, Turkey, Tuvalu, Ukraine, United Kingdom, the United States of America, and Vanuatu need not apply for a visa prior to arrival. All other nationalities must apply for a visa before entering Tonga.

In order to extend a stay beyond thirty days, contact the Immigration Department in Nuku'alofa, or the Immigration Department in Neiafu, Vava'u, which is located inside the Tonga Development Bank. *Nuku'alofa location phone: 26970 or 26969, Neiafu location phone: 71142 or 71149.*

Embassies in Tongatapu

Australia phone: 23244

New Zealand phone: 23122

United Kingdom phone: 24395

China phone: 24554

Netherlands phone: 23654

Sweden phone: 25269

Japan phone: 22221

Americans in need of diplomatic assistance in Tonga should contact the US Peace Corps office, because the nearest US embassy is located in Fiji. The phone number for the Peace Corps is 25466.

Getting Around

INTER-ISLAND FLIGHTS

Currently, one local airline, Chathams Pacific, serves all of the local airports throughout Tonga. Chathams Pacific offers daily flights between Tongatapu, 'Eua, Ha'apai, and Vava'u. About once a week, Chathams Pacific also offers flights to the Niua Islands, with a layover in Vava'u. The Tongatapu – 'Eua flight's claim to fame is that it is the shortest commercial flight in the world, lasting a whopping eight minutes! The flight into the island of Lifuka, Ha'apai is interesting, since the runway runs the entire width of the island from east to west. To first-time visitors, it appears that the plane is landing on water! For that flight, try to get a seat on the left-hand side of the plane flying into Ha'apai in order to see all of the tiny island atolls, sandbars, and reefs from the plane window. The flight into Vava'u is gorgeous as well. On either side of the plane, passengers will see all of the tiny islands, along with the waterway inlets which lead up to the main island.

Three planes operate for Chathams: a small plane, which holds eight people and in which, sometimes, one lucky passenger gets to sit in the co-pilot seat; a medium-sized plane, which holds eighteen people, with passengers sitting on each side of an aisle; and a large plane, which holds up to sixty people, with overhead compartments for carry-on luggage. Although on Tongatapu the domestic airport is located next to the international airport, travelers must nonetheless take a taxi to get from one airport to the other. All of the terminals are fairly basic. Chathams Pacific also recently began to offer scenic flights over Tongatapu, 'Eua, and Vava'u in a restored DC3 vintage aircraft.

Chathams Pacific also offers Kingdom Passes, which offer multiple stops throughout Tonga. Those who wish to visit more than two island groups will want to make the investment: for these travelers, the Kingdom Pass is a good deal. In the off season, prices start at TOP$390 for three destinations and can cost as much as TOP$693 for four destinations during high season.

The following prices are based on all round-trip flights out of Tongatapu.

One-way prices:

Tongatapu to 'Eua: TOP$70

Tongatapu to Ha'apai: TOP$70

Tongatapu to Vava'u: TOP$231

Tongatapu to Niuas: TOP$500

Tickets can also be purchased at any of the airports in Tonga or online at www.chathamspacfic.com and by phone at 28852.

FERRIES

For budget in-country travel, try taking the ferry from one island to another. These are not day trips as the ferry takes approximately twelve hours to travel from Tongatapu to Ha'apai, and eighteen hours to travel from Tongatapu to Vava'u, depending upon weather conditions.

Two ferries operate in Tonga: the *MV Pulapaki* and the new *MV 'Otuanga'ofa*, which was a gift, recently donated to Tonga by Japan. The ferries usually run between the island groups of Tongatapu, Ha'apai, and Vava'u once a week. One of the ferries travels to the Niua Islands, north of Vava'u, about once each month and occasionally the ferry will also stop at the island of Nomuka in Ha'apai.

Those planning to take the ferry should be prepared for substandard conditions, extremely crowded passenger space, and seasickness. People sit on boxes and luggage on the different levels of the ferry. If the weather is nice, passengers can get fresh air by sitting on the outer decks. Locals will bring plastic mats on which they can sit; they also pack meals and snacks for the trip. Usually, the bathrooms are not very clean. Most likely, the newest ferry will have better conditions onboard. Often, the ferries travel at night and, on clear nights, the star-gazing is incredible. Disembarking at the local wharves is an experience in and of itself. It is an organized chaos, of people greeting relatives and friends, others unloading boxes, and general hubbub everywhere—an amount of activity evocative of an anthill. At the smaller island of Ha'afeva, Ha'apai, the unloading sometimes occurs at sea using smaller boats to transport people and cargo to the shore.

The ferry schedules often change at a moment's notice. Therefore, travelers are highly encouraged to simply spend the extra money to take a flight, unless they are operating on a very low budget and have no time constraints. Another

> A major tragedy occurred in August 2009 with the *Princess Ashika* ferry. See page 145 for more details.

thing to note is that local ferries often are not up to code, and they can, in fact, be dangerous. *Cost from Tongatapu: TOP$34/one way to Ha'apai and TOP$44/one way to Vava'u.*

Two additional ferries also operate between Tongatapu and 'Eua once each day: the *MV Alaimoana* and the *MV 'Ikale*. These ferries depart in the early afternoon to go to 'Eua, and return to Tongatapu very early in the mornings. Many currents meet in the channel between 'Eua and Tongatapu, so it is common to feel seasick on this rough voyage. However, this ferry is often the best way to travel to 'Eua, and it is the way that most locals travel. *Cost: TOP$25 - $27/one way*

LOCAL TRANSPORTATION

General descriptions of the many types of local travel available within Tonga follow. More specific information can be found under each island section.

Local Boats

Local boats are a good option for transit within each island group. In fact, riding a local boat can be a great way to experience local life. These boats are small and they often have a little compartment at the front, made from local wood and painted bright colors. These boats have small, slow engines. Tongans crowd into these small boats, and they often use the boats between islands to transport supplies like boxes of food, coolers of fish, trays of eggs, and often live animals. The passengers pack in tightly to fill the boat, sitting on supply boxes or sprawling out on the floor. Finally, when it seems that the boat cannot hold one more person, even more people will jump in and sit along the boat's edges. Boats are always filled overcapacity, and they usually possess no lifejackets or safety gear.

The local skippers are truly amazing. In the past, there have been overloaded local boats, where the boat rim itself sagged down to water level in stormy conditions. Still, the skippers managed to steer the boat through monstrous waves into port, without so much as a drop of water splashing into the boat. They know both their boats and the sea conditions remarkably well.

To find out more information about taking a local boat, visitors can inquire at their guesthouse, the Tonga Visitors Bureau, or the wharf. The skippers usually ask for a small fee from each passenger in order to help pay for gas; fees can range from

TOP$10 - $30 each way, depending upon distance. Unlike commercial boats, local boats usually operate on their own time, so they rarely stick to a strict schedule. Boat travel also depends heavily on the weather; a good rule of thumb is not to venture out on the sea when the wind is blowing above thirty knots. In order to be safe, it pays to do as the locals do, as Tongans generally will not go out on the sea when it is too dangerous to do so.

Buses

There are local buses on Tongatapu, Vava'u, and Ha'apai. Most of these vehicles are privately-owned. Traveling by bus can be a cheap and interesting travel experience, though often frustrating, because the schedules change frequently (that is, if they exist at all). Usually, the buses head into the main cities in the morning—to transport kids to school and adults to work—and return to the villages in the afternoon or evening. The exception to this is on the main island, Tongatapu, where buses run

---

Vaka

One time, we had decided to travel the Tongan way: we would hitch a ride with a *vaka*, a local boat. The boat was headed for an island located just south of an uninhabited island, upon which we were planning to camp. Since some of our neighbor's relatives hailed from that region, we had arranged the ride through his sister. That Friday, we were all packed and sitting at home, waiting to leave. The neighbor had told us that we would leave by mid-morning for the boat, and people kept bustling to and fro over at the neighbor's house, going to church functions in town. (We of course hadn't the slightest clue what was happening.) At one point in the late afternoon, they even said "hurrying" in Tongan, before simply disappearing for several hours.

Then, all of a sudden, everyone rushed back, and our neighbor yelled a loud, urgent, "NOW!" We ran out of the house, caught a ride to the old wharf, and found that the small wooden boats were waiting. (*Who knows how long they had been there?*) By this time, it was about 5:30 pm, leaving us with just enough time to make it to our destination before night fell. That's the disadvantage of traveling the Tongan way—it's always very slow.

At the old wharf, about forty Tongans were scurrying busily around among three boats. We handed our camping gear and bags to people already in the boat, before taking our seats along the outside ledge of the small boat. Due to all of the weight inside, the boats were sagging so low in the water that the ocean was threatening to breach the rims on both sides of every craft. The ocean was fairly rough that day; to me, it resembled a painting, with all of the pointed waves swaying up and down slowly in the glossy last hours of daylight.

The Tongan boat skippers, however, easily overcame the challenge before them. Racing the fast-fading light, they maneuvered among the huge, rolling waves, allowing not so much as a drip of water to enter the boat. Once we reached the island on which we planned to camp, we had to throw all of our supplies out of the boat onto the beach—timing this, of course, between waves in order to prevent all of our camping supplies from being soaked. Since we were the only passengers heading to the uninhabited island before us, we had to simply jump into the ocean and swim ashore while the boat, still loaded with people, continued on to the other islands.

- Kate Asleson

more regularly throughout the day. While all buses are very old, some of the buses in Nuku'alofa are painted to resemble big tins of Palm canned beef.

More specific information about bus travel is located within each island section of this book.

> Often, the buses blast incredibly loud music, and they become quite over-crowded at busy times of the day.

Taxis

There are numerous taxi companies on Tongatapu, and a few on Vava'u. In addition, some private cars operate as taxis in Ha'apai. Taxi meters are nonexistent: the drivers or company will simply quote a price for a given route. When taking a taxi, it is imperative to negotiate the price before the ride begins. Most Tongan taxis are older, run-down cars, although some larger van taxis exist in larger urban areas. In Tongatapu and Vava'u, taxis are marked cars, easily identified as taxis. It is not uncommon to wind up sharing the taxi with other paying customers, or with other Tongans who know the taxi driver.

> Taxi prices from airports into town:
>
> Tongatapu Airport to Nuku'alofa: TOP$40/one-way, 45 minutes
>
> Ha'apai Airport to Pangai: TOP$8/one-way, 5 minutes
>
> Ha'apai Airport to Resorts on Foa: TOP$30/one-way, 15 minutes
>
> Vava'u Airport to Neiafu: TOP$20/one-way, 15 minutes
>
> *There are no taxis in 'Eua or the Niuas.*

Car Rentals

It is possible to rent a car in Nuku'alofa and in Neiafu; drivers need to remember to drive on the left-hand side of the road. It is also possible to inquire about arranging a private, independent car rental in other locations. There is not a single stoplight or stop sign in all of Tonga. The Tongans use roundabouts for traffic control. Gas stations are located in the main cities of each island group; gas prices can be quite high.

Bicycle Rentals

Renting a bike provides a great, affordable opportunity to explore the islands more in-depth without being constrained by anyone else's schedule. Bikers beware, however: some bike rental companies may not keep their bikes in top condition. Average rental prices range from approximately TOP$15 to TOP$30 daily.

Hitchhiking

Suto, or hitchhiking, is very commonplace among the locals; it is also (usually) quite safe. It is not uncommon for a truckload of Tongans to stop and ask pedestrians if they need a lift. Anyone who wishes to try hitchhiking should walk along the left shoulder of the road and wave their right arm in a downward motion to the vehicles approaching them from behind. Women traveling alone should make sure that there are other women in the vehicle into which they are entering.

Walking

What could be better than simply strolling along the beach, or wandering through traditional Tongan villages? The Tongan phrase *aka aka maka*, "just kicking rocks," is a slang term meaning walking; *eva pe* means "just wandering around." In keeping with the laid-back pace of life which pervades these islands, travelers will likely find themselves taking a lot of walks, just wandering around.

Money & Costs

The *pa'anga*, the Tongan currency, comes in denominations of TOP$1, $2, $5, $10, $20, $50, and $100. It can be very difficult to break the $50 and $100 bills in villages, smaller islands, and even in smaller stores in Nuku'alofa. It is best to carry

> All of the prices listed in this guidebook are given in local currency, unless otherwise noted.

Basics

smaller bills if possible, especially when going to the market or taking local transportation. *Seniti*, Tongan coins, come in denominations of 5, 10, 20, and 50.

Local establishments usually do not accept credit cards, only local currency. Some larger resorts may accept credit cards; they will ask for the card either at that time that the reservation is made or at the time when the visitor departs. Rarely will any Tongan business accept foreign currency.

All prices in Tonga include a 15% consumption tax which is almost always built into the cost of goods and services. On occasion, some establishments will give the price without including this tax, so it never hurts to make sure the "CT" tax is included in the cost. There are duty-free shops in the airport, in both the arrival and departure areas.

Several banks operate in Tonga, including Westpac, ANZ, and the Tonga Development Bank. All of these banks are closed on Sundays and close early on Saturdays. There are ATMs in Tonga's main towns: Nuku'alofa, Tongatapu; and Neiafu, Vava'u. In Ha'apai, 'Eua, and the Niua Islands, it is only possible to obtain money from inside of the bank at the counter during the bank's normal hours of op-

> It is not customary to tip for services in Tonga. Tips or donations are accepted only at fundraisers, where Tongans perform dances in order to raise money for a specific cause.

eration. Therefore, it is important to plan ahead for the weekend. Those who use a bank with no ATM machine will need their passport in order to withdraw money with their debit card or to cash travelers' checks. It is also possible to receive money transfers from overseas at Western Union and MoneyGram.

AVERAGE COSTS

For travelers operating on a budget, average costs for accommodation can range from TOP$15 to TOP$50 per night, while daily food costs will average between TOP$20 to TOP$40 per day. Dependent upon individual budget and interests, daily costs for activities and transportation can range from TOP$0 to TOP$15 per day.

For those tourists interested in slightly more luxurious accommodations, dining, and activities, average daily accommodation costs can begin at TOP$200, food costs can range from TOP$50 to TOP$100 per day, and costs for activities and transportation can range from TOP$0 to TOP$200 per day. Finally, for travelers with larger budgets, daily costs can vary widely, depending upon location and activities. However, high budget travelers can expect the cost of traveling in Tonga to be at least TOP$250 per day.

Exchange Rates

1 TOP = 0.56 USD
= 0.39 Euro
= 0.53 AUD
= 0.69 NZD

Electricity

Tonga's electricity system uses 240 Volts and the same type of plugs as in Australia and New Zealand. In the main cities of Nuku'alofa, Neiafu, and Pangai, there is usually electricity twenty-four hours a day. On smaller islands and in more remote villages, electricity may operate more intermittently. On very remote islands, if there is any electricity at all, it will come from a generator and last only a few hours each night.

Communications

The international country code to call Tonga is 676. Local phone numbers may have a different amount of numbers, depending upon the cell phone provider used. While some businesses still use land lines, many Tongans today use only cell phones.

Two cell phone networks exist in Tonga: Digicel and TCC. Digicel is a foreign company operating in many developing countries around the world. TCC, on the other hand, is a Tongan government-owned company. Both companies offer similar coverage, though sometimes one will have a better signal than the other in remote villages. It's not uncommon for calls to be dropped or for service to cut out suddenly. Travelers planning a longer trip in Tonga, or who need an easy connection to communication, may wish to purchase a cheap phone and SIM card to use during their stay. The cheapest cell phones cost around TOP$40, including the SIM card. Alternately, anyone with an unlocked international phone can simply buy a SIM card and use their phone in Tonga.

There are no monthly cell phone plans; cell phone users just purchase prepaid phone cards to add minutes to their phones. Phone cards are available for purchase at most local stores. Since so many Tongans have relatives overseas, there are usually good deals for calling New Zealand, Australia, and the United States.

Internet usage is steadily increasing throughout Tonga, though the connection speed is much slower there than it is in other nations (for instance, in the United States and in Western Europe). There are Internet cafés in the main towns in each island group. Beware, however: many local computers have viruses—virus protection software is not yet common in Tonga—and run very slowly. Some guesthouses and hotels offer Internet service as well. Those who bring their own laptops will find that there are also Wi-Fi connections in the main cities.

A local radio station broadcasts out of Nuku'alofa, featuring Tongan music, older Western music, local news in Tongan, and about twenty minutes of BBC News in English each day. On the main islands, it is also possible to pick up some foreign radio stations, such as Radio Australia and Radio New Zealand. One local TV station broadcasts out of Nuku'alofa, featuring local news, island events, and twenty minutes of BBC news in English daily. Some satellite channels are also available to those who pay for satellite service and a satellite dish. It is usually possible to find satellite TV at restaurants and bars that cater to tourists, as well as at the local *kava* club establishments where Tongans gather to watch rugby.

There are a number local newspapers, several only available in Tongan. The *Matangi Tonga* (www.matangitonga.to) is in English. Another popular newspaper, the *Taimi 'O Tonga* (www.taimionline.com), is very critical of the government, which has caused the paper's editor to be jailed in the past. Another locally published newspaper, the *Faite,* deals exclusively with women's issues.

There are post offices in the main city of each island group. Since all international mail must travel through Nuku'alofa, it is fastest to send and receive mail through there. The post offices usually operate from 8 am to 4:30 pm on weekdays, with a one-hour break for lunch taking place between 12:30 pm and 1:30 pm. Though the mail service is fairly reliable, it may take two to four weeks for mail sent from Tonga to arrive internationally.

There is a DHL courier office (phone: 27-700 or 23-617) in Nuku'alofa.

Tourist Information

For tourist information, suggestions, and booking assistance, the Tonga Visitors Bureau (TVB) is invaluable. The TVB is a government ministry for tourism and it has offices on each of the main islands, including one in Nuku'alofa, Tongatapu; Pangai, Ha'apai; Neiafu, Vava'u; and 'Eua. TVB has brochures, cultural information, and helpful, English-speaking staff members who can make local bookings for travelers. Generally, the main TVB office in Nuku'alofa is the most helpful and knowledgeable. *www.tongaholiday.com, Tongatapu phone: 25334, Ha'apai phone: 60733, Va-*

Best Tongan Non-Required Reading

A few great, quick reads about the South Pacific region are written by J. Maarten Troost: *The Sex Lives of Cannibals* and *Getting Stoned with Savages.* These humorous books detail the author's accounts of living in Kiribati and Vanuatu with his girlfriend. Those interested in the history of Tonga should check out William Mariner's book *An Account of the Natives of the Tonga Islands.* Tourists interested in ancient Oceanic travel techniques may be interested to read *The Last Navigator,* by Stephen D. Thomas. Finally, travelers interested in the astronomy of the South Pacific seas should visit the little Mac store in Nuku'alofa and ask the owner about the astronomy book that he has published. He may even have a few of the books in stock. For information on marine life, many of the local dive shops sell guidebooks on endemic fish species.

va'u phone: 70115, see maps in each island section for locations.

There is also a Tourism Tonga organization in Nuku'alofa. They provide a great deal of helpful information on their website, www.thekingdomoftonga.com.

Accommodations

A range of accommodation types are available throughout Tonga, from high-end resorts to small guesthouses to simple beach shacks. The high-end resorts—on the west side of Tongatapu; in Nuku'alofa; in Foa, Ha'apai; and in Vava'u—will have hot water, private bathrooms, Internet connections, and many more convenient amenities. Most of these resorts accept credit cards. The mid-range hotels and guesthouses may or may not have hot water. Some may also feature shared bathrooms and kitchen facilities, in lieu of having a restaurant. These guesthouses usually accept cash only. Budget accommodations will have shared bathrooms and basic rooms.

Visitors should not come to Tonga expecting accommodations in the style of Western franchise resorts; there are no resorts of this type in Tonga. Each business and accommodation is independent. Some are run by foreigners, while some are owned and operated by locals. It is important to note that the villages and larger cities can be quite bit noisy, so anyone who is sensitive to noise should be sure to pack earplugs. Throughout the night, there are often packs of dogs fighting and barking outside and, beginning in the early morning hours, roosters crow and, on Sundays, church bells chime. While camping is not common in Tonga, it can be done at some budget accommodations on smaller islands.

> In general, high-end accommodations can range from TOP$200 to $1,000 per night; mid-range can range from TOP$80 to $200 per night; and budget accomodation can be as low as TOP$15 per person, per night.

Price ranges vary greatly depending on the type of accommodation and location within the country. Generally, in areas where there are more tourists, like Tongatapu and Vava'u, prices tend to be higher. In more remote locations, it is easy to find cheaper accommodations. However, it is usually more expensive to reach these remote locations in the first place.

Local Business Hours

Tongan businesses tend to operate on "island time," meaning that they do not operate according to consistent, normal hours of operation. Shop owners often live adjacent to their business so it's common for people to walk up and yell "*faifakatau*," meaning "shopkeeper," for assistance. Most foreign-owned stores will operate according to normal business hours, sometimes remaining open late into the evening and opening very early in the morning. Banks, post offices, and other offices are usually open from about 8:30 am to 4 pm, taking an hour-long break for lunch around noon.

Almost all businesses are closed on Sundays. Because they bake all of their bread on Sundays, bakeries are the only type of business allowed to be open that day without special permission. In many places, the bakery will serve as the local hangout on Sundays, as a meeting place for people to talk and socialize.

Other types of businesses must apply for special permits to operate on Sundays. In Nuku'alofa, some Chinese restaurants are open on Sundays. In most other places, however, everything besides the bakery remains closed. So it is important to plan ahead by buying necessary food and other supplies on Saturday.

Water

No one in Tonga drinks water from the tap because it is untreated and not safe to drink. Tap water is used only for brushing teeth, taking showers, and doing laundry. Locals also use the tap water to wash dishes and to rinse food.

Tongans get their drinking water from rainwater tanks, which collect water from the gutters on the rooftops. Rainwater tanks are called *sima vai*, or "cement water." *Sima vai* can be either plastic or cement tanks, which are then connected to houses and buildings. While Tongans drink water right out of the tank, visitors are advised to boil their water before drinking it, in order to kill any parasites that may exist and to reduce the risk of an upset stomach. Since Tongans drink rainwater, it can be difficult to find drinking water during the dry winter season, especially in cases of drought. However, bottled water is available at most local stores.

> Drinking rainwater will help avoid creating extra waste from plastic water bottles on these small islands.

Eating

While food in Tonga is generally very safe, food preparation there may not always fall in line with Western standards. This means that travelers might get sick from the food that they consume, depending on what and where they choose to eat. Because boiling and baking will kill any bacteria which might be living in the food, it is best to eat food that has been prepared in those ways in order to avoid illness. When consuming fresh fruit or vegetables, rinse them in rainwater, not tap water. As anywhere, eating raw fish does carry a risk, even though sashimi is one of the best dishes in Tonga. However, raw fish in Tonga are safer to eat than those in some other Pacific Island nations, where the fish often have ciguatera poisoning. Another Tongan specialty around which to be cautious is 'otai, the local fruit drink. This delicious fresh fruit-based drink is usually made by mixing the fruit with unboiled rainwater, which can easily make the drinker sick.

Anyone who eats with local Tongans will likely be shocked by the unbelievable amount of food that their hosts serve them when they sit down to dinner. The Tongan hosts will, most likely, just sit and watch their guests eat, attending to their every need, before they themselves sit down to eat. When they do sit down, it will be to eat whatever food happens to be leftover after the guests have finished eating. If it is a hot day, the Tongan hosts may even fan their dinner guests. Visitors should keep in mind that, if eating alone makes them uncomfortable, they can always ask their Tongan hosts to eat with them. However, the hosts consider it an honor to have a guest, and so, by allowing their guest to eat first, they are showing that person respect.

It is not necessary to finish all of the food that the hosts set out for dinner; the Tongan family will eat whatever leftovers that their guests do not finish. Because it would be considered an embarrassment for the family to not have enough food to serve to guests, Tongans always put more food on the table than anyone could possibly consume. It is also important to note that Tongans never begin eating as soon as they sit down to a meal; the host first says a prayer before everyone starts eating. At the end of the meal, it is appropriate to make a short thank-you speech, or to give the Tongan family a small gift as a token of appreciation for their hospitality.

> Although more and more Tongans are beginning to use basic silverware and napkins, it is still traditional for Tongans to eat with their hands. Utensils and napkins may not be available at the table.

Eating out in Tonga differs from the standard Western restaurant experience. In restaurants in Tonga, the staff brings the food out from the kitchen as it is prepared, rather than waiting to bring the entire table's food at once. Diners should just start eating as their food comes out, instead of waiting for all of the food to arrive at once. That being said, when eating with Tongans, it is important to wait until the highest-ranking person at the table has received their food before beginning to eat. Someone in the group will then say a prayer, and then everyone can start eating.

Anyone planning to travel to areas outside of the main cities should note that the season will determine the local availability of foods. From October to May, a plethora of fruit is available, including pineapple, mango, passion fruit, avocado, bananas, limes, and papaya. On the other hand, at this time, there are virtually no vegetables available in more isolated areas. From May to October, a great deal of fresh vegetables will be available, including cabbage, green pepper, cucumber, carrots, lettuce, tomatoes, and broccoli. During these winter months, however, less tropical fruit will be available. In the largest city, Nuku'alofa, vegetables and fruits remain available year-round at the market and grocery stores because of shipments from overseas. In fact, Nuku'alofa consistently boasts the largest variety of food products in the entire country. Recommended Tongan dishes include *ota ika*, or raw fish prepared in lime, chili, and coconut sauce; *feke*, or octopus; *puaka tunu*, or roasted pig; and *mei*, or breadfruit chips, which are often sold at *falekoloas*. (See page 42 for more cultural information on local foods.)

Cultural Considerations

As part of their culture, Tongans generally dress conservatively. Nuku'alofa proves the exception to the rule, because it is more influenced by Western norms. However, those heading to areas outside of the capital city should dress conservatively in order to avoid offending the local Tongans. Women should not wear anything which reveals either their leg above the knee, or their shoulders. Men should not go shirtless in public; in fact, this is against the law in Tonga. When swimming or hanging out at the beach in local village areas, women should wear a t-shirt and shorts, even in the water. Men should also wear a t-shirt and swim shorts. In resort areas, however, it is acceptable for women to wear tank tops and shorter shorts, as well as swimsuits, and for men to go shirtless.

On Sundays, physical activities such as running, swimming, fishing, or playing sports are forbidden in Tonga. In strictly resort areas, it is acceptable to do these activities on Sundays, as long as no Tongans can see. Otherwise, in villages or public areas, it is important to respect the culture by observing local Tongan laws, which prohibit any physical labor or activities on Sundays.

In Tonga, it is not appropriate to yell or get angry in public. Anyone who becomes frustrated or upset with a Tongan should not yell or become openly angry with them. Such an incident would be very embarrassing to the Tongan.

Talk the Talk

As in any country, the locals are always very happy and impressed when visitors show an effort to understand their way of life and speak simple phrases in their language. Use our language reference section, on page 219, for some ideas. A little effort in this area will go a long way.

Activities

WATER

Snorkeling

Tonga's reefs are breathtakingly beautiful. In fact, the natural and untouched reefs of Tonga rival those of the Great Barrier Reef in Australia. In Ha'apai, as well as in other remote islands and reefs, visitors will wonder, truly, how many other human beings have actually seen what they are seeing. Colorful soft and hard corals fill the sea, as swarms of intricately-patterned fish—including tuna, parrot fish, eels, clown fish, lion fish, reef sharks, and the occasional sea turtle—paddle lazily past. Many shallow reefs lie close to the shores; their waters provide an ideal atmosphere for snorkeling, due to their incredible visibility and their warm temperatures, which last year-round. It is recommended that no one snorkel alone. Snorkelers should always have someone spot for them, due to the unpredictable nature of currents, marine life, and boat traffic. Anyone who elects to snorkel without a guide should bring their own equipment from home, or rent their equipment from a dive operator. The gear sold at the local stores is cheaply-made, and overpriced.

Diving

Every year, diving enthusiasts flock to Tonga for the incredible scuba diving. Trips are available for all divers of every level, from beginner to advanced, and there are even PADI dive courses offered, for those who wish to learn to dive in Tonga. Divers are rewarded for their efforts with unparalleled views of an amazing diversity of colorful fish, as well as varied reef formations including archways, caves, and walls. Dive operators exist in every island group, except the Niuas. These operators offer dive certification courses, guided dives, and equipment rentals, often at much cheaper prices than in other, more developed countries. Thanks to the warm South Pacific waters of Tonga, diving is possible year-round. Water temperatures range from a high of 28°C (or 82°F) in March to a low of 22°C (or 70°F) in July and August. As mentioned earlier, the water clarity in the reefs of Tonga is unparalleled, with visibility—the diver's Gospel measurement—averaging out around thirty meters.

Swimming with Whales

Tonga boasts one incredibly unique activity: it is one of only two places on earth where it is possible to swim and snorkel with humpback whales. (The other place where people can swim with whales is the Dominican Republic.) Swimming with these magnificent creatures is, simply put, an incredible experience. As visitors jump into the depths of the South Pacific, far away from land, they will feel adrenaline rush through their body, knowing that the whales are swimming somewhere deep beneath them. Then, suddenly, the creatures will silently appear out of the deep blue,

---

Diving in Tonga

The best time of year to dive in Tonga is between November and June, when the water is warmer. While Tongatapu itself offers limited dive opportunities, it does provide access to The Cathedral at 'Eua, a pleasant cavern dive. Ha'apai, on the other hand, has extensive reef systems, boasting more than thirty dive sights, with new ones still being discovered today. It also features a famous underwater coral archway at Ofolonga Island. In the Vava'u group, a wrecked coal ship which sank in the harbor, the *Clan McWilliam*, offers adventurous divers a fantastic wreck dive. Tonga's reefs are very healthy, and they boast a high degree of biodiversity. They feature dynamic characteristics, including drop-offs, swim-throughs, caves, tunnels, walls, and overhangs.

There is an amazing diversity of coral in the reefs throughout Tonga. Hard corals include table and branching acropora, like staghorn and digitate. There are a lot of colorful soft corals in yellow, blue, cream, purple, and green hues. Whip corals and Gorgonian sea fans can also be found, in areas where currents are prevalent. Leather corals coat the reef, and many species of encrusting hard corals color the rocks. Foliose cabbage coral, in green and yellow, is also common.

As a whole, Tonga has a splendid array of marine life (see page 59 for more species of marine life found in Tongan waters). Of course, the big thrill in Tonga is to encounter a humpback whale on a dive. The experience is absolutely jaw-dropping.

- Brian Heagney

their white undersides almost glowing in the contrasting dark water.

Sometimes, this experience lasts only a few seconds or minutes before the whales slip away. Other times, the whales will be curious about the foreign creatures in their midst, and they will hang around for a long time. Whales usually travel in small groups, and there is often a calf in the group. The boat provides a great vantage point from which to watch the whales swim, breaking the surface of the water with their humped backs and fins. Sometimes, the whales will even jump clear out of the ocean, making a backward breach. Every so often, they will poke their heads out of the water to peek around at their surroundings, flap their tails in the air, and slap their fins on the surface of the water. Other times, onlookers can hear the whales' odd clicking, moaning, and singing among themselves. Some operators use an underwater microphone to play the whales' songs and noises from many miles away.

Humpback whales migrate north from Antarctica to the warm waters of Tonga between June and November in order to give birth to their calves. The whales return to the same waters every year. Incredibly, during the duration of their time in Tonga, the adult whales do not eat. Instead, they simply wait until their calves are big enough to make the long, dangerous journey back to the Antarctic waters. Adult humpback whales weigh up to forty tons and measure up to fifty feet long. Though Tongans are no longer allowed to hunt them, the whales are still under attack, both from global warming and from foreign whaling ships.

Humpback whales will permanently leave an area if they feel threatened or disturbed there. This has already happened in other Pacific Island nations. Fortunately, whale sanctuary zones are growing. There are now eleven nations in the South Pacific, including Tonga, which offer protected zones within their waters. These protected areas cover over seven million square miles of ocean.

Whale-watching trips usually last a full day; some will include snorkeling or a stop on a small island for lunch. It is legal to swim with the humpback whales only when accompanied by a licensed operator. Some operators use small local fishing boats, while others use large yachts. All licensed operators should be equipped with safety gear, including snorkel gear and wet suits. Operators must also follow strict guidelines when leading whale-swimming trips. For instance, when boats and people approach a whale in the water, they must leave a distance of at least fifteen feet between themselves and the whale. What's more, only four people, along with a guide, may be in the water with the whales at one time. Boats should also allow plenty of space when passing the whales. Scuba diving with the whales is forbidden.

These guidelines were established for the safety of both the whales and the snorkelers since humpback whales are wild animals and behave in an unpredictable manner. When swimming with the whales, it is important to remember that, fundamentally, the ocean belongs to them. Accordingly, when entering the water, it is best to slip in quietly and remain at the water's surface. It is also wise to avoid diving down with the whales, and avoid splashing around too noisily. At the beginning of the expedition, the tour operator will speak further about important safety issues around the whales.

The best time for whale encounters is usually July through October. Since whale encounters are never guaranteed, anyone who considers this activity a highlight of their trip to Tonga might want to set aside a couple of days for whale-watching trips. This will increase the chances that they will see humpback whales. The best island groups for whale encounters are Vava'u and Ha'apai.

The Tongan Legacy of Whale Hunting

In ancient Tonga, the people hunted humpback whales using spears, until King Taufa'ahau Tupou IV banned the practice in 1976. Before the ban was passed, it was possible to go on whaling tours and watch locals hunt for whales. Although Tongans no longer hunt humpback whales, when a whale washes up on the shore, Tongans will still split the meat among the villages.

Kayaking & Boating

Since the islands of Tonga are surrounded by water, one of the best vantage points to appreciate the islands' beauty is from the sea itself. Kayaks are available for rental from local dive shops. Renting a kayak will allow visitors to paddle around the islands at a relaxing pace. It is recommended that kayakers either have a book or hire a guide for an extended kayaking trip. It is also important to ask the dive shop or local Tongans about areas to avoid when kayaking, since there are some areas between islands with stronger currents. When kayaking, it is best to start with short distances, paddling to nearby islands for a picnic, or simply to enjoy a private stretch of beach. For longer trips, it is best to paddle out against the wind and tides in order to make the return trip easier. It is also possible for kayakers to hitch rides with the local Tongan boats on common routes between small islands; they should just ask the boat how many *pa'anga* they want to help cover fuel costs.

Surfing

Ha'atafu Beach, located on the western end of Tongatapu, is the only well-known surf spot in Tonga. A shallow rocky reef lies just underneath the water there, so the area is not suitable for beginners. Surfers have also attempted some spots in Ha'apai and Vava'u, but these spots are much trickier. In Vava'u, some have tried surfing at Kietahi Beach, near Tu'anekivale village to the east of Nieafu. It is also possible to check with surfers in town about other possible surfing beaches in Vava'u. Because there are no beach breaks in Tonga—where the surf leads simply to a soft, sandy beach, without traveling over treacherous reef to get there—all surfing in Tonga is for intermediate or advanced surfers only. Those who wish to surf in Tonga should bring their own board, since boards are not available for rent on the islands.

Fishing

Fishing has always been a way of life in Tonga. Popular catches include: yellow fin tuna (in fact, locals will even use tuna as bait because of the large quantities available), wahoo, marlin, mahimahi, big sailfish, and more. Some deep-sea fishing operators in Vava'u and Tongatapu will take groups out for fishing expeditions. In the other island groups, it is possible to fish from onshore or from the wharves. Alternately, anyone who wishes to fish can find a local fisherman through their guest-house or through the tourism office. It is important to note that fishing with locals will probably entail fishing with a hand line in a small local boat and trawling. The locals also do a good deal of spear fishing. Yet another local fishing method involves walking along the reefs at low tide in order to find shellfish, sea slugs, and other edible sea creatures. Tongans like to eat these creatures raw, right out of the ocean. Those who end their fishing trips successfully should make sure to ask a local whether they can eat their catch, as some reef fish aren't edible. Fishermen should not plan on preserving any catch, because taxidermy services are not available in Tonga.

LAND

Camping

Camping is not something Tongans do; rather, it is an activity that has been brought to the islands by tourists. Since camping is not very popular, there are no campgrounds in Tonga. Some beach resorts, however, will let guests camp on their grounds and a few even have camping supplies available for rent. Those who bring their own camping gear to Tonga can camp at a few beach resorts, or they can ask the local guesthouses where to camp. Anyone planning to camp in Tonga should bring a lightweight rain-proof tent, a light sleeping sheet or bag, a flashlight, mosquito repellent, matches or a lighter, a rain jacket, and a hammock, in which to lounge or sleep. Campers should not just set their tent up anywhere, however, because all of the land in Tonga is privately owned. Campers will need permission from the property owner in order to camp in any particular location. That said, if campers find themselves in a more remote area, it is acceptable to discreetly camp, if it does not disturb anyone.

Why Octopi Hate Rats

An ancient myth explains the traditional Tongan way of fishing for octopus. The story features a rat and an octopus. One day, the rat got stranded in the water and began to drown. The rat called out to the octopus to come help him. The octopus swam out to meet the rat, then he let the rat ride on his head into dry land. Once the rat was on land, he yelled out to the octopus, "look what I left on your head!" The octopus realized that the rat had pooped on top of his head. By this time, of course, the rat had scampered away down the beach, where the octopus couldn't catch him. Since then, octopi have always hated rats.

Today when the local Tongans fish for octopus, they make and use bait which closely resembles a rat. It is made of shells, and it has a string which looks like a tail—they even tie some feathers on the lure to make it look furry. The fishermen then tie the bait to a string and dangle it in the deep water. As soon as the octopus sees it, he rushes up to the bait. (This bait might also work to capture octopi because the shells tied together make a noise which tends to attract them.) Local Tongans will string the octopi in trees or on poles in order to dry them out.

Biking

Biking is another great way to explore Tonga. Bikes allow people to see the islands at their own pace, to stop and check out all of the little villages strung along the main roads and the coasts of the islands. During the hot summer season, it is generally prudent to limit bike rides to the early morning and late evening; it is also a good idea to bring plenty of water. Local bikes can be in dire condition, so renters should take a good look at the bike before renting it. Anyone who plans to do a lot of biking in Tonga would be well-advised to bring some basic bicycle repair tools over with them.

Ha'apai and Tongatapu offer the easiest, flattest terrains for biking, while Vava'u and 'Eua are hillier. In Vava'u there are also kart tours available. Karts will take tourists to local villages and beaches. Anyone who plans on biking in the evening or into the night should bring a flashlight because most of the local bikes do not have lights or reflectors. Average bike rental prices range from TOP$15 to TOP$30 per day.

Hiking

'Eua offers the best hiking in Tonga and it is also the only place in Tonga where it is possible to hike through natural rainforest bush and rock climb. Many of the trails on 'Eua wind through lush tropical rainforest, thus providing travelers with ample opportunity to spelunk or rock climb. (Although, be warned, most trails in 'Eua are not well marked or maintained.)While there are a few trails in Vava'u and Tongatapu, none are comparable to 'Eua. (See page 129 for more details on hiking on 'Eua.)

Another great option for hiking is walking along the many deserted sandy beaches, or walking all the way around the perimeter of one of the smaller islands. Hikers should make sure to wear sunscreen, and bring either water or a machete, with which to open a green coconut to drink along the trail. During tourist season, a plethora of sights will be visible: whales breaching in the ocean, local fishermen netting fish from the shore, women soaking *pandanus* leaves in the ocean in order to prepare them for weaving, locals gathering shells and seafood at low tide along the shoreline. At other times, the beaches may be completed deserted.

Star-gazing

Due to their distance from main cities, the remote islands provide excellent star-gazing opportunities on clear nights. Since Tonga lies in the Southern Hemisphere, the Southern Cross is clearly visible from the islands. On the smaller islands, it is possible to watch the sun set on the western side of the island and the moon rise on the eastern side.

Horseback Riding

While there are no major horseback riding operations in Tonga, a few resorts do offer horseback riding tours; these tours often offer a ride along the beach. Usually, riders ride bareback or on blankets; there are no saddles.

Cultural Activities

Numerous cultural activities are available throughout Tonga. For instance, it is possible to attend feasts or dances, join *kava* circles, go to local church services, visit Tongan schools, or learn to make traditional island handicrafts. More information can be found in each chapter of this book. In keeping with the country's nickname, "The Friendly Islands," the Tongan people are always more than happy to share their culture with every visitor who arrives on their shores.

Safety

HEALTH & MEDICAL

Western medicine and traditional medicine exist alongside one another in Tonga. Western-style hospitals are available in the capital and in the main cities and because the doctors usually received their training in Fiji or Australia, most of the doctors speak English. There are also traditional Tongan doctors in the villages but most younger Tongans tend to use Western-style doctors and hospitals, leaving the traditional doctors to the older generations. Traditional doctors practice a different kind of medicine, using ingredients like leaves, bark, and other local substances to make medicines to assist patients. Massages are another popular healing technique.

Traditional doctors usually charge a small fee, and they use their own homes as the treatment space. Some locals who could not be cured by modern medicine have found enormous relief in these traditional methods. The Tongans hold strongly to superstitions. For instance, they sometimes believe that if someone falls ill or hurts themselves, it is because that person did something wrong and, thus, they are being punished for that transgression. The major medical issues suffered by Tongans are heart disease and diabetes. The average Tongan life expectancy is 71 years of age.

The main hospital in Tonga, Vioala, is located on the lagoon, just south of Nuku'alofa. There are also hospitals in the main city of each island group in Vava'u, Ha'apai, and 'Eua. They do not, however, offer the same services that the main hospital does. At the local hospitals, patients must bring their own bed sheets, toilet paper, food, water, mosquito coils (the windows are usually screenless), and anything else that they might need for an overnight stay.

Relatives and friends often come visit the patients, bringing food and supplies with them. Most hospital rooms are shared, with beds lining the walls of larger rooms. If someone dies in the hospital, that person's family and friends take shifts, never leaving the body alone. They sit by the body, singing songs and hymns throughout the night. Anyone who becomes sick in Tonga should first try to self-medicate and rest. In severe situations, they should go to the local hospital. If it is at all possible, it is best to go to the main hospital in Tongatapu, which offers a much higher standard of care. *National emergency number: 911, Vioala Hospital phone: 933 or 23200.*

Dengue Fever

Dengue fever is far more prevalent during the rainy season, from October to April, when there are more mosquitoes in Tonga. The mosquitoes tend to be most active at dawn and dusk. Dengue fever is transmitted by a mosquito which is characterized by its black and white-striped legs and body. Only the infected females carry the disease. Dengue causes an extremely high fever of over 104°F, or 40°C. It also causes the bones to hurt so much that it feels as though they will break. This tendency is what gives dengue fever its nickname, "bone-break fever."

No medicine can treat or cure dengue fever. Dengue sufferers can merely rest, drink plenty of water, and take Tylenol or Panadol to alleviate the aches and to reduce the fever. Sufferers should not take Aspirin, because it can cause hemorrhaging in patients with dengue fever. There are four different strains of dengue fever; the worst strain is dengue hemorrhagic fever. Even those suffering from dengue fever only need to go to the hospital if they become dehydrated or suffer a hemorrhage. It is possible to decrease the likelihood of contracting dengue fever by wearing insect repellent (particularly at dusk and dawn), by using mosquito coils, and by sleeping under a mosquito net. Unlike on some neighboring Pacific Islands, there is no malaria in Tonga.

Heat Exhaustion

It is very easy to overlook this safety concern while out enjoying Tonga's beautiful beaches and sunshine. However, in a climate as hot and humid as that of Tonga, the body needs much more water than most visitors may expect or be accustomed to drinking. This is particularly true when out in the sun or on the water, which reflects and magnifies the heat of the sun. The key to preventing heat exhaustion is to drink plenty of water. While the necessary amount varies from person to person, generally two liters of water per day should be enough. Symptoms of heat exhaustion include weakness or vomiting after spending time outside in the sun. In order to recover, it is important to drink plenty of fluids, as well as take rehydration tablets, if they are available, or drink Gatorade or Powerade in order to restore needed electrolytes. Those who cannot hold down any water need to head to a hospital to get IV fluids.

Traveler's Diarrhea

It is not uncommon for visitors to experience traveler's diarrhea while in Tonga, especially if they eat certain foods. More risky food choices include anything made or rinsed with tap water or untreated rainwater; raw fish; and local foods which have been sitting out without refrigeration. Those who experience this illness need to remember to stay hydrated, both by drinking a lot of water and by using rehydration tablets. Traveler's diarrhea will usually pass in one to two days. If it does not, seek medical help.

Motion Sickness

Those traveling by boat may experience motion sickness, or seasickness. Anyone who tends to be prone to motion sickness should prevent the problem before it starts by taking medication. In addition to traditional motion sickness medicines, like

Dramamine, peppermint and ginger can be effective natural preventatives. People who start feeling sick should keep their eyes on the horizon and get fresh air. It's also best to lie or sit down, and avoid walking around. And, as the old joke goes, "If you get seasick, the one cure is to go sit under a tree."

Cuts & Wounds

In the tropical climate of Tonga, cuts and wounds can quickly morph from a small scratch into something much worse. In order to prevent infection, it is very important to wash the wound, apply an antibiotic gel, and cover it with a bandage during the day. If a cut is not healing, or if it is growing deeper, seek immediate medical attention.

Bites & Stings - Land

Barring possible allergic reactions, there is no land animal in Tonga with a deadly bite or sting. There are, however, a few creatures to avoid. Watch out for *molokau*, the centipedes. *Molokau* are very large—reaching up to twelve inches in length and one inch in width; they are black or brown in color and move incredibly quickly. These insects typically emerge with the rain, which forces them out of the ground in which they live. While *molokau* are more common in the bush, they can also live inside of houses and buildings. The most effective way to kill a *molokau* is by chopping off its head, or by completely crushing the body. If a person is bitten by a *molokau*, they will feel a very sharp pain, and the centipede will leave two incision marks on the skin at the site of the attack. Bite victims should take some Benadryl in order to decrease the swelling and help the pain. Wasps are another animal to avoid, although they usually keep to themselves.

Stray and wild dogs live all over Tonga, and they can be quite territorial. The dogs are usually at their worst in bigger towns, such as Nuku'alofa. In case of an encounter with a dog that is barking, or a dog that looks ready to approach or attack, it's best to bend down and pretend to pick up a rock. The dogs

> If you are on a bike and dogs are chasing or barking at you, even though it may be against your instinct, slow down, get off your bike, and walk it.

have a conditioned response to this action: since so many locals have thrown rocks at them in the past, they will assume that the visitor is going to throw the rock at them as well. If this does not work, pick up the rock and throw it near the dog to deter it. Alternately, it may be a good idea to try to make the same noise that local Tongans do, a low throaty hissing noise, to scare away the dogs.

Even if none of these tactics work to scare off the stray dogs, take heart: there is no rabies in Tonga.

Bites & Stings - Sea

While there are sea animals which sting and bite, these creatures usually do not bite or sting unless provoked. Swimmers should watch out for aquatic creatures like stone fish, lion fish, sea snakes, jellyfish, corals, eels, and sharks. In order to prevent a potentially deadly sting from a stone fish, it is a good idea to wear protective shoes or sandals when walking in the ocean, especially in murky water, and shuffle along the ocean bottom. Should anyone be stung by a stone fish, that person should seek immediate medical help and accept any local medicine which may be offered. In order to avoid stings from jellyfish, lion fish, and sea snakes, grant the animals a wide berth and, above all, do not touch them.

Usually lion fish and sea snakes are much more scared of people than people are of them, so they flee at the first sight of humans. Sea snakes do possess very poisonous venom, but their mouths are too small to bite any part of a human, except a little finger. Those stung by a jellyfish may wish to seek medical help, depending on the severity of the sting. Anyone stung by a lion fish or a sea snake, on the other hand, should seek medical help immediately. In order to prevent stings from coral, it is best to avoid any contact between coral and skin. Anyone who gets stung by coral should wash out the infected area and squeeze out any stray coral pieces which may remain stuck in the wound.

Sharks rarely attack humans in Tonga. In fact, most of the sharks which swim in waters shallow enough for snorkeling and diving are probably reef sharks, and they are usually harmless and docile. If a snorkeler feels threatened, they should slowly back away from the shark, always facing it. The larger, more threatening sharks tend to live in deeper water. Snorkelers should be aware of swimming in areas with high boat traffic or in areas where there are deep underwater drop-offs at the edges of shallow reefs. Sharks tend to hang around boats and drop-offs because they can easily find food there.

While the cone shell does not look at all threatening, it can be deadly. Cone shells, which are (surprisingly!) cone-shaped, are generally dark purple or white-and-black in color. Anyone who encounters a cone shell should not pick it up. These creatures have a dagger-like appendage and, if the creature is still living inside of its shell, it can sting and inject its venom into an unsuspecting victim. Anyone stung by a cone shell must immediately seek medical attention.

PERSONAL SAFETY

While Tonga is generally an incredibly safe and friendly nation, crime has recently become somewhat more prevalent in larger cities there. Because many Tongans think that all Westerners are rich, they assume that taking any items which they leave unattended is not a serious offense.

To prevent the theft of valuables, it is best not to leave them lying around in an unattended hotel room. That being said, theft is uncommon in Tonga and when it has happened, sometimes the items have been recovered. (In a small nation where word spreads quickly, unique items stand out, and it's hard to hide them.) In the event of a theft or crime, file a report with the local police. The numbers are listed in each island group section.

Despite the fact that violent crime against foreigners is very rare, solo and women travelers should remain aware of their surroundings nonetheless. Women should not venture to isolated beaches or other deserted areas on their own, and they should try to follow the local dress code in order to avoid unwanted attention. Women should also avoid walking alone at night.

Recently, teenage kids have begun to act against foreigners. Sometimes they swear at the foreigners in English and, on rare occasions, throw rocks at them. Anyone who falls victim to this type of behavior should remember that the teenagers are not trying to hurt them; they are, most likely, simply showing off for their friends. Anyone who encounters this behavior can yell *tuku* or *alu mama'o*, or "stop, go away" at the teenagers. Another potential solution would be finding a Tongan adult and asking them to intervene and assist with the situation.

NATURAL DISASTER SAFETY

Tonga is located in the Pacific Ring of Fire, so its tiny islands are quite exposed to the elements. However, no one should allow this to deter them from planning a trip to the country. Every time the authors experienced a natural disaster in Tonga, their preconceived notions of the event would be far worse than the actual reality of the situation.

Earthquakes

Tonga experiences dozens of earthquakes each year, though many are so minor that they are not even felt on the surface. Since most of the buildings are quite low-lying, most earthquakes do very little damage. Those inside of a building during an earthquake should get outside of the building if possible, staying away from trees. Those who do not have easy access to the outdoors should stand under a door frame or stay under a sturdy piece of furniture until the earthquake is over.

Tsunami

After a major earthquake hits, there can be a chance of a tsunami. Tsunamis usually occur as a set of three large waves. The most devastating tsunami to hit Tonga came from an earthquake in South America, even though there is typically more protection on that side of the islands, due to the natural protection provided by the Tongan

---

Ocean Safety

Though the South Pacific Ocean may be beautiful, it is not without threats. For instance, there are no lifeguards in Tonga. Therefore, travelers should never go into the ocean alone without someone to spot them. Each island always has a safer, calmer coast and a wild, more dangerous coast. Visitors should inquire with the local tourism office, tourism operators, or their guesthouse about where it is safest to swim and snorkel.

Local boats are not very safe; however, tourists who ride on local boats will usually only take them for short distances. Those planning a longer boat trip should ask whether the boat on which they will be riding has safety equipment, such as lifejackets, an eperb (emergency beacon device), and a radio. They should also beware of currents and waves breaking on outer reefs when traveling between islands. Anyone who might happen to get pulled out to sea should swim in a diagonal direction toward the shore in order to get back.

Trench. In 2009, a tsunami hit the northern Niua Islands, and smaller waves reached some of the other island groups.

If there is a tsunami warning via local radio, television, or word of mouth, head to the highest ground available. If there is enough lead time, it is also possible to get into a boat and head out into the deep sea. Boats in deep water will ride right over the large tsunami waves. While there is no official national emergency plan to deal with tsunamis, after a destructive storm or event, local communities and governments will come together to provide relief and rebuild the towns.

Cyclone

Cyclone season in Tonga lasts from November through April, during the hot and rainy summer. On average, one cyclone hits Tonga each season, out of the average eight to ten cyclones which hit the Southwest Pacific region each season. A cyclone is marked by gusts of wind, heavy downpours, coastal flooding, and rough sea conditions. Usually, there are a few days warning before a cyclone hits. If a cyclone is approaching, the best course of action to take is to stock up on food and water before the storm hits. Once it hits, stay inside of a safe, secure building, away from windows. During a cyclone, most of the destruction affects crops, trees, shorelines, and unstable older buildings.

Volcanoes

Most volcanoes in Tonga are dormant or, if they are active, they are only active infrequently. In Ha'apai, the Tofua Volcano is occasionally active, releasing small plumes of smoke, which are visible on the horizon from the main island of Lifuka. The Tofua, however, poses no threat, and it is a unique sight to see. In 2009, a volcanic explosion occurred in the southern islands of Ha'apai, forming a new island, and sending out huge plumes of smoke. The volcanoes pose a small risk to boats at sea, though, if the boats are near one of these volcanoes when it erupts.

Giving Back

There are numerous ways to help the local communities in Tonga while visiting, or even from home. Many Tongans can live on next to nothing and, in fact, may be considered poor by Western standards. Strong community and family ties compensate for the relative lack of material wealth. That is, Tongans take care of each other. For instance, no orphanages or nursing homes exist in Tonga. Despite their infinite readiness to assist one another, the Tongan people may be in need of certain supplies or technical expertise, neither of which are readily available in the country.

One great way to help the local schoolchildren is by supporting fundraisers. This can be done by locating and attending a fundraising event, such as a feast or dance. No one is expected to donate a huge amount of money at such events, but even a few *pa'anga* help. In addition, on occasion, schoolchildren walk around and ask people to sign up to give monetary donations to assist their school. This provides another avenue for contributions. Another way to contribute to the local Tongan community is by buying locally-made crafts and goods. There are markets in all of the main cities, where local artists and women's groups sell handicrafts. Alternately, it is possible to inquire with the guesthouses about local village women's groups.

It is also possible to donate books to the schools or libraries. Tongans love books, and it is considered a privilege to have books in their schools. Not all books are created equal for donation, though: it is vital that the donated books are actually useful to schoolchildren. If the books are for adults, they should either be educational or useful for business. Schools are also always in need of other types of school supplies, such as paper, stickers, maps, and other small items. One item not to donate is old computers since in the humid environment of Tonga, computers break down very quickly, and they are difficult to fix. It is also hard to recycle old computers, and they usually wind up polluting the environment. Other items which can potentially be donated include sports balls, notebooks, pens, maps, flash cards, and other educational materials.

Basics

A Uniquely Tongan Fundraiser

One peculiar fundraising event which has sprung up all over Tongatapu is the car wash. For a Tongan car wash, instead of actually washing cars, Tongan children will simply stand on the side of a busy road and hold up a sign saying "car wash." Cars will then pull over onto the shoulder, hand the children money, and drive away.

Several volunteer organizations have worked in Tonga for quite some time, including the United States Peace Corps, the Japan International Cooperation Agency, and two Australian volunteer programs. The Australian volunteers work only in Tongatapu and Vava'u, while the Japanese and American volunteers are spread across all of the island groups. Visitors who encounter one of these volunteers can also ask them about opportunities to assist with their projects. In conjunction with one of these volunteers, visitors may be able to visit a local school, give the kids a quick English lesson, or assist employees at a local business with computer skills.

Another way to help Tonga and Tongans is by being aware of the environment while traveling. For instance, be sure to take batteries and other toxic waste out of the country when leaving. Also avoid buying plastic bottles, bags, tin cans, glass bottles, and other such materials on the smaller islands. Recycling does not exist in Tonga, and it is too costly to ship these pollutants off of the islands. Therefore, use less, reuse more, and take as many recyclables as possible off of the island upon departure.

Above: A group performing the ma'ulu'ulu dance for a special occasion.
Below: You can still see traditional Tongan *fales* today, used as weaving huts or gathering places for *kava* circles.

Below: A Tongan bride and groom at their first Sunday church service together.

Below: School kids at a fundraiser dance.

Above: A rugby match at the sports stadium on Tongatapu.
Below: A typical Tongan house.

Above: Local boat in Tongatapu. Below: Outside the Talamahu Market in Nuku'alofa, full of fruits, veggies, handicrafts, and second-hand goods.

Tongatapu

Introduction

Tongatapu, home of Tonga's capital, Nuku'alofa, houses the country's international airport. Tongatapu is also a necessary stop on journeys between the various islands of Tonga. Though the airport is located here, visitors should not merely arrive and then hop on the next plane to Ha'apai or Vava'u. With numerous must-see sights, Tongatapu definitely merits a visit.

From the waves crashing against the immense cliffs of the southern shore, to the beautiful sunsets that bathe the sandy beaches of the west coast in golden light, Tongatapu possesses near-unearthly beauty. What's more, the vast array of natural wonders spread throughout the island, along with the incredible diversity of sights and activities there, will leave no one unimpressed.

In order to fully appreciate Tongatapu, it is best to take a few days to roam the island, spending time on each coast, eating world-class cuisine and sightseeing in Nuku'alofa, and taking day trips to snorkel and sunbathe on nearby outer islands.

HISTORY & MYTHS

"Tongatapu," located in the southern island group, literally translates to mean the "sacred South." Both the largest island in the nation and the most populous, Tongatapu houses over two-thirds of the Tongan population. The capital city, Nuku'alofa, serves as the central hub of commerce and government; it's also home to one-third of the entire population of Tonga.

Many places on Tongatapu attest to the country's long, rich history, from Nukuleka, the village where archaeologists unearthed three thousand year-old Lapita pottery; to Nuku'alofa, the city which bore witness to both civil war and the recent, bloody political riots, all of which have shaped Tonga's future as a nation state. Clearly, there is no shortage of history on Tongatapu; the island offers something to pique anyone's interest.

Historians believe Tongatapu was first settled by the Lapita people. As a matter of fact, in 2007, a Canadian archaeologist found pottery in the small fishing village of Nukuleka which carbon dates to approximately three thousand years ago. Based on this finding, Tongatapu now claims the title of "Cradle of Polynesia," much to the disdain of the Samoans, the previous title-holders. In fact, archaeological evidence suggests that the people of Melanesian ancestry remained in Tonga for some time creating their own distinct culture, before venturing out to populate various islands of the rest of contemporary Polynesia.

Centuries passed before the Europeans "discovered" Tongatapu. In 1643, Abel Tasman, of the Dutch East India Company, landed upon the shores of Tonga en route to chart unknown territories of the South Pacific. Upon landing, he laid claim to the island, naming it Amsterdam Island, due to the abundance of goods he found there. Strangely, although the Dutch claimed the island as their own, they never returned. In 1777, Captain James Cook reached Tongatapu, and it is his journals which first refer to a place called "Tongatapu." Captain Cook did misspell the name, however, recording it as "Tongataboo," with the word taboo meaning "sacred" or "forbidden," depending upon context. It is thus that Tongatapu came to be known as the "sacred South." "*Tapu*," or "taboo," is also the only word in English which is known to have Tongan origins.

ORIENTATION

For orientation purposes, Tongatapu can be divided into four regions: the main city of Nuku'alofa, the western region, the eastern/southern region, and the central region. Each area offers its own unique blend of sights and activities. Nuku'alofa caters to the cosmopolitan, offering a wide array of restaurants, accommodations, and shopping. A trip to Nuku'alofa's large market, a stroll along the Ocean Boulevard and the Royal Palace, and dinner on the town are some of the distinct highlights which only the city offers. The western side of Tongatapu beckons the adventurer, boasting excellent beaches, including a world-class surfing beach. The western side of the island also houses a number of resorts catering to tourists.

The aesthete will love the eastern and southern part of Tongatapu, which features incredible natural landscapes, such as the famous blowholes and caves. History buffs will find themselves attracted to the central section of the island, which houses historic locales, such as the current King's residence. Furthermore, Nukuleka, believed to be the oldest village in all of Polynesia, is located there, along with the celebrated *Ha'amonga 'a Maui*, an ancient limestone archway. The north-central coast of Tongatapu features a large lagoon. Much of Tongatapu is very flat, with beaches dotting the west coast and interspersed throughout the rest of the island. The south and east coast, on the other hand, feature rocky cliffs.

TRANSPORTATION

Arrival

Tongatapu is the easiest of all the island groups to reach, since all international flights come through Fua'amotu International Airport in southeastern Tongatapu. Three major airlines offer flights there. Flights arrive in Tonga every day of the week, except Sunday, when no planes are allowed to fly in Tonga. Air New Zealand offers direct flights from Auckland five days a week. Pacific Blue, a subsidiary of Virgin Airlines, offers flights twice per week from Sydney and Auckland. Finally, Air Pacific offers flights to Tongatapu three days a week from Los Angeles, Sydney, and Brisbane, with a layover in Nadi, Fiji.

Flying High

Want to arrive in Tonga in style? Fly Air New Zealand. The Air New Zealand planes feature movies on personal video screens, gourmet food, and alcoholic beverages on all international flights. In fact, Air New Zealand was voted Airline of the Year for 2010 by the leading airline industry magazine, *Air Transport World*.

Upon arrival at Fua'amotu International Airport, the best way to get into Nuku'alofa is by taxi. No buses serve the airport, but there are always plenty of taxis just outside the baggage claim area. The cab ride from the airport to town takes about forty minutes and it usually costs around TOP$40. Many of the hotels and resorts offer shuttle services to pick up guests upon arrival; the shuttle then ferries them directly to the hotel or resort. However, this service typically requires advance booking, and the cost varies depending upon the hotel or resort.

That's Just How He Rolls…

On the ride into Nuku'alofa, visitors will pass the King's mansion in the village of Pe'a, just across from the lagoon. The mansion will be obvious, because it is huge, not to mention set back from the main road behind a vast, green open space. If the flag at the end of the driveway is raised, that means that the king is home. When he travels around the island, he rides in an old black Rolls-Royce with a license plate emblazoned with three crowns on the front. A small motorcade precedes him on these trips around the island.

GETTING AROUND

Taxis

There is an extensive network of taxi companies on Tongatapu; using this network of taxis is the easiest way to travel around the island, besides walking. Taxis are identified by a sign on top of the car, or simply by a "T" at the beginning of the numbers on their license plate. There are both car taxis and larger taxi vans. Tongan taxis are not metered, so it is very important to agree upon the price of any given ride before the taxi departs. It is also important to have the right amount of cash to make change when paying the cab fare. Taxis are available for hire simply to get around Nuku'alofa for TOP$2 to TOP$5 a ride. Taxis can also offer tourists an all-day guided tour, which will take them to sights all over the island. There are a few taxi stands around town, but patrons can call the taxi company directly for a ride. *Holiday Taxi phone: 25655, Wellington Taxi phone: 24744, Atelaite Taxi phone: 23919, Fiemalie Taxi phone: 24270.*

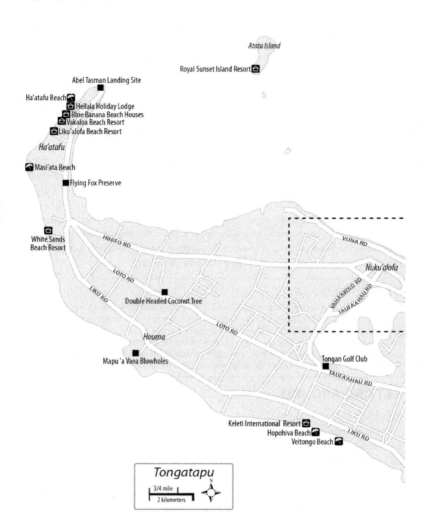

Atata Island

Royal Sunset Island Resort

Abel Tasman Landing Site

Ha'atafu Beach
Heilala Holiday Lodge
Blue Banana Beach Houses
Vakaloa Beach Resort
Liku'alofa Beach Resort

Ha'atafu

Masi'ata Beach

Flying Fox Preserve

White Sands
Beach Resort

HIHIFO RD

VUNA RD

Nuku'alofa

LOTO RD

LIKU RD

Double Headed Coconut Tree

VAHA'AKOLO RD
TAUFA'AHAU RD

LOTO RD

Houma

Mapu 'a Vaea Blowholes

Tongan Golf Club

TAUFA'AHAU RD

Keleti International Resort
Hopohiva Beach
Veitongo Beach

LIKU RD

Tongatapu
N
3/4 mile
2 kilometers

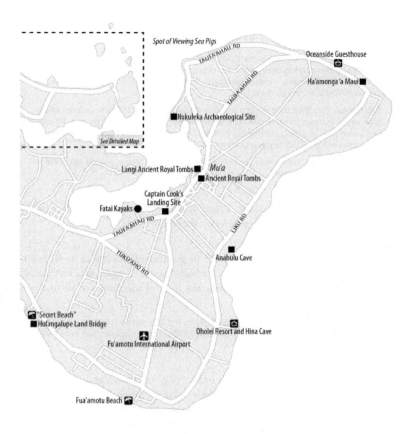

Tongatapu

Fafa Island Resort

Spot of Viewing Sea Pigs

TAUFA'AHAU RD

TAUFA'AHAU RD

Oceanside Guesthouse

Ha'amonga 'a Maui

Nukuleka Archaeological Site

See Detailed Map

Langi Ancient Royal Tombs

Mu'a
Ancient Royal Tombs

Captain Cook's
Landing Site

Fatai Kayaks

TAUFAKAHAU RD

LIKU RD

TUKU'AHO RD

Anahulu Cave

"Secret Beach"
Hufangalupe Land Bridge

Oholei Resort and Hina Cave

Fu'amotu International Airport

Fua'amotu Beach

Bus

Many private buses operate on Tongatapu; most head from the western and eastern sides of the island into Nuku'alofa, though others simply operate around the outlying Nuku'alofa area. There is a bus station for more central destinations on Vuna Road across from the Tonga Visitors Bureau. The bus station serving the eastern or western sides of the island is located slightly further northwest on Vuna Road. Inside of the bus, there will usually be a person at the front collecting fare money, usually about TOP$1 – 3, depending on the destination. Buses run throughout the day, from 7 am until around 5 pm. Because are no posted bus schedules and departure times can be unreliable, it is usually a good idea to arrive at the bus stop by 3 or 4 pm in order to catch the last bus ride of the day.

Car Rental

In order to rent a car on Tongatapu, it is necessary to obtain a Tongan driver's license from the Ministry of Transport. Remember, fuel is very expensive in Tonga.

Avis Those who seek a new car with air-conditioning will find it here. Avis provides, essentially, the service that might be expected from an international car rental chain. *Open Mon-Sat, morning to evening. Located on the Main Road in the Fund Management Building, next to Café Escape. Phone: 21179, avis@tonfon.to*

Fab Rental For those who don't mind driving something a little less *palangi* and a little more Tongan, the friendly staff at Fab Rental can help. The cars may be old, and some may lack air conditioning, but the price is right. *Open Mon-Sat morning to evening. Located on Salote Rd, just a block from the wharf. Phone: 23077*

Pasifika Rentals Pasifika Rentals also offers rental cars at reasonable rates. *Phone: 27718, pasifikarentalcars@tonfon.to*

Hitchhiking

Suto, or hitchhiking, is common in Tonga. It is not as common, however, in Nuku'alofa as it is in the smaller villages around the island.

Biking

Biking provides a great opportunity, both to get around Nuku'alofa itself, and to venture out to see more of the island as a whole. Because Tongatapu is very flat, it's ideal for biking. Bikers beware: cars have the right of way, and not all roads are paved.

Niko's Bicycle Rental This shop, located next to the International Dateline Hotel on Ocean Road, has bike rentals for about TOP$15. Other guesthouses and hotels will also have bikes available for rental use.

Walking

It is very easy to see most of Nuku'alofa on foot. The Ocean Boulevard, along Vuna Road, provides a beautiful setting for leisurely walks. Occasionally, dogs on this road can present difficulties, especially at night. Anyone who is approached by a barking dog should bend over and pretend to throw a rock at the animal. This should drive the animal away.

BANKING

ANZ A large bank which operates out of Australia and New Zealand, ANZ has a couple of branches in Nuku'alofa. Because these banks are brand-new, they offer standard Western banking services, including ATMs. *Located on the Main Road next to the Fund Management Building, and on Vuna Road just down from Faua Wharf. Both locations open Mon-Fri, 9am – 5pm.*

Westpac This Australian bank also has two branches in Nuku'alofa. These branches offer the standard banking services; Westpac also has a few ATMs scattered around town. *Branches are located on the Main Road where it turns into Vuna Road next to the Royal Palace, and on the Main Road next to the Si'i Kaeola Store and Te'ufaiva Stadium. There is also an ATM located next to Vaiola Hospital. Open Mon-Fri, 9am - 5pm.*

COMMUNICATIONS

Many cafés in Tongatapu offer free wireless Internet, including Friends, Café Escape, and Reef Café. Those who did not bring their own laptop needn't fret: all of these cafés also have desktop computers available for an hourly fee. Many guesthouses and hotels also have free Wi-Fi, or computers with Internet. Internet cafés are also scattered throughout Nuku'alofa.

Both cell phone companies, TCC and Digicel, have offices in Nuku'alofa. In general, both companies provide good coverage throughout Tongatapu, except in a few scattered areas around the eastern and southern parts of the island. *Digicel has a store on Taufa'ahau Road right across from Friends Café. TCC has a store right down the street from there. Both open Mon-Sat, morning to evening.*

The main **post office** is located at the center of town, on the corner of the Taufa'ahau Road and Salote Road. It offers most shipping services. It is also very reliable, because most goods leave Tonga from nearby Fua'amotu Airport.

There is also a **DHL office** (phone: 27700 or 23617) in Nuku'alofa.

TOURS

Café Escape Tourist Center Located in the same space as the café, the Café Escape Tourist Center offers a wide range of information about booking tours and accommodation throughout Tonga. The center also offers Internet access, printing, copying, faxing, and other helpful services. *Open Mon-Sat, morning to evening. Main Road in the Fund Management Building. Phone: 21212*

Friends Tourist Center Located right next door to the café, the friendly staff there can help make any kind of booking, from tours to accommodation to diving and fishing trips. Friends Tourist Center also has computers for Internet use and souvenirs for purchase. *Open Mon-Sat, morning to evening. Located on the corner of the Main Road and Salote Road, Phone: 26323, www.friendstonga.com*

Rising Sun Tours and Travel This agency offers a range of services, including airport transfers, tours, accommodation, flights, and pretty much everything else a traveler might need. Rising Sun Tours and Travel is a one-stop shop. *Open Mon-Sat, morning to evening. Located on the Main Road across from Friends Café. Phone: 28463, www.risingsuntourandtravel.com*

Tonga Visitors Bureau For general information on sights, activities, and accommodations throughout Tonga, visit the Tonga Visitors Bureau. Built in the style of a traditional Tongan *fale*, the TVB office really is a sight in and of itself. *Located on Vuna Road next to the International Dateline Hotel. Phone: 25334, info@tvb.gov.to, www.tongaholiday.com*

Tongatapu

EMBASSIES

A few foreign government entities exist in Nuku'alofa. The Japanese Embassy is located in the Reserve Bank Building on Salote Road, while the Australian High Commission sits facing it, across the street. The New Zealand Consulate is located on the corner of Salote Road and the Main Road, while the Chinese Embassy is located on Vuna Road, a few doors down from the International Dateline Hotel. (See page 64 for contact information.)

EMERGENCIES & MEDICAL SERVICES

For any emergency requiring police, fire, or medical services, dial 911. The main police station is located in the center of town on Salote Road, next to the main market. Vaiola Hospital is located south of town on the Main Road, across from the Tonga Cultural Center. This facility offers the best medical services in Tonga. *Hospital phone: 21200, main police station phone: 21222.*

Nuku'alofa

"Nuku'alofa," which literally means the "abode of love," is a city like no other. Although one-third of the population of Tonga lives there, the city itself is still in the process of rebuilding after political riots in 2006 left half the city in ashes (see page 24 for more on the riots). Given this recent turmoil, along

> There is a public saltwater swimming pool. The pool is located along Vuna Road on the ocean, near The Billfish Bar on the eastern side of town.

with the profusion of Western influences there, Nuku'alofa is a blend of old and new, rustic and cosmopolitan, traditional and modern. Fishermen bring their daily catch to the wharf, while eager sellers hawk their wares at a huge, buzzing market in the center of town, selling produce and handicrafts. Nuku'alofa also offers plenty of restaurants and cafés, which offer not only local fare, but also various types of ethnic cuisine. Nuku'alofa is best seen by foot or by bicycle, because it is small enough to cover quite easily. The scenic walkway along the water, which stretches from the wharf to downtown, is particularly worthwhile.

While Nuku'alofa boasts a number of different sights and activities, there is even more to see around Tongatapu itself. So enjoy the city, but get out of town and explore!

ACTIVITIES

Diving and Deep-Sea Fishing

Both diving and deep sea-fishing are available on the main island of Tongatapu. These attractions can be enjoyed either at nearby inner reefs, near further, more distant reefs; or even around 'Eua, which features the famous underwater "cathedral" cave (pg 128). Snorkelers too can enjoy these underwater wonders. Fishing enthusiasts can go deep-sea fishing for marlin, tuna, mahimahi, and other varieties of tropical fish. One operator, Deep Blue Diving, offers both diving and deep-sea fishing. Alternately, the hotels and tour companies can offer more information on fishing opportunities around the waters of Tongatapu.

Deep Blue Diving Deep Blue Diving offers introductory diving courses for beginners, as well as all of the PADI courses. The operator also guides fishing trips and offers boat charters. *Located on Tongatapu, at Faua wharf. Dives begin at TOP$245/inner reef and TOP$340/outer reef or 'Eua Island. Full-day fishing starts at TOP$565, whale swims start at TOP$208. Phone: 26203 or 16268, www.deepbluediving.to*

Rugby Game at Teufaiva Stadium

A rugby game at the main stadium can be an amazing event. Teams from all over the Pacific and Europe come to Nuku'alofa to play against Tonga's *Ikale Tahi*. Rugby season typically lasts from March through August. While there are seats on one side of the stadium, in order to get a true local experience, the best place to sit is on the grassy hillside, where it's easy to catch all of the game time action. Tickets usually sell fairly cheaply, and the proceeds from ticket sales benefit youth sports organizations. The stadium also hosts multiple other sporting events, as well as cultural activities, throughout the year.

Ocean Boulevard

Ocean Boulevard provides the picture-perfect setting for a beachside stroll, offering a pristine waterfront pathway and a beautiful view of Nuku'alofa. A good place to begin is at the fish markets on the wharf. From there, it's easy to walk or bike to the center of town on this pedestrian pathway. The path offers gorgeous views out over the Pacific Ocean, as well as beautiful vantage points of the nearby islands. It is a nice, leisurely walk. For those who wish to bike along Ocean Boulevard, there is a rental shop next to the International Dateline Hotel on Vuna Road.

> A chilled coconut from one of the many street vendors makes a delicious treat for the walk.

Rain Tree

While walking around town, keep an eye out for a very large banyan tree in the central town square near the Westpac Bank. This tree, nicknamed "Rain Tree," is a beautiful old tree, and it makes a great gathering spot.

Sunday Church

Because Sunday is such an integral cultural touchstone for Tongans, attending a service at one of the many churches around town is a great way to "do as the Romans do," as it were. Most services are conducted in Tongan, with the beautiful singing being an obvious highlight. Three of the main churches are situated across the street from the Royal Burial Grounds: the Catholic Basilica, the Free Church of Tonga, and the Free Wesleyan Church. A few (typically Catholic) churches offer services conducted partially or totally in English.

For church, Tongans wear their Sunday best and visitors should do the same. Modest, conservative norms of Tongan dress are discussed in the Cultural Considerations section (pg 75). There will typically be services in the early morning, late morning, and afternoon. The 10:00 am service is popular in almost all of the churches. So, when the bells start chiming, head to church!

SIGHTS

Tonga National Museum and Cultural Center

Although the National Museum and Cultural Center is nothing like the museums of Europe or the United States, it does display some interesting artifacts and exhibits. From small models of the original Tongan *kalia* boats, to photographs of ancient Tonga, to artifacts from the Royal Family, the Tonga National Museum has a little bit of everything. The Cultural Center next door features a traditional Tongan dinner show, which offers visitors a taste of the local food and dancing. *Located just on the outskirts of town on the Taufa'ahau Road, across from Vaiola Hospital. National Museum open Mon-Fri, 9 am – 4 pm. Museum entry is free, though donations are welcome. Cultural Center open Tuesday and Thursday evenings. The dinner show costs TOP$30. Phone: 23022 or 886-8338,*
www.tonganationalculturalcentre.com

Langafonua Handicrafts Center

The brainchild of a royal family member, Princess Pilolevu Tuita, the Langafonua Handicrafts Center sits right in the middle of town and displays photographs of the

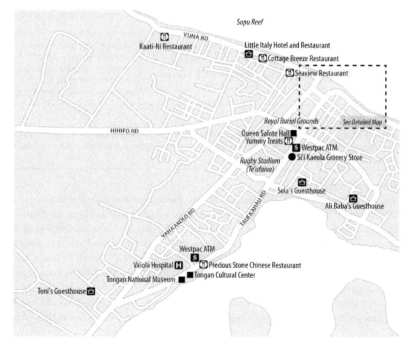

Tongan monarchs, along with traditional artifacts donated by the royal family. The Village Park also offers the opportunity to walk through traditional Tongan *fales*, or houses, as well as watch live demonstrations of craftmaking, such as weaving and

> The Langafonua Handicrafts Center added the Royal Art Gallery and Village Park in February 2011.

tapa-making. Handicrafts are also for sale inside of the handicraft center. *Located on Taufa'ahau Road, next door to Friends Café. Phone: 21014*

Royal Burial Grounds

A vast, open green space with large tombs and statues in the center, the Royal Burial Grounds, are as beautiful as they are culturally significant. This is where the line of modern kings is buried, along with their very close relatives. Kings from earlier times lie buried in the *langi*, or tombs, in Mu'a. Pines—once deemed to be the "royal trees"—line the perimeter of the Royal Burial Grounds; they were planted when the grounds were first designated as the burial grounds of the royalty in the late nineteenth century. In fact, Tongans designated this area as the Royal Burial Grounds after King George Tupou I, the first king of the united Tonga, died. In the middle of the twentieth century, expatriates and tourists used the green space around the tombs as a public golf course. *Located opposite the Free Church of Tonga, just before the central business district,*

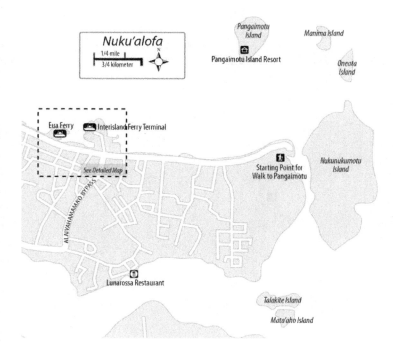

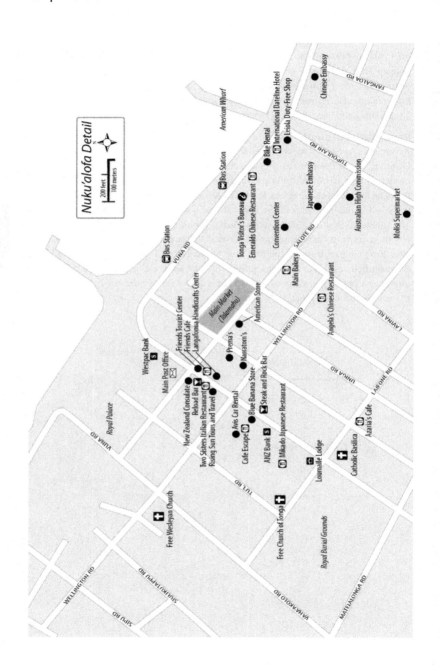

Nuku'alofa Detail

Tongatapu

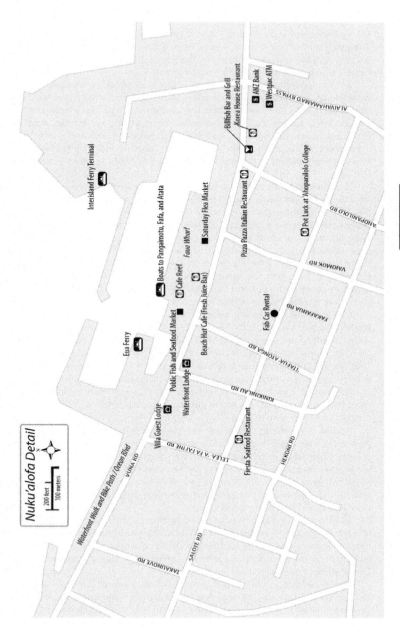

Nuku'alofa Detail

200 feet
100 meters

Waterfront Walk and Bike Path / Ocean Blvd

TAKAUNOVE RD

VUNA RD

SALOTE RD

LELEA 'A FA FAI FINE RD

KINIKINILAU RD

'ITA'FLA-'ATONGA RD

HE KONI RD

FAKAFANUA RD

VAIOMOK RD

'ANOPANILOLO RD

ALA'AIVAHAMAMA'O BYPASS

Villa Guest Lodge

Waterfront Lodge

Fiesta Seafood Restaurant

Public Fish and Seafood Market

Beach Hut Cafe (Fresh Juice Bar)

Cafe Reef

Fua'a Wharf

Saturday Flea Market

Boats to Pangaimotu, Fafa, and Atata

Eua Ferry

Interisland Ferry Terminal

Pizza Pazza Italian Restaurant

Fab Car Rental

Pot Luck at Ahopanilolo College

Billfish Bar and Grill

Korea House Restaurant

ANZ Bank

Westpac ATM

Sounds of the City in Nuku'alofa

The air is cool, peacefully silent as Tongans rise to a new morning. Suddenly, from far away, the sound of two roosters' crowing contest travels in on the breeze. Many families in the city keep pigs and chickens in their yard, but most of those who do this live farther out in the country, not in the downtown area.

As the morning progresses, car noise gradually escalates, as everyone drives to work. In order to get to work, most people drive or ride in cars, while others take buses from outlying areas. This means that the only adults who can be seen walking or biking are foreigners. Not only do Tongans consider driving a status symbol, but, much like Americans, Tongans highly value convenience. For those who can afford to drive, walking is simply out of the question. A bit later, we begin to hear children leaving for school, calling dispirited good-byes before boarding buses or sleepily walking to school.

By mid-morning, the cell phone company has set up their promotional booth, blaring a loop of Shakira, Akon, and other pop songs through the streets throughout the day. Suddenly, the music cuts off, and a wailing karaoke singer takes control of the loudspeaker, belting out what can partially be identified as Cher. In fact, erecting a music-blaring booth serves as the two cell phone companies' main advertising technique. Akon songs are particularly popular, along with repetitive polka-beat Tongan dance songs. Tongans love blaring these songs from cars, blasting them at clubs, broadcasting them from speakers at feasts, or roaring them from sound systems at fundraiser concerts. Our personal favorite repetitively sings the phrase, "Go next to my choo-choo." *Maybe the composer was a fan of trains?*

Late afternoon is by far the loudest hour of the day, as cars idle and stall, trucks motor down the road, and jubilant kids stroll to their bus stops on their way home from school, shouting and laughing together. Many families from the outer islands send their kids to live with relatives in Nuku'alofa, so they can attend better schools there. Thus, you will find an unusually large population of children here. The kids stroll along in coloured jumpers and *tupenu* skirts, the hue varying with the wearer's school. (I like to think that if, for some reason, all of the kids in Tonga got mixed up in a giant stadium, they could easily be returned to their rightful school within minutes, because of the colors that they were wearing.)

As dusk slowly starts to settle, the brass band across the street starts warming up. A while later, the band—which practices on folding chairs behind a shipping container—has gotten into full swing, playing familiar classics. We truly enjoy hearing these songs as we read, write, cook, and play on the computer. The bands, which are composed mainly of young male musicians, are much more common here than we had expected. These bands play at feasts and perform at other venues, in order to raise money for their school or community.

Dusk begins to fall, and young adult voices float up from the street. They *'eva*, or wander. Tongans use "wandering" as a time to stroll and socialize; *'eva* most often happens at twilight, as the sun is fading. Although most young women try to avoid walking alone, because doing so is generally viewed as inviting and improper, they are free to wander if they are accompanied by a friend.

By 8:00 pm, though, the city falls silent: the street is suddenly completely devoid of cars and people. Then the city dogs start roaming, challenging each other, barking at people and other animals. Their faraway barks echo in the night, the lights go out, and the city sleeps.

- Elena Borquist Noyes

Royal Palace

The palace was originally built by King Tupou I in the mid-nineteenth century. Constructing the Royal Palace was, in part, Tupou's way of modernizing Tonga. Though the royalty no longer reside there, the Royal Palace is still used for various functions for the monarchy today. Many events also take place on the vast greens outside the building. *Located at the corner of Salote and Vuna Roads, near the ocean.*

Performances at Queen Salote Hall

A range of performances, from the Heilala Festival Dance, to music competitions, to "Tonga's Next Top Model," take place at Queen Salote Hall throughout the year. This is the ideal place to check out a local event, or perhaps even to contribute to whichever organization happens to be hosting the event occurring at the time. *Located across (south) from the Royal Burial Grounds, on the main road.*

Secret Spot: Snorkeling at Sopu Reef

Seeking incredible underwater life? Look no further than Sopu Reef. Although getting there requires a trek out to the reef edge, and it is necessary to visit the reef at mid-tide, the unbelievable snorkeling is well worth the trouble. Due to the reef's location within the city area, snorkelers need to be sure to dress appropriately, meaning that both men and women must wear shorts and a t-shirt. Since snorkelers have to walk over coral and rocks to reach the reef, reef shoes are a must. They also need to bring snorkel gear. One key fact to remember: snorkeling and all other physical activities are prohibited on Sundays. While expats and travelers can enjoy themselves on Sundays at more secluded locations, Sopu Reef is located right in front of the big church on Vuna Road.

SHOPPING

Food

In addition to the larger, more official markets listed below, roadside stalls are also interspersed throughout town. The stands dot Vuna Road along the ocean, as well as the roadside between Nuku'alofa and the route leading to the airport. The stalls sell a variety of produce, and sometimes even strings of fish. They offer cheap prices, and the fruit and vegetables are incredibly fresh. There are also roadside BBQ stands, selling chicken, fish, and mutton curry.

Falekoloa, or small local stores, are also found in abundance, both in Nuku'alofa and in the villages throughout the island. These stores stock basic food supplies, along with other odds and ends, such as shampoo, soaps, and toys. Shoppers never really know what they will find on these shelves. Some of these small stores are Tongan-owned, some Chinese-owned (see page 23 for more on Chinese immigration).

American Store The American Store, which sells a variety of non-perishable items from the United States, is a great place to pick up items such as cereal, and pasta, along with other foods which may remind American tourists of home. *Located just across the street from the main market. Open Mon-Sat, morning to evening.*

Bakery The main bakery boasts piping hot fresh bread and pastries. The Bakery is the only bakery in Tonga which sells whole wheat bread; it also offers a variety of cakes and delicious sweets for sale. Since it is open on Sundays, the Bakery is quite the local hang-out spot. *Located on Salote Road, just down the street and east of the main market. Open 7 days a week, morning to evening.*

Fish and Seafood Market Because Tonga is surrounded by ocean, there is plenty of fish and seafood to be had there. On Tongatapu, the majority of the daily catch is brought into the main wharf, where it is sold at the public markets. There are two seafood markets at the wharf: one fish market sells crab, lobster, octopus, a variety of smaller whole fish, and whatever else may have been caught that day. The other sells larger fish.

There are no fixed prices at either of these markets. However, the locals are honest, and they will charge a good, fair price, especially to anyone who buys several items from them. In order to procure quality seafood, it is important to arrive at the market early, when everything is freshly caught. This is especially crucial because the seafood for sale is simply put out on tables, not in coolers (there are no refrigeration units).

The market at which the larger fish are sold is located next door to the small fish market, inside of the building where the commercial fishermen bring their catch for processing and export. In this market, gourmands can purchase beautiful pieces of freshly-caught tuna, swordfish, mahi-mahi, and other large fish. *Both markets are open Mon-Sat; the Saturday morning market offers the freshest catch and the widest variety of food options.*

Talamahu Market Shoppers seeking fresh fruit and vegetables should visit the main market in the center of town. Depending on the season, this market can feature anything from freshly-picked bananas to coconuts to papayas to a range of vegetables. Shopping at the Talamahu Market is a great way to do something "Tongan," while supporting the local farmers. Nothing beats seeing the huge smiles of the locals who work there. *Open Mon-Sat, morning to evening.*

Molisi This store had to be rebuilt from the ground up after the old store burned down during the 2006 riots. Now that its reconstruction is complete, this brand-new grocery store is the closest thing to an American-style grocery store. Molisi sells everything from fresh dairy products and meats to a wide range of packaged foods and other goods. It also has a small liquor store, which sells wine and beer. Although the prices are not the cheapest, the products offered there are both the highest-quality and the most varied in Tonga. *On Tupoulahi Road, a couple of blocks off Vuna Road. Open Mon-Sat, 9 am-6 pm.*

Si'i Kaeola Offering a range of products, spanning both refreshments (food, wine, and beer) and other small essentials (toiletries, household items), Si'i Kaeola is a decent place to shop. The store's prices, which are consistently lower than those at some of the larger stores in town, make it worth the visit. *Located on the main road just opposite Te'ufaiva Stadium. Open Mon-Sat 9 am- 9 pm*

Men at Work

Since 2009, the city of Nuku'alofa has been undergoing major renovations. For the most part, Tongans are rebuilding the sections of downtown which were destroyed in the political riots of 2006. Today, in the downtown area, some large, new buildings are being erected to house stores and businesses. Despite reconstruction efforts, many empty cement lots remain, attesting to the vast number of buildings destroyed in the riots.

Beer, Wine and Spirits

Molisi Just to the left of the main entrance of the grocery store, there is a small liquor store which sells a selection of wines and beers. *Open Mon-Sat, 9 am-6 pm.*

Leiola Duty-Free Located inside of the International Dateline Hotel, this is the place to get top-shelf imported liquors for the same price that the airport duty-free shops charge.

Si'i Kaeola The section for beer and wine is located at the back of the store. It usually has cheaper prices than the other stores in town. *Open Mon-Sat, 9 am- 9 pm.*

Handicrafts

Blue Banana Although this shop may be small, Blue Banana sells many unique souvenirs, including carvings, paintings, t-shirts, and more. *Open Mon-Sat, morning to evening. Located on Taufa'ahau Road next to Café Escape, in the Fund Management Building, Phone: 22662*

Langafonua Handicrafts Center The proceeds from the sale of all of the traditional handicrafts at this store help support the local women's organization. From carvings and paintings to traditional clothing and seashells, Langafonua Handicrafts Center offers an unbeatable selection. A trip to the shop supports not only the talented women artisans, it also supports their efforts to continue practicing the traditional arts on a rapidly-changing island. *Located on Taufa'ahau Road next door to Friends Café, Phone: 21014*

Talamahu Market Half of the main market, along with most of the second floor, features traditional handicrafts, including wooden carvings, *tapa* cloths, postcards, woven baskets, fans, purses, and jewelry. This is a must-visit place for souvenir shopping, as well as for sightseeing in general. Talamahu Market is also a great place to meet local artists and to learn about traditional handicrafts. *Open Mon-Sat, morning to evening. Located in the center of town on Salote Road.*

Clothing, Electronics, & Other Goods

Flea Market Just as the name suggests, the Flea Market offers everything, from clothing and food to sporting equipment and electronics. Most items sold here are imported from the United States, Australia, and New Zealand. Some items are new, some second- and third-hand. Anyone who sees something that they want at Flea Market should buy it there, because it is unlikely that that particular item will be available anywhere else in Tonga. Because the Flea Market serves as a main gathering spot for locals on Saturdays, it's also a great place to people-watch. *Open every Saturday morning to afternoon. Located at Faua Wharf.*

Narratom's Offering products which range from packaged foods and clothing to electronics and appliances, shoppers can find many of the things that they might need here. With a brand-new location in the center of town, Narratom's is also a very convenient place to shop. *Open Mon-Sat, morning to evening.*

Prema's Located right next door to Narratom's, this store has a decent range of electronics, clothing, cooking, and household supplies. *Located in the center of town on Railway Road. Open Mon-Sat, morning to evening.*

CAFÉS & RESTAURANTS

Unsurprisingly, Nuku'alofa has more cafés and restaurants than any other spot in Tonga. With a wide variety of restaurants, Nuku'alofa offers fare to assuage every craving, from a hankering for mu shu pork to a craving for chicken tikka masala, from a need for eggplant parmagiana to an urge for a cheeseburger.

Most restaurants offer both eat-in and takeout options, and most do not require reservations. One way to enjoy consistent delicious local delights is to check out the

Tongatapu

daily specials, because these dishes usually feature the freshest catches and the ripest produce which the island has to offer.

Angela's Chinese Offering a range of Chinese dishes and seafood, Angela's is a great place to eat. It has regular tables for small groups, private rooms for larger ones. Adventure-seekers who would like to try something different should order one of the spicy hot pots. Main dishes start at around TOP$6, so it's a good value as well. *Open for lunch and dinner, seven days a week. Near the center of town on Wellington Road, Phone: 23930*

Azaria's Café For those craving curry, Azaria's is the place to go, as the portions are large, the flavors fantastic. The restaurant also offers tasty pizzas, burgers, and fish dishes. Main dishes start around TOP$9. *Open Mon-Fri for breakfast, lunch and dinner. Located just behind the Catholic Basilica on the corner of Laifone and Railway Road.*

Beach Hut Café (Fresh Juice Bar) After a stroll along the waterfront, Beach Hut Café serves as a perfect place to stop for bite to eat, or perhaps simply for a caffeine refill. It offers a range of dishes, hot and cold coffee drinks, and delicious smoothies. Beach Hut Café also has a great café atmosphere, both for those who wish to relax and for those interested in socializing, with locals and fellow travelers alike. Dishes start around TOP$10. *Open Mon-Sat for breakfast and lunch. Located at Faua Wharf on Vuna Road. Phone: 27808*

Café Escape When the weather grows hot and humid, Café Escape is the place to beat the heat. With a modern atmosphere and very efficient air conditioners blasting, Café Escape offers the (rather unusual) opportunity to sit on a leather sofa and enjoy a hot espresso in the middle of a summer day in Tonga. Café Escape has a great menu for breakfast, lunch, and dinner, including sushi rolls and delicious dessert pastries. Free Wi-Fi is also available. Dishes start around TOP$8. *Open Mon-Sat for breakfast, lunch, and dinner. Located in the Fund Management building on the main road in the center of town. Phone: 21100*

Café Reef With burgers, fish and chips, pizza, hot and cold coffee drinks, beer and wine, and free Wi-Fi on the menu, what's not to love about Café Reef? Add in the friendly staff and the social vibe and it's obvious that Café Reef has it all. To top it off, this restaurant is open on Sundays. Dishes start around TOP$8. *Open Mon-Sat for breakfast, lunch, and dinner, and Sundays for dinner. Located at Faua Wharf, next to Beach Hut Café on Vuna Road. Phone: 26777*

Cottage Breeze With an intimate setting and a fantastic location, Cottage Breeze has proven to be a favorite among locals and travelers alike. Located on the quiet side of Vuna Road looking out over the ocean, Cottage Breeze has a decidedly peaceful location and a great menu and wine list. Specials usually include the fresh catch of the day, but the steaks are superb as well. Raw fish lovers should try the impeccable lightly-seared tuna salad. Dishes start around TOP$10. *Open Mon-Sat for lunch and dinner, and Sundays for dinner. Located on the western side of Vuna Road, just before Little Italy Hotel. Phone: 28940*

Emeralds Chinese Between the plethora of traditional Chinese dishes, the fresh seafood, and the great lunch specials offered, Emeralds is a good place to grab a bite to eat. Emeralds Chinese offers alcoholic beverages as well. Dishes start around TOP$6. *Open Mon-Sat for lunch and dinner. Located on Vuna Road, next to the International Dateline Hotel. Phone: 24619*

Fiesta Seafood For seafood, look no further than Fiesta: they have it all. From fresh tuna sashimi to lobster, visitors can fulfill any and every seafood craving here. The restaurant also has a nice, cozy atmosphere, and their prices are fairly reasonable. Dishes start around TOP$12. *Open Mon-Sat for lunch and dinner. Located on Salote Road in Ma'ufanga. Phone: 27935*

Friends Café If there is one place visitors absolutely must visit during their stay on Tongatapu, it is Friends Café. As the unofficial meeting place for locals and tourists alike, Friends is the perfect place to grab food and a drink, chat up the super friendly staff, and meet locals and fellow travelers. Friends Café has a fantastic menu, offering a wide range of caffeinated and alcoholic beverages. They also have free Wi-Fi for all web browsing needs. Dishes start around TOP$8. *Open Mon-Sat for breakfast, lunch, and dinner. Located in the center of town on the corner of the Main Road and Salote Road. Phone: 22390, www.friendstonga.com*

Kaati-Ni Anyone seeking succulent swordfish or juicy steak will love this restaurant, as these two entrées are the house specialties. Kaati-Ni does have a couple of other choices on the menu, but diners needn't bother. The surf and turf is where it's at there. Situated a short distance from downtown on the southwest side of Vuna Road, Kaati-Ni boasts beautiful ocean views and quiet surroundings. Dishes start around TOP$25. *Open Mon-Sat for lunch and dinner. Located on Vuna Road in Sopu. Phone: 28560*

Korea House As the only Korean restaurant in Tonga, Korea House offers a delicious variety of authentic dishes, such as *bulgogi* and *kimchi*. It also has a fresh tuna sashimi platter, a dish well worth its cost. The lunch specials, in particular, are a great bang-for-the-buck. Dishes start around TOP$10. *Open Mon-Sat, for lunch and dinner; Sundays for dinner. Located on Vuna Road, just east of Faua Wharf, next to The Billfish.*

Little Italy For Italian food in Tonga, this is the place to go. Little Italy serves delicious pasta and pizza dishes in an upscale, yet comfortable, atmosphere. Due to its fantastic location, the restaurant also offers excellent ocean views. Dishes start around TOP$12. *Open for lunch and dinner, Mon-Sat. Located just outside of town on the western side of Vuna Road. Phone: 25053*

Lunarossa Although Lunarossa is located a bit out of town, those diners who do make the journey will be rewarded with authentic Italian cuisine, including mouth-watering steaks and seafood, all served in a delightfully upscale atmosphere. Dishes start around TOP$25. Since the restaurant is in an odd location, it's best to travel to Lunarossa by cab. *Open Mon-Sat for lunch and dinner. Located at the Lagoon Lodge. Phone: 26324*

Mikado Japanese For tasty Japanese food, from sashimi to cooked dishes, this is a sure bet. Though the restaurant may be small, sitting cross-legged on floor pads and eating with chop sticks makes dining there a fun and unique experience. *Open Mon-Sat for lunch. Located on the Main Road, just behind the Free Church of Tonga. Phone: 25705*

Pizza Pazza For delicious pizza made-to-order, along with a cozy atmosphere, this is a good spot. With second-story patio seating looking out over the wharf, the location can't be beat. While Pizza Pazza doesn't serve alcohol, diners can BYOB. Pizzas start around TOP$15, but they are large enough for two people to split. *Open Mon-Sat for dinner. Located on Vuna Road, just opposite Faua Wharf. Phone: 25939*

Pot Luck at 'Ahopanilolo College Those who would like to try something different, and support the local youth while doing so, should check out Pot Luck at 'Aho-panilolo College. This is the training restaurant for students at the college. It opens its doors to the public for lunch once each week. The *prix-fixe* menu usually consists of two to three courses, and costs around TOP$25. *Located on Salote Road, behind St. Mary's Cathedral in Ma'ufanga. Phone: 25091*

Precious Stone Chinese Located slightly out of town, this restaurant has a nice menu of Chinese dishes. Precious Stone Chinese is perfect for lunch after a visit to the Cultural Center and National Museum. Prices start around TOP$7. *Open Mon-Sat for lunch and dinner. Located on the Main Road just past the hospital. Phone: 878 8999*

Seaview Recognized as one of the best restaurants in Tonga, Seaview offers a range of seafood and other dishes to suit any diner's fancy. The tasty food and cozy atmosphere make for an enjoyable meal. Dishes start around TOP$30. *Open Mon-Sat for lunch and dinner. Located just outside of town, on the west side of Vuna Road. Phone: 23709*

Two Sisters Italian With a perfect central location, delicious Italian food, and a second-floor vantage point to watch all the passersby below, this is a great place to eat. Dishes start around TOP$15. *Open Mon-Sat for lunch and dinner. Located in the center of town, opposite Friends Café. Phone: 26097*

Waterfront This restaurant boasts one of the nicest atmospheres of all of the restaurants in Tonga. Waterfront embraces Polynesian art and design, and it offers delicious gourmet food to complement the beautiful surroundings. Add a bottle of wine for a perfect dinner night out. Dishes start around TOP$25. *Open Mon-Sat for breakfast, lunch and dinner. Located on Vuna Road, opposite Faua Wharf. Phone: 24692*

Yummy Treats For backpackers on a budget, or for anyone looking for a quick, cheap lunch, this is the place to go. Yummy Treats serves sub sandwiches, burgers, and barbecue plates which are tasty, filling, and easy on the wallet. Prices start around TOP$5. *Open Mon-Sat for lunch. Located on the Main Road, just behind Queen Salote Hall.*

NIGHTLIFE

Billfish Bar and Grill If there is one place in all of Tonga guaranteed to provide a wild night out, it is definitely the Billfish on a Friday night. Though Tonga is an incredibly conservative country overall, Billfish is the exception to the rule. Only there is it possible to see locals and tourists getting down and dancing the night away. Interesting note: guys might want to take a closer look at the "woman" with whom they are dancing, as the Billfish is a popular hangout for the *fakaleiti* (pg 30) in town. *Open Mon-Fri until late, and Saturday until midnight. Located on Vuna Road, opposite Faua Wharf.*

Reload Those seeking simply a cold beer and friendly conversation will enjoy Reload. It's a bit small, but the prices are very reasonable, with beers starting around TOP$4. The central location is ideal. *Located opposite Friends Café. Open Mon-Fri until late, and Saturday until midnight.*

Steak and Rock For live music, pool tables, and a (mostly) local scene, Steak and Rock is worth checking out. If a is band playing, there is usually a TOP$5-$10 cover charge. *Open Mon-Fri until late, and Saturday until midnight. Located on the Main Road in the center of town, opposite the Fund Management Building.*

ACCOMMODATION

Accommodations are abundant in and around Nuku'alofa, from budget backpacker-style accommodations to hotels offering every comfort imaginable. Most facilities have hot-water showers, and most can also assist in arranging activities and transportation on the island. Some of these accommodations also provide either a free breakfast or kitchen facilities for guest use.

Guesthouses & Backpacker Accommodations

Ali Baba's Guesthouse Located just a short walk from the center of town, Ali Baba's is a great place for those looking for clean private rooms at a good price. *Prices range from TOP$60 for a single to TOP$120 for a family room; this includes breakfast. Phone: 25154 or 878 6076, info@alibabaguesthouse.com*

Sela's Guesthouse A little off-the-beaten path but only a short walk from town, Sela's is an affordable place to stay, with clean rooms and a friendly atmosphere. A popular spot with local ex-pats and international travelers, Sela's has a solid reputation. The guesthouse also offers a large common area with a guest kitchen at no extra charge. The wonderful buffet-style breakfast spread will fuel guests for half the day (breakfast is not included in rate). *Prices range from TOP$20 for a shared dorm to TOP$80 for a private ensuite room. Phone: 25040 or 15617, mettonga@kalianet.to*

Toni's Guesthouse A favorite among backpackers, Toni's is clean and affordable. It also offers a fun atmosphere in which it is easy to meet other travelers, especially on *kava* nights. Just a short ride from town, the guesthouse is situated in quiet surroundings. Toni himself is also famous for his island tours, which can be arranged for TOP$40/person. Rides to and from Nuku'alofa cost only TOP$1/person. *Rooms range from TOP$15/person for a shared room to TOP$50 for a private room; there are also two family houses for TOP$150/night. Phone: 21049 or 48720, www.tonisguesthouse.com*

Hotels & Lodges

International Dateline Hotel For those who want to relax poolside, this is the spot: International Dateline Hotel is the only hotel in town with a swimming pool. Between the large rooms, restaurant, bar, salon, and duty-free gift shop, there is little need to go elsewhere to obtain any necessities. The hotel offers a perfect location, looking out over the ocean along Vuna Road, and lending easy access to every part of town. *Prices range from TOP$100 for a single to TOP$600 for an executive suite with an ocean view. Phone: 23411, www.datelinehotel.com*

Little Italy Hotel If luxury and comfort is the name of the game, Little Italy is the place to stay. Located just outside of downtown on the quiet side of Vuna Road, Little Italy features large private balconies overlooking the ocean. In a nutshell, it is a little slice of urban living at its best. Combine that with a full-service Italian restaurant, and it will be hard to leave the building. *Prices range from TOP$230 for a standard room to TOP$260 for an ocean view, not including 15% GST. Phone: 25053, www.littleitalytonga.com*

Loumaile Lodge With large modern suites which spare no possible luxury and a complex which houses restaurants, gift shops, a café, bar, and beauty salon, Loumaile Lodge offers a level of convenience matched by nothing else on the island. It's also ideally located in the center of town on Taufa'ahau Road, across from the royal tombs, close to everything else. *Prices range from TOP$217 for a standard suite to TOP$350 for an executive suite. Phone: 28444, www.loumaile.com*

Villa Guest Lodge With only five rooms, Villa is small. However, it still offers every amenity that anyone might need for a great stay. Each room has an ensuite bathroom, and the lodge also has a large common living area that guests can share. It has a central location on Vuna Road, right across from the wharf, and the New Zealand owners live on-site, ensuring that all guests are provided with the best stay possible. *Rooms range from TOP$167/$120NZ for a single to TOP$245/$176NZ for a triple, not including 15% GST. Phone: 24998, www.tongavilla.com*

Waterfront Lodge Situated in an ideal location, featuring a fabulous café and restaurant, the Waterfront is boutique at its best. Because the hotel has only eight rooms, the owners are able to pay incredible attention to detail. The Waterfront's list of amenities is staggering: each room has a private balcony, air-conditioning, an ensuite bathroom with hot water, and a mini fridge. Best of all, Waterfront provides this level of perfection in an excellent location, just across from the ocean on Vuna Road. Breakfast is included. *Prices range from TOP$200 for a garden view to TOP$210 for an ocean view. Phone: 25260, www.waterfront-lodge.com*

Tongatapu

Portrait of a Modern Artist in Tonga

Last year, Mele saw an old, grainy picture of a woman's dance costume from the 1800s. She was inspired. Today, no one makes the fine woven comb which she saw in the dancer's hair; instead, the dancers simply wear simple bundles of flowers tied on to palm sticks for performances. And so, after seeing the picture, Mele went home to experiment. She returned to her craft co-operative several days later with a traditional Tongan comb, crafted using modern kabob sticks she had found at the local grocery store. Upon seeing the comb, everyone laughed. *What business did this woman have making an old, obsolete costume piece, crafted from kabob sticks?* Less than a week later, an American scout from the Field Museum in Chicago visited the downtown craft shop. She bought the piece. "Now it's on display in a museum," Mele says with a smile.

When I met Mele in the small, corridor-like Langafonua Craft Shop in downtown Nuku'alofa, I was immediately absorbed by her stories and her creative spark.

The craft shop is actually the business arm of the largest women's association in Tonga. The shop acts as a gallery for members who come, sometimes as often as every week, to collect commissions from the sale of their crafts. Although the items might not normally be termed "modern art," it seems almost a disservice to label them "crafts," as a quick look down the aisles reveals ornate carvings, intricate bark cloth paintings, and finely-woven tapestries.

Mele and I walked along dusty tables while she pointed out the items that she had made. She picked up a pair of woven bracelets from a huge stack, and said, "No one else made these in Tonga before I started." She slipped several bracelets on her upper arms and grinned at my camera.

Mele has been weaving since 1986, and she sells her pieces at the Langafonua Craft Shop. Although she focuses on traditional finely woven mats and formal men's *ta'ovala* (waist mats), Mele also creates bracelets, woven necklaces, baskets, traditional hair combs, and purses. She is the only artisan in Tonga to make woven earrings and woven tissue boxes.

Mele is unique in that she reintroduces ancient styles of traditional Tongan crafts and makes them into modern Tongan crafts. She brings a fine craftsmanship to her work: her traditional items are finely done and well-produced, and her more modern pieces are creative and original. Her items often start a flurry of lesser-quality reproductions among the other craftspeople.

Along with her comb, several of her pieces are on display in the Field Museum, including a women's formal belt, or *kiekie*, woven from tiny strips of pandanus fiber. As we walk up and down the craft-filled tables, she points out a woven basket shaped exactly like a miniature Tongan *fale*, or traditional house.

Having had a lifelong career in teaching, Mele is a natural educator, and she loves explaining her craft. She is a charismatic speaker and a captivating storyteller, punctuating her sentences with charged pauses and quick grins. Her opinion is that "handicrafts make a lady powerful," allowing the artisan to use her own mind and hands to support herself and her family. She says, "Women here [in Tonga] are strong people." She certainly fits the description.

- Elena Borquist Noyes

Western Side

With idyllic South Pacific beaches—perfect for surfing, soaking up the sun, and enjoying beautiful sunsets—the western side of Tongatapu is the perfect place to spend a Tongan vacation.

SIGHTS AND ACTIVITIES

Abel Tasman Landing Site
The very northwestern tip of Tongatapu marks the spot where Abel Tasman first landed in Tonga in 1643. A monument, located in a nice clearing overlooking the ocean, commemorates the occasion. On a clear day, it is possible to see all the way across the large bay over to Nuku'alofa.

Double-Headed Coconut Tree
Located in the middle of the island, en route to the island's western side, on Loto Road just past Liahona, there stands a coconut tree which simply isn't the same as the rest. At the top, it splits into two separate heads! This is quite rare and remarkable; in fact, locals believe that this tree is the only one of its kind in all Tonga.

Flying Fox Preserve
Along the main road, passing through the village of Kolovai, a certain group of trees beckon, demanding further attention. While at first it's not clear why, the trees feel different, in some way, from all of the other trees, in a way that's nearly impossible to classify. Upon further inspection, however, curiosity will pay off, as there is something hanging in these trees, something which definitely is not fruit. Stranger still, the things in the tree seem to be making quite a bit of noise. *But what are they?*

The mysterious sight in the tree is actually a colony of fruit bats, or "flying foxes," as Tongans lovingly call them. The flying foxes are the only indigenous mammal in Tonga. This is a great spot to take a close look at these interesting creatures as they hang upside down, talking among themselves in their own funny language.

Mapu'a Vaea - Blowholes
On the island's rocky southwestern shore, near the village of Houma, lies one Tongan sight which is an absolute must-see. It is the famous blowholes, or "Whistle of the Noble," as the blowholes are called in Tongan. When the tide hits just right, the waves crash into the rocks, travel through tiny channels in the coral, and then spray up to twenty meters into the air as water plumes. This sight is truly spectacular!

Masi-ata Beach
Anyone seeking the perfect spot for a bonfire or camp-out will love Masi-ata Beach. Complete with long stretches of sand and excellent shade trees, Masi-ata Beach has plenty of room for everything. Better yet, Good Samaritan Inn—located just down the beach—sells food and drinks, a plus for those who may have packed too lightly for the trip.

Surfing at Ha'atafu Beach

Surf-worshippers can head to the beach on the very end of the western side of Tongatapu to catch the waves. Because this area features a large reef break, this spot is recommended only for intermediate and advanced surfers. In addition, surfers need to BYOB (bring your own board), as there are no rental places on the island.

ACCOMMODATION

Blue Banana Beach Houses Managed by the same people responsible for the downtown arts and crafts store, this fantastic little resort is a great spot. With only three *fales* (traditional Tongan houses), Blue Banana Beach House is quite private—perfect for a romantic getaway. *Rates start at TOP$185/$100AUD per fale per night. The hotel also has specials for weekly bookings. Phone: 41575, bluebanana@kalianet.to, www.bluebananastudios.com*

Good Samaritan Inn This resort is located on the beach, near the village of Kolovai, a place which enjoys wide fame for its flying foxes. Good Samaritan Inn stands out as more of a budget option among the many higher-end resorts on the western beaches. It features small bungalows scattered across a grassy field, each with a beautiful ocean view. Camping is also available there. The inn also boasts a bar/restaurant, and there are floor shows every Friday evening. *Bungalows start at TOP$30/night per person; additional people pay TOP$20 per person per night. Camping costs TOP$10/night. Phone: 30112, info@goodsamaritan.to, www.goodsamaritan.to*

Ha'atafu Beach Resort Established in 1979 and located on the best surfing beach on the island, the Ha'atafu Beach Resort has a staff of surf experts, making it the perfect place for anyone looking for a surfing holiday. As such, the resort caters almost exclusively to this crowd. The accommodations are traditional *fales* strung along the beach. *Rates start at TOP#140 ($75AUD) for a fale; TOP$120 ($65AUD) for shared dormitory. Rates include breakfast and buffet dinner. Phone: 41088, steve@surfingtonga.com, www.surfingtonga.com*

Heilala Holiday Lodge Previously located just outside of Nuku'alofa, Heilala Holiday Lodge sits in a gorgeous new site, just steps from beautiful Ha'atafu Beach, the best surfing spot in Tonga. Heilala Holiday Lodge features a restaurant and bar onsite. *Rates start at TOP$70 for a single room and TOP$105 for a private fale; both include breakfast. Phone: 29910, www.heilala-holiday-lodge.com*

Liku'alofa Beach Resort This resort features a number of wonderful amenities: an amazing bar and restaurant, an incredible ocean overlook—a perfect spot to take in the magnificent sunsets—, and brand-new *fales*, featuring every amenity anyone could want. Better yet, the resort offers a fantastic dinner show, including traditional singing and dancing. This show will certainly keep everyone fully entertained. *Prices start at TOP$190/$105AUD for a standard cottage. Phone: 41967, www.likualofaresort.com*

Vakaloa Beach Resort Given the excellent location—right on the beach—and the immaculate facilities, Vakaloa Beach Resort is definitely one of the nicest resorts on Tongatapu. The quality facilities and location virtually guarantee a pleasant stay. The resort has a restaurant and bar on-site, as well as weekly floor shows, accompanied by a buffet dinner. *Rates range from TOP$100/fale per night up to TOP$195/fale per night; this includes breakfast. Free transportation into Nuku'alofa. Phone: 41234, vakaloabeachresort@yahoo.com.au, www.vakaloabeachresort.com*

White Sands Beach Resort For those who don't love swimming in the ocean but who do want to enjoy the beautiful western sunsets, White Sands is the place as it is the only resort on the western side of the island with a proper swimming pool. There is also fantastic private beach, a café/bar on-site, and a kitchen for guest use. *Rates start at TOP$165 per night for a standard room; breakfast is included. Phone: 878-9383 or 772-0098, www.whitesandstonga.com*

Eastern & Southern Side

The eastern and southern sides of Tongatapu feature many cliffs and rock formations, including caves and a natural land bridge archway. There are also a few beaches interspersed throughout these regions of the island.

SIGHTS AND ACTIVITIES

Anahulu Cave

On a hot, humid day, nothing beats a dip in the cool fresh waters of this limestone cave. A local guide can be hired for around TOP$5 to light the pathway through the cave to the swimming spot. Incredibly, the water inside the cave is so deep it is even possible to dive off of the sides into the water.

Beaches

Although the southern and eastern parts of the island consist mainly of huge cliffs, which drop straight down to the ocean below, the area does have many fantastic beaches. These beaches are perfect for soaking up the sun, for swimming in the crystal-clear waters, or, simply, for relaxing.

Fua'amotu Beach, the easiest beach to access, allows great views out to the massive, mountainous 'Eua Island. And with the long stretches of sand at Fua'amotu Beach, there is plenty of room for everyone.

Veitongo Beach, named for a nearby village, is much smaller than Fua'amotu Beach but with lots of locals hanging out there, Veitongo Beach is a great place to meet Tongans, as well as to see a more relaxed side of the culture than is usually on display elsewhere in Tonga. Because it is enclosed by a large reef break, Veitongo Beach is, essentially, a giant natural swimming pool. In addition, the waves crashing up over the rocky reef make for an incredible sight.

While **Hopohiva Beach** is more difficult to access than the other beaches, it certainly merits the effort necessary to make the trip. It is located just next to Keleti International Resort; there are a couple of ways to get there.

One way to reach Hopohiva Beach is by walking across the coral from the beach next to Keleti International Resort. The other way to reach it is by heading down the road just west of the resort. Upon reaching the end of the road, visitors will then climb down the rocks to reach the beach. The reward for the trip, is great: the sand is white, the water crystal-clear. And because, like Veitongo Beach, Hopohiva Beach is protected by a large reef break, it also acts like a huge, salty swimming pool.

Hufangalupe Archway

Once upon a time, the repeated motion of waves crashing against cliffs carved out a sea cave. However, the roof of that cave eventually collapsed, creating a natural land bridge. Today, the natural land bridge is a must-see attraction. Looking through the bridge, it is possible to see from the inside of the bridge out to the ocean. It is also possible to walk across the land bridge and then watch the waves crash inside of it. The view from the cliffs above is magnificent—it is easy to see all the way down the coast to the blowholes—and the high vantage point makes it a great place to watch the sunset.

Oholei Resort and Hina Cave

Always rated as the best traditional dinner and cultural show in Tonga, this event at Oholei Resort is a must-do for anyone visiting Tongatapu. Merely glimpsing the resort itself—built into the side of a cliff, made from all local materials imitating the traditional Tongan style—takes visitors on a trip back in time. Between the delicious buffet, the traditional dancing and singing, and the amazing atmosphere inside the spectacular Hina Cave, guests will feel that they should have paid at least double the price for such a wonderful experience. *Dinner shows take place on Wednesday and Friday nights around 6 pm; on Sunday afternoons, the cave is also open, but only for the buffet. Costs begin around TOP$30.*

ACCOMMODATION

Keleti International Resort This resort offers virtually the only accommodation in the southern and eastern part of the island. Sitting atop the cliffs, Keleti International Resort offers a fantastic view of waves crashing against the reef break. With a small private beach for swimming, this place is as far from any metropolis as it gets on Tongatapu. There is also a restaurant, a café, and a bar, open to both resort guests and to day-trippers. *Private fales start at TOP$85 for a single, prices go up to TOP$155 for a family unit; this includes free airport transfers. Travel to and from town costs TOP$5. Phone: 29400, www.keleti-resort-tonga.com*

Interior & Northern Side

From the time-worn tombs of kings past in Mu'a, the ancient capital; to the Tongan version of Stonehenge, there are many sights to see in this part of the island. Therefore, it should not be missed on any visit to Tonga.

SIGHTS & ACTIVITIES

Captain Cook's Landing Site

Located on the main road along the lagoon, en route to the northeastern side of Tongatapu, there sits a monument commemorating the site where Captain James Cook first landed in Tongatapu in 1777. This is a great place to sit and imagine what the natural landscape and people of Tonga must have looked like hundreds of years ago, from the beaches to the rainforests to the culture to the clothing.

Ha'amonga 'a Maui

Often referred to as "Stonehenge of the South Pacific," this ancient monument certainly merits the trip out to the northeastern tip of the island to see it. The monument itself consists of three massive limestone sections, each weighing around twelve tons and standing over five meters high. Gazing up at the monument, it's hard not to wonder how the workers could possibly lift the top section over the other two sections supporting it in order to place it on top, especially since the structure was built in the thirteenth century. *Ha'amonga a Maui* served as a gateway for the King during that time, but legend also states that the spot has astronomical significance relative to the Solstice and Equinox. This may explain why the monument is surrounded by long paths in different directions, each of which leads down to the ocean.

Kayak the Lagoon

For a little exercise, along with views of the local sights from the water, head to **Fatai Kayaks**. Located in the village of Holonga, this kayak rental shop offers hourly rentals, as well as kayak adventure packages to some of the local islands. Fatai Kayaks also makes delicious iced coffees and other beverages, which can help get kayakers jazzed up before their trip. *Single kayaks start at TOP$18/hour or TOP$55/day, double kayaks cost $28/hour or TOP$85/day; guides are also available. Phone: 45832, www.fataiglobal.com*

Langi Terrace Tombs

History buffs who wish to get a glimpse into Tonga's early years should head to the village of Mu'a, the original capital of Tonga, where they can see the burial grounds of the ancient kings. These burial grounds consist of huge layers of coral rock; they resemble the beginnings of pyramids. Upon seeing these structures, it's impossible not to wonder how the ancient Tongans could possibly carve out such huge slabs of rock and line them up so perfectly.

Tonga Golf Club

The only golf course in Tonga is located a short distance outside of Nuku'alofa, en route to the airport, near the village of Veitongo. It has nine holes, and club rentals are sometimes possible.

Nukuleka

Although, on the surface, Nukuleka appears to be little more than a simple fishing village, this place is actually incredibly significant. In fact, it's the site of the first human settlement in Tonga. Furthermore, based on discoveries by a Canadian archaeologist in 2008, it is quite possibly the first settlement in the entire South Pacific. That is, pottery found at Nukuleka during the last excavation proved that the Lapita people lived there at least three thousand years ago. Like Captain James Cook's landing site, this village is also a great place to sit by the ocean and imagine what Tonga must have been like long ago.

Tongatapu

Sea Pigs

Driving down the main road in the northeast of the island, visitors may wish to take a look out to the ocean and see if there are any unusual animals out in the water. Yes, that's right: this is the area favored by the famous sea pigs! The sea pigs go out into the ocean in order to fish; they eat whatever seafood they can find. With the sun shining and the islands sitting pretty in the background, this makes for a great picture.

ACCOMMODATION

Oceanside Guesthouse This is the only place to stay on this part of the island. Oceanside Guesthouse consists of six guestrooms, ranging from a standard room to a master suite. As the name suggests, Oceanside Guesthouse is beautifully-situated, alongside the ocean. It's a great place to relax, enjoying the soft sound of the sea right outside the window. *Rates start around $90 per night. Phone: 33009, www.oceansideguesthouse.com*

Nearby Islands

Just off of the coast of Nuku'alofa, there are many islands to explore. Three of them feature resorts, all of which offer plenty of potential activities, from soaking up sun to snorkeling around colorful reefs. For both the day-tripper and the overnighter, these islands are a definite slice of South Pacific paradise. Boats bound for these islands leave from the wharf in Nuku'alofa just behind Café Reef.

ATATA

Royal Sunset Island Resort, on the island of Atata, is a perfect place to go, whether for a day trip or for a couple of nights. It boasts a spectacular reef for snorkeling and a nice beach for relaxing. The resort also offers deep-sea fishing charters, along with scuba diving for certified divers. There is also a local village on the island, for those who want to get a taste of Tongan life off of the mainland. *Private beachfront* fales *start at TOP$250 per night, including breakfast; dives start at TOP$163; and day trips cost TOP$52/person for the boat trip, lunch, and snorkeling. Phone: 24923, www.royalsunset.to*

FAFA

Fafa Island Resort is one of the most picturesque spots in all of Tonga. Although it's located just off of the coast of Nuku'alofa, the luxurious Fafa Island Resort is situated on the north side of Fafa. Despite its proximity to civilization, Fafa Island Resort offers amazing, unobstructed views of the blues and greens of the crystal-clear ocean surrounding the island. These views are some of the best in Tonga. The buildings, decorated in traditional Tongan style, contribute to the feeling of living inside of a postcard. Activities offered include snorkeling around the colorful reef; chartering the resort's private yacht, *Sea Star* (www.seastar.to); and simply relaxing on the beach, admiring the view. *Transfers from the wharf TOP$25/one way for day trips; private* fales *start at €170 Euro (TOP$430)/per night. Phone: 22800, www.fafaislandresort.com*

PANGAIMOTU

No trip to Tongatapu is complete without a day trip to Panagaimotu. The unofficial Sunday party spot for tourists and locals alike, this small island is the perfect place to grab a cold drink at the restaurant/bar and meet people from all over the world. For those who seek activities outside of the bar, a quick walk around the island provides a great way to search for shells and see different views of the ocean. Snorkeling around the iconic shipwreck, which literally juts out of the ocean in the water in front of the resort, is another must-do activity. A mind-blowing array of colorful fish paddle around the shipwreck at all times. Round-trip boat rides to Pangaimotu cost TOP$20, while more adventurous travelers can actually walk out to the island at low tide from the easternmost point in Nuku'alofa.

Pangaimotu Island Resort is located on this small island; it also operates a restaurant/bar on the beach. There are four basic *fales*, beach huts, as well as shared sleeping facilities. All have cold showers. This is a great offshore option for those on a budget. Camping on the property is also permitted. Fales *start at TOP$60/night, dormitory TOP$35/night, and camping TOP$10/night, with tent rentals for TOP$5. Phone: 23759, pangaimotu@kalianet.to*

Tongatapu

'Eua

Introduction

Sometimes considered to be part of the Tongatapu island group, sometimes considered its own island group entirely, 'Eua is an enigma. In any case, the island is markedly different from the rest of the country.

'Eua rose from the ocean forty million years ago, making it four times older than the rest of the kingdom and, arguably, the oldest island in the entire Pacific region. The island's rocky landscape and rainy, cooler climate make it distinct from the rest of Tonga.

Many consider 'Eua to be the "Forgotten Island." Its population is smaller than any other island group and, due to its close proximity to Tongatapu, 'Eua is often overlooked. For instance, when King Tupou I established the national governmental

> One claim 'Eua can make unquestionably, though, is the title of Highest Coral Island in the World.

system, he gave every island its own noble...except for 'Eua. Even today, both the national government and private businesses consider 'Eua last. Amenities are sparse, on-island transportation difficult, off-island transportation even harder. However, anyone who spends a few days exploring 'Eua will enjoy an amazing experience, an experience which many miss completely.

Above all, the most stunning feature of 'Eua is its nature. Though 'Eua is the second largest island in Tonga, it has the largest amount of uncultivated land (leaving many areas ripe for exploration). 'Eua has many things not found on the other islands, such as large banyan trees, the Koki parrot, a natural waterslide, geologic abnormalities, and unfarmed forest tracks.

HISTORY & MYTHS

The island has, until recently, been very sparsely populated by humans. Only three of the fifteen villages on the island have existed since 'Eua was first settled: 'Ohonua, Tufuvia, and Houma. Initially, Tongans used 'Eua as an agricultural island in order to supply food, *tapa*, and *'umea*—clay for dye—to Tongatapu. In the 1890s, shortly after King Tupou I took over the kingdom, he discovered that European ships were landing upon the remote southern island of 'Ata. There, the Europeans kidnapped

Tongans to sell as slaves. To counteract this, Tupou I decided to move the entire island's population to 'Eua for their own protection, creating the village of Ha'atu'a. Later, during the 1940s, the remote northern island of Niuafo'ou suffered violent volcanic eruptions, so Queen Salote moved the entire population of that island to 'Eua, where the transplants settled all of the villages between 'Ohonua and Ha'atu'a. They named these villages after their home villages on Niuafo'ou. Since then, many families have moved back to their home island. Just as many, however, have decided to stay on 'Eua. Today, there are fifteen villages stretched in a line along the island.

Due to the abundance of food and the rough nature of the island, the men of 'Eua have long been renowned as the strongest, fiercest warriors in the land. As a matter of fact, the warriors of 'Eua played a vital role in assisting King George Tupou I in uniting the kingdom. Two brothers, both chiefs of 'Eua, were invited to serve as generals under the command of King Tupou I. So impressive was their bravery that, once Tupou had acquired power over the kingdom, he had both generals killed so that they would never rise up to threaten his newfound power. The king also refused to assign a noble to the island; that way, he reasoned, the 'Euans would never be able to mount a challenge to his unilateral power. Even though all of this happened over one hundred years ago, this same attitude towards 'Eua persists, to a degree, within the government ministries today.

'Eua

ORIENTATION

Outside of the bush, 'Eua is fairly easy to navigate. In terms of obtaining needed articles from towns, there is, essentially, one road, which runs the length of the island from north to south. Visitors should remember that, wherever they land on 'Eua, they will not be able to simply walk around and find accommodation, restaurants, or tourism information. 'Eua simply is not set up for this. As a result, almost everyone books lodging in advance, and they arrange transport to the island either by boat or by plane.

Those who arrive by boat will come in to the main town of 'Ohonua, a town with an estimated population of 1,000. By this point in the journey, many travelers will feel seasick. However, since few *palangis* are arriving on the boat, representatives from the guesthouses will be able to find their guests right away and help them on their way. Arriving passengers who have not established lodging reservations beforehand will likely be approached by a hotel proprietor to see if they need a place to stay. Those who arrive by plane will find that the same thing occurs (without the motion sickness).

Why Rats Hate Octopi

A king once left his daughter on a beach of Tongatapu, hidden in a cave; he asked a rat to protect her. After a while, the rat grew hungry, and he left in search of food. While the rat was absent, an octopus came and kidnapped the maiden. Just as the octopus was leaving, the rat returned and tried to fight the octopus. After biting off one of the kidnapper's tentacles, the octopus escaped with the princess out to sea, bound for the rugged island of 'Eua. "'Eua," in Tongan, means "of two."

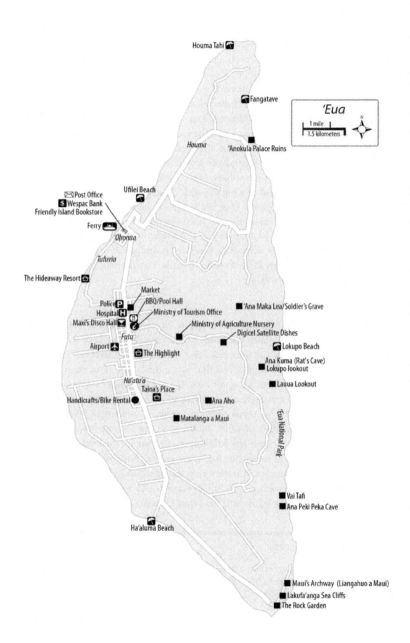

Houma Tahi

Fangatave

'Eua

1 mile
1.5 kilometers

'Anokula Palace Ruins

Houma

Post Office
Wespac Bank
Friendly Island Bookstore

Ufilei Beach

Ferry

'Ohonua

Tufuvia

The Hideaway Resort

Market
Police
BBQ/Pool Hall
Hospital
Ministry of Tourism Office
Maxi's Disco Hall
Futa

'Ana Maka Lea/Soldier's Grave

Ministry of Agriculture Nursery
Digicel Satellite Dishes

Airport

Lokupo Beach

The Highlight

Ana Kurna (Rat's Cave)
Lokupo lookout

Ha'atu'a

Lauua Lookout

Taina's Place

Handicrafts/Bike Rental

Ana Aho

'Eua National Park

Matalanga a Maui

Vai Tafi
Ana Peka Peka Cave

Ha'aluma Beach

Maui's Archway (Liangahuo a Maui)
Lakufa'anga Sea Cliffs
The Rock Garden

GETTING THERE

Even though 'Eua is closer to Tongatapu than either Vava'u or Ha'apai, 'Eua itself is surprisingly difficult to reach. Though the journey there is not actually difficult, finding a boat or plane heading to 'Eua can be. Most Tongans are accustomed to *palangis* traveling to the other islands of Tonga, and so they give visitors information directing them to *those* islands, instead of directions to 'Eua. Furthermore, 'Eua-bound vessels often get rerouted due to weather, or other random issues. Thus, anyone heading to 'Eua should be prepared for complications and delays.

Like the Hotel California, You Can Check In, but...

A brief warning about leaving 'Eua: although most travelers have no problems at all, visitors occasionally cannot leave the island when they want to. This can happen because the boat requires repairs, or because, perhaps, the captain simply cannot be found. Flights can get rerouted because a noble wants to hire the plane for a private trip, or simply because of bad weather. Therefore, it's not uncommon to miss, or very narrowly miss, a flight out of the country after getting stuck on 'Eua. It is imperative that all travelers plan to leave 'Eua at least one day before they need to be anywhere in Tongatapu.

By Air

Chatham's Pacific (www.chathamspacific.com) is the only air carrier serving 'Eua. Tickets and flight information can be found either online or in person at the Chatham's desks, one located in Nuku'alofa inside of the Air New Zealand office, the other inside of Friend's Café. Chatham's offices are also located at any of the airports throughout the country. Do note that flights to 'Eua depart exclusively from the airport on Tongatapu. It is also wise to buy the return ticket at the same time as the departure ticket, since purchasing a ticket in 'Eua can prove extremely difficult. This is because, on 'Eua, no one is at the airport unless the plane is there. *Tickets cost TOP$75 one way.*

By Boat

In terms of reaching 'Eua, the boat is the way to go. It's cheap, and it's an adventure. Those who do not feel up to long boat rides to the other islands can make the trip to 'Eua in about three hours, and they will assuredly return with a story to tell. Boat tickets are available either at the boat at the time of departure from Nuku'alofa, or at the time when the boat arrives on Nuku'alofa from 'Eua. Two boats serve 'Eua: these boats leave Nuku'alofa for 'Eua between noon and 12:30 pm, and they leave 'Eua for Nuku'alofa at 5 am. In Nuku'alofa, the easiest way to locate the boat headed for 'Eua is to hire a taxi. However, it's also possible to walk to the wharf from downtown Nuku'alofa. To do this, simply walk to the waterfront and head east, towards The Roadhouse Bar. The ferry leaves from the dock across the street from The Roadhouse. Leaving 'Eua is simple: the guesthouses usually give their patrons a ride to the dock for a small fee.

GETTING AROUND

'Eua is fairly easy to navigate. One main road runs from the town of Houma in the north, all the way to the southern tip of the island. This road totals about seventeen kilometers in length. All of the villages on the island are located along this road, with the exception of the town of Tufuvai. The main road is (usually) paved, as is the road to Tufuvia and Telefoni Road; most of the other roads are composed of crumbling pavement, dirt, or gravel. Although there are no street signs, walking from one place to another within the villages is fairly easy. True, the walks can be a bit long, but hey—it's Polynesia, what's the hurry? In addition, locals often stop and ask travelers if they'd like a ride. This helps not only in terms of speeding up the commute, but also in terms of obtaining information in order to locate key sights. Time spent in the car also offers a brief, welcome escape from the hot, beating tropical sun. Most Tongans walk or hitchhike to reach the places where they want to go, so it's not hard to do the same. However, because Tongans don't go for hikes, it can be more difficult to get rides to many of the trailheads.

Taxi
Even though there are two cars on 'Eua that are labeled "taxi," these cars are not actual taxis. There are no taxis on 'Eua.

Guesthouse Transportation
Any of the guesthouses will arrange transportation for their guests, but the guesthouses will do this based upon their own schedule, rather than upon the guests' schedule. Travelers need to simply work with their guesthouse's plans and be patient. Waiting is a cultural experience in Polynesia. *Hiring a ride usually costs TOP$10-$20.*

Suto
Hitchhiking here is very safe. It may be uncomfortable for single women, because Tongan men can be very forward. Generally, however, people are very friendly.

Car Rental
While there are no official rental car companies on 'Eua, any of the guesthouses can arrange for car rental from a local villager for TOP$50-$100 per day. The type of car rented can vary widely. Those who do not wish to operate on the guesthouse's schedule may want to rent a car. A rental car will offer more freedom, allowing visitors to explore the island at their own pace.

Bike Rental
'Eua is much larger and hillier than most anticipate before arriving, so walking from one place to another can take much longer than expected. Biking can provide a great solution to the vast, hilly terrain. Any of the guesthouses can arrange for bicycle rental. *Prices vary, but they should average at around TOP$20 per day.*

BANKING

There are a **Westpac** and a **Western Union** available in 'Ohonua; both operate during normal Tongan office hours. There are, however, no ATMs on 'Eua, so it is vital to make sure to have enough money on hand before leaving Tongatapu since there is no way to access cash on 'Eua. In addition, never expect the bank to be open when needed. Although The Hideaway accepts credit cards, no other business on 'Eua does so.

Because most visitors depart on either the early boat or the morning plane, the guesthouses like to settle fees the night before their guests plan to depart. This can lead to problems, for instance when travelers forget to get cash ahead of time, or when the hotel fees turn out to be higher than expected. Planning ahead and having plenty of cash on hand to pay the guesthouse is highly recommended.

COMMUNICATIONS

All of the villages have adequate cell service, and it is possible to buy a phone at the **Digicel Office** in 'Ohonua if necessary. However, one caveat about cellular reception on 'Eua: no matter how well the phones may work in town, they will not get service on most of the hiking trails around the island.

At the time of this printing, two of the guesthouses—**Hideaway** and **Taina's**—had Internet service available, and there were a few Internet cafés. The most reliable location with the longest opening hours was the nameless Internet/video rental/pool hall in Futu.

There is a **post office** in 'Ohonua, just around the corner from the bank. It operates between 8:30 am and 4 pm, with an hour-long break in the middle of the day for lunch. The post office can provide stamps and send letters and packages, but they have no packing supplies. Those who need to purchase a box should head back around the corner to the **Friendly Island Bookstore/Digicel Office** to buy it.

MEDICAL & EMERGENCY SERVICES

In general, 'Eua is not the ideal place to receive medical attention. It does have a hospital, but the facilities are sparse, and the staff is only minimally prepared to help with the most basic of medical care. Care for real medical issues should be handled only in Nuku'alofa. It's imperative for anyone traveling to 'Eua to bring all of the medications and first-aid supplies that they might need. Travelers should also take good care of themselves, and they should exercise caution in order to avoid accident, illness, and injury on the island. There are both a police station and a firehouse located in Angaha, in order to handle other emergencies. One important note: any visitor who must file a police report in 'Eua should make sure to file the same report in the Nuku'alofa Police Station, because it's quite common for reports to get "lost" on 'Eua. *National emergency phone: 911, Hospital phone: 50111, Police station phone: 50112*

Sights & Activities

'Eua offers a variety of wonderful activities, especially for the adventurous, outdoorsy traveler. It's simplest to arrange most activities through the guesthouse. Despite the fact that many of these activities can be done independently, many require either a great deal of legwork or a large chunk time to arrange and execute.

WHALE-WATCHING

Anyone who eschews the allure of swimming with the humpback whales in Vava'u (see page 148), electing instead to go whale-watching in 'Eua, will no doubt be pleasantly surprised. 'Eua is the only island where whales will come in very close to the beach. Often, shore-bound whale watchers can be as close to the whales while standing on the rocky shoreline as they would be in a boat (not to mention that onshore whale-watching is free!). Those who do want to go out in a boat should speak with their guesthouse to arrange it. The cost is usually about TOP$150 per person. Whale-watchers will share the boat with only a few other people and the boat will most likely be the only boat out on the water.

DIVING

'Eua has some excellent dive sights, including one named "The Cathedral," which was discovered in 2001. The Cathedral is about one hundred meters long, fifty meters wide, and thirty meters deep; it also features three large holes on the top of the cavern, where sunlight shines through, filtering down through the water onto the coral below, creating a sublime underwater vision. The Cathedral also features tunnels, drop-offs, and an incredible variety of coral and colorful fish. One dive shop operates in 'Eua.

Deep Blue Diving, a dive shop based out of Tongatapu, operates dives in the waters around 'Eua. Deep Blue Diving offers introduction courses for beginners, all the way up through the PADI courses; it also offers fishing trips and boat charters out of Tongatapu. *Dives in 'Eua TOP$340, Phone: 26203 or 16268, www.deepbluediving.to*

Cultural Tourism

'Eua offers sundry opportunities to learn about Tongan culture. Above all, there is church. Tongans are very religious, and they welcome guests who would like to attend services with them. Other opportunities, for men to drink *kava* and for women to cook Tongan food and make Tongan crafts, can easily be arranged through the guesthouses.

HORSEBACK RIDING

Horseback riding can be arranged through your guesthouse for TOP$40. However, it should be noted that the horses are in poor condition, and saddles are rarely used. The owner will most likely come along on the trip, walking alongside the horses the entire way. The departure point for the trip might vary, but riders usually go down the road or to a beach. While horseback riding is available, it is not a recommended activity.

FISHING

There are no established fishing charters available. But, like most activities on 'Eua, any guesthouse should be able to make arrangements for those interested in going out fishing with a local fisherman. It is important to note that these fishing trips will be local-style: the participants will be traveling out to sea on a small fishing boat with a bad motor, no radio, and maybe a life jacket. All of the fishing will also be done local-style…with a hand line. While it may not be everyone's cup of tea, it is certainly an adventure.

Hikes

While 'Eua may be lacking in amenities, the island more than compensates for its rustic atmosphere through all of the wonderful places it offers to explore. 'Eua is an incredible island, filled with caves, rivers, banyan trees, sinkholes, and hidden beaches. While not all of these remarkable features are easy to find, it is possible to hire a guide to point the way there. It typically costs between TOP$60 and TOP$150 to hire a guide, depending upon the area of the island visited, and the length of the trip. Anyone who wishes to go off on their own should know that it is crucial to have an excellent sense of direction and to bring along plenty of water for the trip. While maps of the island are available from the Ministry of Lands and Surveys in Nuku'alofa, they are rarely available in 'Eua. Nonetheless, even with a map, it's still easy to get lost.

There is no cell service on many of the trails, so it is important for visitors to be careful, and to make sure that their guesthouse knows where they are going, as well as the time when they plan to return. While this is always good practice while traveling, it is especially important in 'Eua. It is very difficult to gauge exact distances and times simply by studying a map, so the following numbers are averages based upon various individual hiking experiences. The distances and times listed are all round-trip, assuming that hikers start and finish their journeys in 'Ohonua, unless otherwise stated. Times and distances can be greatly reduced by hitchhiking to the trailhead for each hike.

DANGERS WHILE HIKING

Getting Lost

It is inevitable: everyone who hikes on 'Eua, without a guide, will get lost, if only for a short time. The "trails" are usually two-tracks or old roads that are often in poor condition, and there is very little signage. It is advisable to hire a guide, although maps can often be borrowed from the guesthouses, from the Ministry of Tourism Office, or from the Ministry of Lands and Surveys in Nuku'alofa. Hikers need to bring plenty of food and water with them on their excursions. (Remember that cell phone service is not reliable on any hike.)

Bulls

Although bulls very rarely prove to be an issue for hikers, they have occasionally presented a problem in the past. Some of the bulls on 'Eua are not tied up, and they are not always happy to see people. Those hikers who do happen to encounter a bull should show no fear, then throw something at the bull. At this point, the bull will usually mind its own business or leave the area. Another important thing to note is that many cows have horns, but they are not bulls. The horned cows are not aggressive. In order to distinguish a bull from a horned cow, hikers can look for the humped shoulders and the obvious other parts.

Salato

There is a plant on 'Eua called *salato*; it is a large, heart-shaped leaf with a serrated edge. *Salato* is actually a tree, with leaves which grow too high to be of concern to hikers. However, when the tree is still a sapling, its leaves are at human height. If touched, the *salato* produces no visible rash, but the area which has been contacted begins to hurt immediately. The contact causes an intense burning heat, and this sensation takes a few weeks to subside. There is no known cure or relief. The *salato* is not prevalent on most trails; there is, however, quite a bit of it around the Viefefe Trail. That said, those who stay on the trails should be fine. Even those who have the misfortune of touching the plant need not worry much; it won't cause any real damage. They will just be very uncomfortable for a while.

FANGATAVE HIKE

Distance: 15 kilometers round-trip
Time: 6 hours return, with some time at the beach
Physical difficulty: Hard
Route-finding difficulty: Very challenging

Fangatave is the name of a beach on the northeastern tip of the island. It's usually deserted, except for the occasional fisherman or guided group. The beach is a great place, and the trail leading to it provides plenty of adventure. In order to reach the trail, hikers will head north, to the town of Houma. About one-half kilometer past the town, the road will turn right and uphill into a pine plantation. Hikers should then follow that road to the point at which the road starts to level out, where they will see a dirt/mud road through a grass field to the right. They should follow that road through the field and up a small hill. The road then splits; hikers will follow the road heading downhill to the right. In a short time, this road will dead-end. At this point, trekkers will find a marked footpath leading downhill. At the bottom of the hill, they will find Houma's water supply at Kahana Stream. They should then follow the road past the water tanks, to a locked gate. On the left, there is a beautiful lookout to Fangatave Beach.

After admiring the view, hikers should return to the gate and get past it somehow, then follow the road out to a clearing above the cliffs and beach. Upon reaching the cliff, they should follow the cliff line all the way to its northernmost end, where the trail reenters the cover of trees. Within one hundred meters, there is trail access to the beach. The trail is, however, extremely difficult to find. Once under the tree canopy, hikers will need to follow a faint trail which skirts about twenty meters inside of the cliff edge, and then look for a tree with a giant fan of roots with many names carved into it. (The tree should be fairly easy to spot; it looks much like an upside-down whale tail.)

Looking out toward the cliff, it is just possible to see a small, flat overlook. Just to the right of that spot, there is a body-sized notch in the rocks. Hikers should proceed to this point, pass through the notch, and grab the rope leading down. Now, the adventure begins! After following the trail down to more ropes, hikers will enter into the caves which lead down to the beach. For the return trip, travelers need to make sure to remember the path that they took to get down to the beach and follow that path back to the top of the cliff and out to the road beyond.

> **'Anokula Palace Ruins**
> With some amazing views 120 meters above the sea, it's easy to see why a royal palace was to be built on this site. Construction began in 1983 but, unfortunately, only a concrete foundation was poured. Today, the 'Anokula site still offers spectacular views on top of a sheer cliff.

HOUMA TAHI HIKE

Distance: 15 kilometer round-trip
Time: 5 hours return
Physical difficulty: Moderately hard
Route-finding difficulty: Challenging

Houma Tahi is a deserted beach on the northernmost tip of 'Eua. In order to reach this trail, hikers will need to travel north to Houma and go about one-half kilometer beyond it, at which point they will reach a fork in the road. The path to the right leads uphill into the pines, but hikers will take the left fork, heading straight through farmland. They should then simply follow the road, keeping to the road most-traveled by, if there are options. After about ten minutes of walking, the road will curve uphill, and there will be a small rock ledge on the right. At this spot, hikers will find a road leading off to the left; they should follow that left-hand road, continuing in that general north-by-northwest direction, as the road becomes narrower and narrower. Eventually, there will be a footpath branching off to the left. Hikers should continue to head north-northwest on the footpath, until they find a tree slashed with a machete. At this point, the trail cuts down through a rock, requiring hikers to down-climb. Hikers should follow this trail, climbing down through the rocks. After completing the climb, they should follow the trail to another small down-climb on a log, then scramble down to the beach. To return, hikers should retrace their steps back to Houma, and beyond.

FOREST LOOP HIKE

Distance: 20 kilometer round-trip
Time: 6 hours return
Physical difficulty: Moderate
Route-finding: Moderate

On the Forest Loop, hikers will have the chance to delight in the many amazing sights which the heart of 'Eua has to offer. They can begin the loop trail either at the road located near the Ministry of Tourism Office, or on Telefoni Road. (Telefoni Road is the road on which Taina's Place is located.) For the best overall experience, starting the journey on Telefoni Road is recommended; however, the trail can be done either way. Also, since there are many sights along the trail, it is possible to see a few of them one day, and to then start hiking the trail beginning at the other end on a different day.

Travelers will begin by climbing the steep Telefoni Road to the top. Just beyond the telephone tower, there will be a small dirt road. This road leads to a group of banyan trees; the trees will begin appearing within the first two hundred meters. After admiring the trees, hikers should return to Telefoni Road and continue east. Telefoni Road will then make a ninety degree turn to the right. About one hundred meters past this corner, there is a small dirt crossroad, with a road heading to the left, following a line of pine trees. Hikers will follow this road about one hundred meters, until it starts to curve uphill. At this point, hikers will see a dirt/mud trail leading downhill to 'Ana Aho, Smoking Cave. After standing at the cave entrance and peering into the depths of 'Eua, hikers will backtrack to Telefoni Road and return to the sharp right turn that they had previously passed.

At the sharp right, there is a bad, overgrown dirt road leading east. There the hikers should follow that road and continue east. After this, hikers will come to several crossroads. First, there is a road which joins the road from the left. At this point, hikers should continue straight through the mud, up and down hills, until they reach a very large crossroad, with a good dirt road. At this point, they should continue straight east onto the pine-covered road. In a short while, there will be a road less-traveled, which veers to the left of the main road and opens into an even more beautiful pine forest. Hikers will then follow this road until it dead-ends in a T-intersection, with the better path leading left. They should then go right about thirty meters, until seeing a sign for the trail down to Lauua Lookout.

After admiring the beautiful view at Lauua Lookout, hikers should backtrack to the T-intersection and follow the road north. They will then continue north, ignoring all of the roads which lead off to the left. After about four hundred meters, there will be a trail leading to the right (east), which leads up Lokupo Lookout, perhaps fifty meters from the dirt road. From the steps of Lokupo Lookout, a small trail leads north about one hundred meters, to Rat's Cave. From Rat's Cave, they should follow the more prominent trail back to the road.

From this road, they will head to the right (north) up the hill, before taking the first decent road which heads off to the left. They will then follow that road until it intersects another, better road at a T-intersection. Hikers will then follow that road north, until it runs into an east/west road at yet another T-intersection. At the T-intersection, visitors will go right, following a good road which will quickly lead to the Digicel tower. They should then head downhill, until they reach an abandoned Ministry of Agriculture nursery. From there, it is possible to follow the main road down to reconnect to the village of Mata'aho.

Alternately, adventurous hikers can go through the fence on the right and follow that road up to a rock pool and waterfall. Those who cross the pool and head uphill for fifteen or twenty minutes will find another large banyan tree and cave. From there, it is possible to backtrack down to the nursery and continue on down to the town of Mata'aho.

VAIFEFE HIKE

Distance: 24 kilometers round trip
Time: 8 + hours return
Physical difficulty: Very difficult
Route-finding difficulty: Very difficult

> This is an extremely difficult hike. The use of a guide is highly recommended.

Vaifefe Hike leads to Lokupo Beach, through the national park, and down below the lookout on top of the cliffs. In fact, the hike through the forest is better than the beach itself. The beach, however, is a beautiful spot to stop for a coconut before doing the beautiful (yet grueling) hike back up to the cliff top.

To access the trailhead, hikers will head up the road in Mata'aho, which runs next to the Ministry of Tourism Office and leads to the Digicel satellite dishes. They will pass the satellite dishes, staying on the main road until they come to a nice dirt road leading to the right. There should be a sign on the corner. There, hikers will take a right, then take the first road leading off to the left; this road is a bit overgrown. When this overgrown road hits a T-intersection, hikers should turn left on a very muddy/rutty road, then look for a sign which says "Lokupo 1 km." At that sign, there will be a trail leading downhill. Hikers should then follow that trail, as well as they can, to the beach. While almost everyone will lose the trail a few times, as long as they continue to head downhill, the hikers will eventually reach the beach.

Hikers can return via the same trail; they simply need to follow the beach south about one kilometer. After reaching the end of the sandy beach, it is necessary to do a bit of rock-hopping. Following this scramble, visitors will reach a large, mushroom-shaped boulder, with a little sandy beach and pool behind it. At the back of this beach, a trail leads up between the rocks. This is a great, technical trail; it leads hikers through some of the most beautiful parts of the park. Again, it is easy to lose the trail at times, but those who keep their eyes open will see markers. Eventually, the trail climbs a steep hill, dead-ending into a rock wall. Hikers will then climb the rock wall, which will lead to the top of the ridge. They will then follow a short trail to a small farm plot, and then head through the left side of the farm for fifty meters. At that point, they will reach a dirt road which goes north/south. Hikers should follow this road north (right); this will lead them to larger, better roads leading north, and, eventually to the Digicel satellites.

SOUTHERN TIP

Distance: 25 kilometers round-trip
Time: 2-3 hours return (for hikers who travel to the Southern Tip by car)
Physical difficulty: Easy
Route-finding difficulty: Easy

The Southern Tip is the most beautiful part of the whole island. Heading south on the main road, hikers will come to a gate. Upon reaching the gate, they should go through the gate and follow the road to the Lakufa'anga Sea Cliffs. After appreciating the beautiful panorama, hikers will head north on the road to Maui's Archway, a beautiful two hundred-meter natural archway which opens onto the Pacific. To reach Maui's Archway Lookout platform, hikers will look for a trail leading uphill to the left, which enters a wooded section. A slashed tree on the right-hand side of the road marks the trail. After seeing the archway, hikers will head north on the same road to the next set of beautiful sea cliffs.

> Hitching a ride to the trailhead is highly recommended, since the trail itself is a road the whole way.

Hiking Secret Spots

The following spots are not pushed by the guesthouses, so they see very little traffic. Anyone who ventures to these places most likely won't see a soul—Tongan or *palangi*.

'ANA PEKI PEKA/VAI TAFI

Distance: 5 kilometers round-trip (starting at Maui's Archway)
Time: 2-3 hours return (from Maui's Archway)
Physical difficulty: Moderate, with some scrambling
Route-finding difficulty: Fairly easy

From the Southern Tip, hikers should head north on the dirt road, following the road until it dead ends. After that, they will follow any trail leading north from the road's end. After a short while, the terrain will steepen, with cliffs encroaching on the left. These cliffs eventually give way to 'Ana Peki Peka Cave. After exploring the cave, visitors will follow the faint trail leading north, until it dead ends into heavy brush. At this point, the sound of running water should be clearly audible. From there, hikers will scramble uphill, keeping the sound of the running water on their right. Eventually, they will come to *Vai Tafi* waterfall and pool. It is important to be extremely careful while exploring this area, because it is very close to large cliffs which drop over one hundred feet down to the ocean below.

For a better view of the larger falls, hikers can cross the small pool and scramble uphill and climb onto a small grassy clearing. This serves as a great vantage point from which to look back at the falls. Travelers will then return using the same trail, following it all the way to Maui's Archway.

World War II Tragedy

During World War II, some Allied troops were stationed in Tonga. In an unfortunate game of hide-and-seek, a New Zealand soldier was shot and killed. The 'Euan people felt so remorseful that they chose to bury the soldier at the highest point of the island. Although the spot itself is hard to find, it's definitely an interesting piece of 'Eua's history.

'ANA MAKA LEA/ SOLDIER'S GRAVE

Distance: 2 kilometers, round-trip (from Forest Loop Trail)
Physical difficulty: Easy
Route-finding difficulty: Moderate

After they have walked past the Digicel satellite towers, hikers will head back on the good dirt road. When the road turns right, and the option which heads straight ahead becomes difficult to follow, hikers should follow this bad road straight ahead. Eventually, this road comes to a T-intersection,

> *Safety Warning:* This is a treacherous scramble, and it should not be attempted if the rocks are wet.

where hikers will head left (north) for one-quarter of a mile. At that point, there will be a clearing, where there will likely be animals tied to the trees.

Travelers will then follow the road through the clearing for approximately one hundred yards, until they reach a sign on the right indicating the 'Ana Maka Lea Cave. After peering into the hole leading into the cave, the more adventurous (and extremely brave) can head up to the left about sixty feet, where they will find a tunnel which leads to a climb down into the cave.

MATALANGA A MAUI

Distance: 8 kilometers round-trip
Time: 3 hours, return
Physical difficulty: Easy
Route-finding difficulty: Easy

The Matalanga a Maui is a strange, arch-like rock formation, hidden in the bush near the southernmost village on the island. Although the hike is easy to access, very few people go out of their way to do this hike, even if know about it. In order to access the trail, it's easiest to head south on 'Eua's main road, passing through the village of Ha'atu'a. Hikers will then head past the nice paved road on the left with a sign for Taina's Guesthouse, Telefoni Road. After passing Telefoni Road, they will take the next decent dirt road on the left. Hikers should then follow that road back perhaps half of a mile, until they reach a sign on the right. Then follow the trail down about one hundred meters to Matalanga a Maui. They can then return via the same route.

Shopping

'Eua is not known for its shopping. However, the stores on the island should carry basic necessity items, such as food and toiletries.

Tongan-Owned Stores
There are *falekoloa*, or stores, spread throughout every village, except, ironically, in the areas near the guesthouses. There, shops seem to be nearly non-existent. All of the small shops are Tongan-owned, their product selection limited. The three most notable stores on the island are Anna's Store in 'Ohonua, Mosimani in Angaha, and the green store in Ha'atu'a. At these three stores, the inventory is always something of a pleasant surprise because the shopkeepers stock their shelves with the supplies they receive in shipments from their family members overseas. Because no one knows what these family members will choose to send, shoppers never know exactly what they will find on store shelves in 'Eua.

Chinese-Owned Stores
The Chinese stores offer both the widest selection and the best prices. This doesn't really mean much, except that shoppers can choose between five different brands of crackers or canned fish, as opposed to just one brand at the smaller stores. There are five Chinese-owned stores on island: three in 'Ohonua, one in Mata'aho, and one in Fata'alua.

Bookstore
The Friendly Islands Bookstore/Digicel Office is located in 'Ohonua. The store carries basic stationery, a few books, and other assorted odds and ends.

Market
There are two markets in 'Eua. The main one is located in Mata'aho, along the road. Those who simply drive by this market will probably miss it. The market is fairly small but during the wintertime, it should carry a decent selection of produce, by Tongan standards. Shoppers can usually find lettuce, carrots, onions, and, sometimes, eggplant there. Occasionally, there is also a market across from the Westpac Bank in 'Ohonua.

Fresh Fish
Those craving fresh fish should ask their guesthouse to take them to the wharf in the early morning around 7 am. At that time of day, those who are lucky may catch one of the fishermen just returning from a trip. In that case, the visitors can purchase extremely fresh fish for an extremely cheap price. Although it can be hit-or-miss to find a fisherman there, it is definitely worth trying to find one before the rest of crowd flocks down to the wharf to buy up all of the fresh fish caught that day.

The other way to find fresh fish for purchase is to listen for the sound of someone driving around town blowing a whistle. That whistle is the "fish truck." Despite its official-sounding name, the "fish truck" can be any vehicle. Whatever the vehicle, it is always selling fish. Those who wish to buy fish should flag down the fish truck. The truck will sell a string of fish for about TOP$40. These fish can then be cooked, either by travelers themselves, or by their guesthouse upon request.

Handicrafts

There is one handicraft store in 'Eua; it's located in Ha'atu'a, near Taina's Guesthouse. Just south of the Mormon Church, there is a large sign on the road indicating the shop, which sits just a block off of the main road. The shop features quite an array of local handicrafts, from sandalwood carvings to jewelry, tiki masks to *tapa*. Nearly all of these crafts were made by local 'Eua producers.

Eating

'Euans eat at home or with friends. Tongans won't buy something that they can otherwise cook for themselves, and they generally don't like foods that they can't prepare themselves. This means that every place on the island which sells prepared meals has been established specifically to cater to tourists.

Guesthouses

Anyone who would like for their guesthouse to prepare a meal for them should make sure to let the staff know in the morning, in order to afford them adequate time to prepare the food. These are not short-order places. Although Hideaway has very limited breakfast and lunch options, it does serve a variety of Western and Tongan dishes at dinner time. Taina's Place is much less formal; diners will eat whatever the staff feels like making. Luckily, they usually feel like making delicious homemade Tongan food.

Take-away

There are a few takeaway stands, also called BBQs. However, BBQs don't usually offer any food that has actually *been* barbequed. Usually, the liberal use of ketchup on an item more than qualifies that item as "BBQ." In most cases, TOP$5 suffices to buy a plate of food containing any number of meats—mutton, chicken, hot dogs—along with a root crop—taro, ufi, manioke, or kumala. There are always new takeaway shops, and other takeaways which have closed. However, there is one takeaway which is consistently operating: it is the one located in Futu, attached to the pool hall.

Feasts

Tongans eat and eat and…eat. Feasts are a very common way to celebrate any event. Weddings, funerals, school test days—just name the holiday, and there is probably a feast in honor of it.

Those who wish to have an up-close, personal encounter with a distinctly Tongan experience should ask their guesthouse about any upcoming feasts which might be occurring during their visit. Attending a Tongan feast is an important cultural experience.

Nightlife

In 'Eua, the only nightlife option (besides *kava* circles) is **Maxi's Disco Hall** and a visit is an experience not to be missed. Maxi's, open most evenings, is located in Futu, across from the Golden Success Chinese Store. Although there is no alcohol available there, customers can purchase ice cream at Maxi's. Do beware, though, of dancing too close: the old woman who owns the place has been known to chase down dirty dancers with a flashlight!

Accommodation

Before planning a trip to 'Eua, it is important to note that the island possesses by far the fewest amenities of any of the four island groups of Tonga. While some of the outer islands of Ha'apai and Vava'u possess even fewer facilities, many people expect more lodging choices on a beautiful island located so close to the capital, on an island which a population of nearly five thousand people call home. While all of the places listed here are adequate, no one should arrive expecting four-star accommodations.

The Hideaway Resort Want to watch whales swim by during morning coffee hour? Care to consult with expert staff who know their way around every trek on the island? If so, head to The Hideaway. The Hideaway has eight rooms, each of which can accommodate four people. Six rooms have their own bathroom and solar hot water; two separate small houses share an outside bathroom with cold showers. There is also a general lounge area available: it features wireless Internet, dining, and a gorgeous view. Visitors are free to use the resort kitchen. However, they must wait until the hotel staff are not using it. *Prices range from TOP$55/single to TOP$100 for four people, and camping is TOP$25 for a tent site. Phone: 50255, hideawayeua@gmail.com, www.kalianet.to/hideawayeua*

Taina's Place Those who favor hidden, quiet lodgings, tucked away from the island hubbub in a nice garden, will love Taina's Place. At this guesthouse, visitors stay close to a Tongan family, since Taina—along with her daughters and nieces—runs the guesthouse. Each room is a separate house, and guests use two shared bathrooms. There is usually hot water available for showers. A guest lounge, kitchen facilities, and Internet service are also available. *Prices range from TOP$40/single to TOP$100 for four people, camping is TOP$20/person. Phone: 50186 or 65002, tainasplace@gmail.com, www.tainasplace.com*

The Highlight This place is a four-bedroom home; it will rent out either single beds, or the entire house. It is possible to rent a bed, or the house, for any length of time. There are no services, staff, or hot water. However, The Highlight is very centrally located on the island. *Phone: 50143 or 888-4626, highlight_guesthouse@hotmail.com*

Ha'apai

Introduction

Want to walk around the inside of a travel poster advertising the South Pacific? Head to Ha'apai. The island features endless sandy beaches fringed with palm trees, pristine reefs filled with marine life, and aqua waters teeming with humpback whales. Better yet, there is no need to fight for a spot on the beach on Ha'apai. Oftentimes, in fact, travelers will find that they have the entire beach to themselves.

What's more, the views are unmatchable. It is possible to watch both the sunrise and the sunset (without moving a foot!) on these small, low-lying coral islands. To the west, views of stunning volcanoes add to an incredible sense of a South Pacific adventure. Inland, on the islands themselves, the fascinating local Tongan culture thrives in traditional villages. Those who travel to Ha'apai will also enjoy hiking to historical sights, such as the spot where the unification of Tonga began. As the local saying goes, "Don't worry, be Ha'apai!" It would be hard to be anything but happy there.

It is easy to get "off-the-beaten track" in Ha'apai. The island group is still relatively undiscovered; visiting thus affords a rare opportunity to glimpse the local island culture as it has been for centuries. Since the island group does not cater to tourism, Ha'apai lacks certain conveniences and entertainment. In fact, in Ha'apai, visitors will likely find themselves spending most of their time relaxing on the beaches, swimming in the warm Pacific waters, soaking in the fascinating local culture, and exploring the small villages which dot the islands. Those seeking active pursuits should look to the water. Ha'apai offers myriad opportunities for diving, snorkeling, and fishing. On the land, it is actually possible to *bike* between islands (yes, that was not a typo), exploring local village life from an intimate, close-range perspective.

Excluding the resorts, one restaurant/bar exists in the entire island group. There is also one main road, which covers only two of the sixty-two islands in the Ha'apai chain. Fourteen of the islands in Ha'apai are inhabited. Most travelers will probably divide all of their time between the islands of Lifuka, Foa, and Uoleva. These locales boast guesthouses, resorts, and endless sandy beaches. Visitors in Ha'apai will immediately notice that they stand out and draw attention from locals. This is because

Ha'apai residents are not as accustomed to seeing *palangis* as the residents of Tonga-tapu and Vava'u are.

HISTORY

Even in a nation as historically rich as Tonga, Ha'apai boasts an especially eventful past. It is home to many historical sights and significant happenings. In fact, the villages of Uiha and Hihifo may be some of the oldest settlements in all of Tonga. Historians have found ancient Lapita pottery in some of the excavation sights on Ha'apai, and they have carbon-dated it to the years between 1300 BC and 3000 BC. Interestingly, on Uiha Island, archaeologists have unearthed curious rocks in the old housing foundations, rocks which are not original to Tonga. This evidence suggests great oceanic voyages in ancient times.

Both the current royal lineage and the unification of Tonga owe their beginnings to this island group. Captain Cook also made one of his first landings here in 1777; it was on that visit that he nicknamed Tonga the "Friendly Islands." Furthermore, the famous mutiny on the *Bounty* occurred in Ha'apai waters in 1789, between Lifuka and Tofua. Another famous incident occurred in 1806, when the *Port au Prince* was destroyed at anchor, and young William Mariner's life was spared. Mariner would go on to live with a local Tongan chief for four years, an adventure he would later detail in his book, *An Account of the Natives of the Tongan Islands*. That book remains one of the best documentations of ancient Tongan life.

MYTHS

One of Ha'apai's most infamous myths springs from the island of Mo'unga'one. Once, a long time ago, there was one spirit in the form of a shark, and another spirit in the form of a puffer fish. The shark ate the puffer fish. The puffer fish, however, became so angry that he kept puffing himself up, growing bigger and bigger inside of the shark. In pain, the shark pleaded with the puffer fish to leave him, but the fish wouldn't stop. The shark then met a man from nearby Mo'unga'one, who was traveling in a canoe. The shark begged the man for help. The shark told the man that, if he helped him, the people of Mo'unga'one would never again need to worry about sharks, that they would be forever protected. Tempted by this offer, the man agreed and pulled the puffer fish out of the shark.

From that moment on, the people of Mo'unga'one have never feared sharks. In fact, the people who live in Mo'unga'one believe even today. Recently, the Fisheries Office sent a crew on a diving expedition to measure coral growth. Once the crew got near Mo'unga'one, the water was absolutely infested with sharks. No one wanted to enter the water, but a local from Mo'unga'one who was on the boat offered to help. He went into the water with a few of the researchers, and he pushed away any of the sharks that got too close to the other divers.

Another famous myth born in Ha'apai concerns the volcanic islands of Kao and Tofua, both of which can be seen on the horizon, to the west of Lifuka. According to legend, a Samoan god was angry that Tonga had a higher mountain than Samoa. In order to fix this problem, he came to Ha'apai to steal some land. He ripped off the top of Tofua, and he began flying away with it. However, a Tongan god chased him and caught him in the act. Frightened, the Samoaon god dropped the land into the sea, thus forming the volcanic island of Kao. There is now a lake in the center of Tofua, where the piece of land which became Kao Island was broken off from the island.

ORIENTATION

Of all the island groups in Tonga, Ha'apai is spread out across the largest area of ocean. However, most of the people and businesses are concentrated on the islands of Lifuka and Foa. Several other population hubs are located on Nomuka, to the

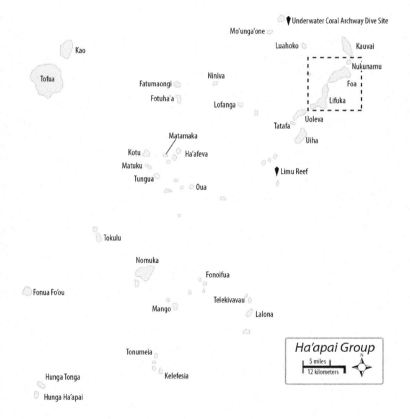

south; as well as in the Lulunga group, in the middle; and upon the islands of Ha'afeva, Tungua, and O'ua. To the west lie the volcanic Islands Kao and Tofua. On clear days, these small islands are visible from the Lifuka and Foa.

Those who arrive by plane will land on the northern tip of Lifuka Island in Koulo village. From there, it takes about five minutes by car to arrive in the main town, Pangai. Heading into town, the road passes through both Holopeka village and the bush area—fertile Tongan farmland bursting with crops, shaded by tall coconut trees. Along the right side of the road, between the stands of coconut palm, brief snatches of blue sea beckon, and scattered views of sandy beaches.

Travelers who arrive on the ferry will first stop at Ha'afeva Island, in Ha'apai's middle island group, Lulunga. After unloading passengers and cargo there, the boat will continue on, docking at the main wharf on the northern side of Pangai, the main town on Lifuka. Straight across from the wharf sits one of the tallest buildings in Pangai, stretching an impressive three stories high. The road one block inland from the wharf is Ha'apai's main road. This road travels from the southernmost tip of Lifuka to the northern tip of Foa Island, where the resorts are located.

GETTING THERE

As the plane prepares for its approach to Ha'apai, it passes over myriad tiny dots below—uninhabited, palm-fringed islands; sand bars; isolated reef systems, all surrounded by pristine turquoise blue waters. Finally, the plane drops low over the reefs, just before touching down on Lifuka Island. Since Lifuka Island's main road actually cuts through the middle of the runway, a "railroad crossing"-style gate comes down in order to stop traffic when the flight lands. After it touches down, the plane coasts across the runway, traveling all the way from the west side to east side of the island, at the narrowest stretch.

Travelers, beware: this tricky maneuver tends to give the illusion that the plane will continue right off of the edge of the island into the ocean. (But this hasn't happened yet!) Disembarking from a climate-controlled airplane into the hot, tropical air, it is impossible not to feel the certain air of timelessness pervading Ha'apai, both in the slow island pace of life, and in the unmistakable feeling of having stepped back centuries in a moment. Truly, it is an amazing experience.

Inside of the small airport, there are no security checks whatsoever, food and liquids welcome. In fact, locals often pass off packages to passengers to carry with them to other island groups. When passengers check in to fly out of Ha'apai airport, the staff members check the travelers' names off of a handwritten list—upon which names are often misspelled. After this, the airport staff hand each passenger a handwritten ticket stub with their seat number. Passengers flying into Ha'apai should ask for a seat on the left side of the plane, while those flying back to Tongatapu should ask for a seat on the right side of the plane. These seats provide passengers with the best possible views of the small islands and reefs below.

It is possible to fly to Ha'apai every day, except for Sunday. The only carrier currently running this route is Chathams Pacific (www.chathamspacific.com). During the peak tourist season, flights might happen a couple times a day; during the off-season there might be only one flight a day. A one-way ticket from Tongatapu to Ha'apai costs TOP$149, if purchased at least two weeks in advance. The price increases to TOP$179 if the ticket is purchased last minute. It is best to either buy tickets online or from the main office in Nuku'alofa, because it can prove more difficult to purchase tickets in Ha'apai. Although flights are usually pretty reliable, they can sometimes be delayed or canceled due to weather. It is best to arrive at the airport forty-five minutes before the flight is scheduled to depart. Anyone who shows up earlier than that will, more than likely, find the airport empty and uninhabited. There is a small handicraft and snack shop located inside the airport, but prices are higher there than elsewhere on the island. *Chathams Pacific Phone: 878-8898 (local office), 28852 or 877-7328 (main office), www.chathamspacific.com.*

Ferries run between the island groups on a weekly basis. In Ha'apai, the ferry lands at the main wharf in Pangai. Because the schedule depends upon the weather, it can be very irregular. Furthermore, the ferry cannot operate on Sundays due to local religious laws. Tickets are available for purchase at the small office building on the wharf. The schedule is also sometimes posted there, but it usually changes. The schedule is also announced on the radio. However, the best way to find out the actual ferry schedule is to ask a local. Sometimes, the ferry will come in during the day, other times it may arrive in the middle of the night.

The ferry begins its journey in Tonga's capital, Nuku'alofa, makes a quick stop in Ha'afeva—an outer island in Ha'apai's Lulunga group—and then finally stops in Pangai, Ha'apai. After unloading all of the Ha'apai-bound cargo and passengers, then reloading with Va'vau-bound cargo and passengers, the ferry continues on to Vava'u. As on Ha'apai, the ferry unloads and reloads there, before returning to Pangai the following day, en route back to Nuku'alofa. Although ferry times vary, it usually takes about twelve hours to travel from Nuku'alofa to Pangai; it takes another eight hours to travel from Pangai to Vava'u. Those who decide to travel by ferry should be prepared for both delays and rough sea travel. Furthermore, they should know that there have been inquiries into ferry safety recently, following the sinking of the *Princess Ashika*. However, despite its drawbacks, ferry travel is the best way to travel as the locals do in the island archipelagoes of Tonga. What's more, it's interesting to watch the buzz of activity around the wharf as the ferry unloads its cargo, and families and friends greet one another after a long journey. *Phone: 23855, local office is on the main wharf in Pangai.*

All those who arrive by private yacht need to check in with the customs department at the post office, even if they have already registered their yacht in another island group. Yachts tend to anchor either in the small bay of Uoleva Island or near the main wharf in Pangai. Many yachts also stop at Ha'afeva, Uiha, and Kauvai, along with some of the smaller uninhabited islands of the Ha'apai group. Mariner's Restaurant is a popular gathering place for tourists and yachties alike; the restaurant even has its own yacht registration book at the bar.

GETTING AROUND

Navigating the main islands of Ha'apai is fairly easy, since the islands are very small, and there are only a couple of main roads. Because there are no marked street names, it can, at times, be difficult to get directions. Therefore, it's best to navigate by using landmarks, along with the map in this guidebook. At a few intersections, hand-painted wooden signs point in the direction of some of the sights or guesthouses. Throughout Ha'apai, there are no stoplights, stop signs, or roundabouts.

A handful of taxis operate in Ha'apai. Usually, one or two will sit waiting at the airport when flights arrive. It costs TOP$8 to travel from the airport into the town of Pangai, and it costs around TOP$20 to ride from the airport to the resorts on Foa. Another way to travel into town from the airport is to make arrangements with the guesthouse—most guesthouses offer airport transfers as part of their packages.

There is one bus in Ha'apai, and it runs from the middle of Pangai up to the wharf in Faleloa on Foa Island. The bus is primarily used by local schoolchildren to go into Pangai for school in the morning and to return home in the afternoon. The bus schedule is irregular; fares cost $1 for a one-way trip.

For inter-island travel within Ha'apai, local boats are one possible mode of transportation. The more popular boat routes run between the main island of Lifuka and the islands of Uoleva, Kauvai, and Uiha. Because the boats that run these routes are smaller, they follow no set schedule. In order to

> Travelers who want to see the small islands of Ha'apai on their own time may prefer to bike or walk to their destinations.

obtain further information about traveling by local boat, it is wise to talk to the local skippers by the wharf in Pangai, inquire at the Tourism Bureau, or speak with guest-house staff. On these local boats, each passenger contributes money to defray fuel costs. In order to determine how much money to give the skipper, it's best to inquire either with the Tourism Bureau or with a guesthouse. The contribution amount varies, depending upon the length of the boat ride. If the other passengers don't seem to pay on the boat ride, those passengers probably made other arrangements with the skipper in advance. Visitors should compensate the skipper for the transporta-tion provided.

Suto, or hitchhiking, is another option for transportation. This practice is very common on the main road between Pangai and Foa. While hitchhiking is generally quite safe, women traveling alone should make sure that there are other women in the vehicle in which they will be riding. It is easiest to catch a ride heading into Pan-gai in the morning, and a ride going out toward Foa in the afternoon or evening. That being said, there are usually vehicles traveling in both directions throughout the day.

It is polite for hitchhikers to offer TOP$5-10 to help with fuel costs, depending on the length of the ride. Should the driver decline the money proffered, travelers can use their own judgment—they can either take the free ride, or leave the *pa'anga* on the seat next to the driver as they exit the vehicle. The driver will appreciate the extra money since fuel costs are astronomically high on these remote islands.

BANKING

Westpac Bank is located on the main road in Pangai, near most of the stores. There are two ways to obtain money at the bank: by withdrawing money at the counter, using a credit card; or by exchanging currencies. Either way, a passport is required for every transaction. Because there is no ATM machine in Ha'apai, it is only possible to obtain money when the bank is open. The hours of operation are Monday to Fri-

Princess Ashika Tragedy

In August 2009, a tragedy at sea occurred in the Ha'apai island group, near the island of Nomuka. The government ferry, *Princess Ashika*, sank at sea, killing over seventy people who were onboard. Because many reports had deemed the ferry to be unseaworthy, these deaths were senseless and preventable.

The Tongan ferries are important for several reasons. First of all, they are the main mode of inter-island transportation for the local people. Furthermore, the ferries also transport food and supplies to the islands of Ha'apai and Vava'u. In fact, the *Princess Ashika* was an interim ferry, substituting for a brief period after the old *Olovaha* ferry had been removed from operation. The Tongans had purchased the *Princess Ashika* from Fiji, where the boat was already known to be in a state of major disrepair. At the time of the accident, the *Princess Ashika* had only been operating in Tonga for a few months.

The problems arose due to the design of the *Princess Ashika*: the boat was never designed for voyages on the open sea. During the ship's final voyage, water had begun leaking into the cargo hold area, and the crew started bailing water as fast as they could. The passengers, however, were never warned that anything was amiss. This occurred during the middle of the night and, as usual on a long ride, the women and children were sleeping on the inside of the boat, while the men were gathered around the outer decks. When, in the final moments, the boat suddenly overturned, it all happened so fast that there was no time for the passengers on the inside of the boat to escape. The *Princess Ashika* sank immediately.

With Tonga's small population, everyone had family or friends onboard. It was a national tragedy. To make matters worse, the royal family made no public statement about what had happened. In fact, the king actually left the country the next day on a planned vacation to Europe. After the accident, a major inquisition was conducted, and some government officials resigned their posts. In terms of safety, all of the ferries and aircraft in Tonga have come under intense scrutiny since the *Princess Ashika* tragedy. In early 2011, five of the people involved in purchasing, and granting operating approval to the unseaworthy ferry were brought to trial in Nuku'alofa. Just recently, in November 2010, the government paid $1.2 million in damages to the next of kin of fourteen of the victims who perished in the accident. Because the next of kin of other victims had already filed civil claims against the government, they now can choose between continuing to pursue their civil cases and collecting this government handout.

day 8 am – 4 pm; the bank is closed on Saturday or Sunday.

There is also the **Tonga Development Bank**. It is located across the street from the gas station, and it has the same hours of operation as Westpac Bank. An important item to note: while there are banks in Pangai, it is still wise to bring Tongan currency when arriving in the islands of Ha'apai. Most businesses accept only local cash. Another perk of any visit to the bank is the lobby air-conditioning—the guesthouses on Lifuka do not have air conditioning, so the banks are the only places which provide this luxury.

Finally, there is a **Western Union Money Transfer Office,** connected to the Tourism Office on the main road in Pangai.

COMMUNICATIONS

Internet connections are available at several locations in Ha'apai. Mariner's Café has one computer with Internet available, along with a separate Internet café next door. However, the connection speeds tend to be much slower at the Internet café than at Mariner's Café itself. The dive shop on the main road in Pangai, Fins 'n' Flukes, also has its own Internet connection. At Fins 'n' Flukes, travelers can either pay to use the shop computer or pay for a wireless Internet connection on their own laptop. The resorts on Foa provide Internet service for their guests. Since the Internet connection is satellite, it can, at times, be unreliable in these remote islands. Another important item to note is the fact that, outside of the main islands of Lifuka and Foa, there is no Internet access. Prices for Internet usage vary, but usually run from TOP$3 – $6/hour.

There is typically good cell phone coverage in Ha'apai on Lifuka, Foa, and Ha'afeva, where the cell phone towers are located. However, cell phones in Ha'apai are not entirely reliable, and calls frequently get dropped for no apparent reason. Furthermore, cell phone connections may not always work as well on Uoleva, Kauvai, and the other outer islands. Both cell phones and phone cards are available for purchase in Pangai, at the Digicel and TCC stores. Digicel is located on the main road in Pangai; TCC is located on a small dirt road behind the Wesleyan church.

The **post office** is located on the Ocean Road in the main part of Ha'apai, just south of the wharf, near the flag pole. Hours of operation are Monday through Friday, 8:30 am – 4 pm, with an hour long break for lunch. It can take anywhere between two weeks and one month for mail sent from Ha'apai to arrive at an overseas destination. Although Ha'apai mail service is fairly reliable, it is usually quicker and more reliable to send mail from the main island, Tongatapu. There are no mailing supplies for sale at the post office; however, mailing supplies and postcards are available at nearby **Friendly Islands Bookstore**. The post office also acts as the local customs office for yachts, so all yachties should check in there when they arrive in Ha'apai.

TOURISM OFFICE

The Tonga Visitors Bureau is located on the main road in Pangai, near the market, across the street from Fins 'n Flukes. The Visitors Bureau is open from 8:30 am – 12:30 pm, and 1:30 pm – 4:30 pm Monday through Friday, and Saturday 8:30 am – 12:30 pm during tourist season. These official hours are not always followed—it is quite possible to show up at the Tonga Visitors Bureau and find that no one is there. The Tonga Visitors Bureau can assist in making accommodation and transportation arrangements; the staff can also provide suggestions on good sights to see and activities to do. The Tonga Visitors Bureau also has brochures available, along with a small section of handicrafts and display items from the old museum. *Phone: 60733, haapaitourism@gmail.com*

MEDICAL EMERGENCY SERVICES

The local hospital, Niu'ui, is located in the town of Hihifo, just south of Pangai on Lifuka Island. It offers basic services, but it has no pharmacy. Therefore, travelers headed to Ha'apai need to bring a first-aid kit, along with any medications they may need, along with them on their trip. In an emergency, if at all possible, it is best to return to Nuku'alofa, Tongatapu, for care at the main hospital. The quickest way back to Tongatapu is by plane; there are flights several times each day, except on Sundays. *Niu'ui Hospital Phone: 60203*

The police station for Ha'apai is located on the main road in Pangai, just south of the Tourism Bureau. There is also a minimum-security prison on the edge of the town of Pangai, en route to the bush to the east. The fire station sits on the ocean road, near the post office. *Police station Phone: 60222, Fire station Phone: 60771*

Lifuka & Foa Islands

Lifuka, the main island in Ha'apai, is home to three thousand Tongans, approximately half of the population of the Ha'apai island group. Housing the main wharf in Pangai, along with the airport in Koulo, Lifuka is also the point of entry into Ha'apai. There are four villages on Lifuka: Hihifo, Pangai, Holopeka, and Koulo. As the capital city of the Ha'apai group, Pangai has both the largest population and the largest number of stores and guesthouses of all the Ha'apai islands. Pangai also houses the hospital, banks, tourism bureau, post office, police station, and other services. Hihifo and Pangai are neighboring towns, while Holopeka and Koulo merge into each other on the north side of the island. All of the villages are situated on the more protected west side of the island. A sandy beach runs the entire length of the island; some reefs lie just offshore. The east side is the wild, uninhabited side of the island, and the waters are more dangerous there, with bigger waves and stronger currents. The Tonga Trench is located to the east of the island.

The island of Foa is located just north of Lifuka, connected to Lifuka by a causeway. Travelers searching for traditional Tonga will find it here, in the gorgeous little

Ha'apai

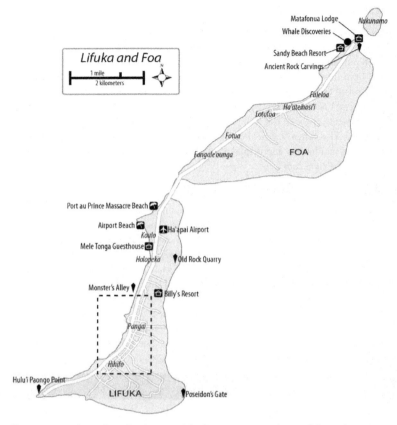

villages strung along this island. One of the best ways to explore Lifuka and Foa is to bike from the south to northern tip of the islands. The main road meanders through each of the five villages: Fangale'ounga, Fotua, Lotofoa, Ha'ateihosi'i, and Faleloa. Riding from the north side of Pangai on Lifuka to the northernmost tip of Foa will usually take between forty-five minutes and one hour.

ACTIVITIES

Swimming with Whales

Fins 'n' Flukes is currently the only operator offering an incredibly unique activity: the chance to swim with humpback whales. The whales migrate to Tonga in June and remain there to have their calves, before migrating back to Antarctica in November. Since there aren't many tour operators in the area, the islands of Lifuka and Foa are ideal locations for whale encounters, as visitors often find themselves on the only boat in the whole area. Trips take a full day: groups will spend time boating around the area to find the whales, and there may be snorkeling along the way. Lunch is typically included on these excursions.

Diving/Snorkeling

Ha'apai offers unbelievable snorkeling and diving opportunities. Since there has not been a lot of tourism or development in this island group, the reefs are pristine and untouched. The waters surrounding the islands house a wide variety of colorful fish and coral and, sometimes, sting rays and reef sharks. There are also walls of coral and caves, not to mention one of the largest underwater coral archways in the Pacific. Those who

> The dive shop Happy Ha'apai Divers/Ocean Blue Adventures closed in 2011, but it recently re-opened under new ownership as Whale Discoveries (ww.whalediscoveries.com). There may also be sailing or whale watching soon thorugh Mariner's Café in Pangai.

are not already certified scuba divers can take courses to become PADI-certified in Ha'apai, or they can plan shore dives or beginner courses there. However, it is also possible to do advanced courses and dives in Ha'apai.

Fins 'n Flukes This outfitter offers a million ways to enjoy the stunningly pristine reefs of Ha'apai, with scuba diving, PADI dive courses, snorkeling, island trips and transfers, and kayaking all year-round. From July through November, Fins 'n Flukes can take travelers out to swim with the majestic humpback whales. Because the guides ensure that snorkelers are in small groups at all times, it is sure to be a very personal and unforgettable experience. Even better, the ex-pat owners (Brian and Sabine, who are Irish and German, respectively) spice up the trips with their fun, friendly personalities. Brian is also a marine biologist, so he can share a lot of knowledge on local marine life. *Located on the main road in Pangai, across from the tourism bureau. Dive trips starting at TOP$245 (2 dives), discounted packages available for multiple days, snorkeling trips TOP$75 - $120, equipment take-away available, whale watching trips TOP$230 (full day). Phone: 887-0141 or 73-13549, info@finsnflukes.com, www.finsnflukes.com*

Fishing

It is possible to go deep-sea fishing on Ha'apai. Another way to enjoy the seas around Ha'apai is to either go fishing with some of the locals from shore or to go fishing for octopus in the traditional way. There are several ways to arrange fishing trips: by speaking with the local dive shops, inquiring at the guesthouses, or asking at the Tourism Bureau. There are no official deep-sea fishing outfitters in Ha'apai.

Kayak

Kayaking provides yet another great way to see these small islands; the sport also enables travelers to get to some smaller uninhabited islands they might not see otherwise. Kayakers can pull up on isolated beaches for a picnic lunch, or perhaps just paddle along the shores of the main islands. Because there is often wind, it is best to row out against the wind.

> A great option for paddling around this area is to head across the channel to the King's island, Nukunamo (pg 158), or go south along the coast of Lifuka.

That way, on the return trip, tired travelers can count on the wind to carry them back to shore.

Fins 'n Flukes Sit-on kayak rentals are available at Fins 'n Flukes: these are meant for short trips, not open ocean travel. They have three of these boats available, two singles and one double. *TOP$30/full day, TOP$20/half day.*

Friendly Islands Kayak Company Based out of Vava'u, this outfitter offers guided kayak/camping tours throughout the islands of Vava'u and Ha'apai. *13 day all-inclusive guided tours in Ha'apai. Phone: 70173, www.fikco.com.*

Kite Surfing

Both Foa Island, near Matafonua Lodge, and Uoleva Island, offer some great spots for kite surfing. Interested travelers need to bring their own gear, or Matafonua Lodge offers kiteboarding for the experienced to the novice with lessons available.

Biking

Biking is not only one of the best ways to see all of the villages in Ha'apai, it's also the easiest way to travel between Foa and Lifuka. Best of all, the bike trail through Koulo village, on Lifuka, crosses the runway, so bikers get to go across the airport runway en route to Lifuka! It is also easy to see many of the sights by bicycle.

When renting a bike, it is imperative to check the bicycle in advance to make sure that it is in good working order. On Foa, the resorts have bicycles available for guest use.

Guesthouses may have bicycle rentals available; visitors should check with their guesthouse. Most bike rentals cost about TOP$15 – 20/day.

Fins 'n Flukes offers new bicycles for rental (TOP$20/day), along with bike combination locks. These bikes are in the best shape of any of the bicycles on the island. They are also the easiest to pedal around.

New Life Church has several older, rusted bicycles available for rent. These bikes may be in rough shape and difficult to manage, and they will not come with locks. Renting a bike from the church is a bit different from renting a bike elsewhere. In order to rent a bike there, visitors should simply show up at the church and yell for someone for assistance. *The church is located on the main road to the south of all the stores, about ten minutes, just past the Catholic Church. Costs TOP$15/day.*

Horseback Riding

There is horseback riding available for guests staying at the resorts on Foa. Adventurous travelers can gallop along sandy, isolated beaches, enjoying the gorgeous scenery from a completely different point of view. They can also explore the villages and bush roads.

Wildlife-Watching

Though there's little bird-watching here, on the northern tip of Foa, travelers can bat-watch. The famous "flying foxes" migrate between Nukunamu and Foa Islands, and it's easy to observe them from the beach on Foa, or from Matafonua Lodge. At dusk, the bats return from Nukunamu to Foa. At dawn, they return to Nukunamu, just across the channel.

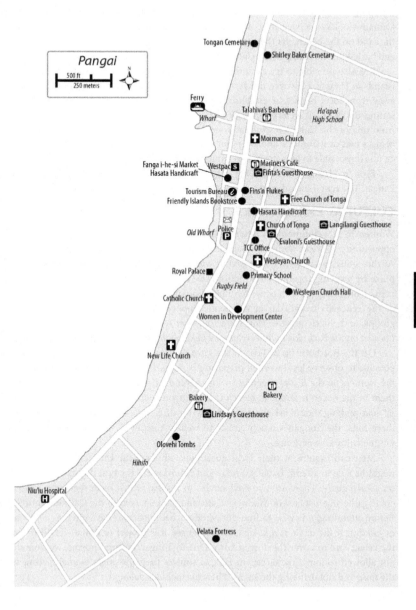

Ha'apai

Camping

Camping is allowed at two of the accommodations on Uoleva Island: Taina's and Captain Cook's (see page 167). At these guesthouses, travelers can pitch their tents in the sand on the beach, yet they can still enjoy access to a bathroom, shower facilities, and basic kitchen. Campers can, alternately, just cook out over an open fire.

It is also possible to try camping on some of the more isolated beaches on other islands in Ha'apai. However, it is best to make an effort to find places that are located away from local houses or establishments; it is also wise to ask permission before setting up camp. Travelers can either bring their own tent, or they can rent a tent from one of the Uoleva resorts or from the dive shop. Alternately, visitors can just bring a mat or hammock and sleep out under the stars, weather permitting. However, it is impossible to buy any of this equipment in Ha'apai.

Fins 'n Flukes offers camping gear rentals (TOP$30/day) from their office in Pangai. The rental includes tent, self-inflating sleeping mat, and sleeping bag.

CULTURAL EXPERIENCES

Women in Development Handicraft Center (WID) in Pangai grants travelers the opportunity to create their own handicrafts and souvenirs for a small fee of TOP$8. At the center, participants try weaving with pandanus leaves, or making their own purse by weaving together dried palm leaves. WID also offers locally-made handicrafts—including *tapa* mats, woven mats, bookmarks, and purses—for purchase. All of the proceeds from sales at the center support local women's groups, disabled groups, and elderly groups. *Hours are 10:00 am – 3:00 pm, Monday through Friday. Located on the back side of the large rugby field, by the Wesleyan Church.*

On the northern tip of Foa, in the cove next to Matafonua Lodge, it is usually possible to observe local women preparing pandanus leaves for weaving. To do this, the women tie the leaves together in long strands, tie weights on them, and throw them in the ocean in order to bleach them. Anyone with a keen interest in weaving or *tapa*-making should ask their guesthouse for directions to a local weaving hut. At these huts, the Tongan women gather to weave. Visiting a weaving hut is truly a unique cultural experience.

Men can inquire at their local guesthouse about local **kava circles** that they might be able to attend. Usually, Friday and Saturday are the best nights to "drop in" on a *kava* circle. There are two *kava* circles in Ha'apai which meet regularly: a *kava* circle gathering just east of Mariner's Café, and another next to the Catholic church. Before attending, it is wise to find out whether that particular kava circle is a *kalapu* or *faikava*. If the circle is a *kalapu*, or fundraiser, it is proper to donate TOP$10 for the cause, and to cover the cost of *kava*. Due to Tongan cultural norms, women are not allowed to join *kava* circles in Ha'apai (unless they are single women acting as the *tou'a* and not drinking the kava). This rule includes *palangis*.

TOURS

Fins 'n' Flukes, the local dive shop, is the only operator which offers island tours. They will drive travelers around Lifuka, taking them both to the historical sights and to some of the more isolated beaches. An alternate way to find a guided driving or walking tour around the island is by asking at a guesthouse; the staff can usually provide this type of information.

Lifuka Sights

Wesleyan Church

The Wesleyan Church, one of the largest churches in Ha'apai, is white, with a large bell tower. Church services there fairly radiate life, as schoolchildren in their blue and white uniforms stream through the door, and a brass band plays along with the choir. This church is also marked by a concrete cross in the front lawn. It is believed that this cross marks the spot where some locals once saw a burning cross appear. The islanders decided to commemorate the incident by erecting a permanent cross in its place.

Royal Palace

The Royal Palace is located on the main road in Pangai, across from the rugby field near the Wesleyan church. This is the building where royalty and nobles stay when they are visiting Ha'apai, though it is not their permanent residence. Visitors should not get too close, however; they are only permitted to look from the roadside. None-theless, they shouldn't fret: there is not much to see.

Afi Historical Museum/Tonga Visitors Bureau

The Afi Museum in Pangai was founded by an ex-pat who invested an enormous amount of work into gathering items and historical pieces before she died. However, since that time, no one has scheduled hours for the museum, or taken over the task of maintaining the facility. It is a unfortunate, since the museum contains a room full of interesting Tongan artifacts. Fortunately, however, many artifacts and pieces from the museum still sit on display at the Tonga Visitors Bureau.

Hulu'i Paongo Point

At the southern tip of Lifuka is Hulu'i Paongo Point: this is the spot where the island comes to a narrow, sandy point. From this vantage point, it is possible not only to see across the channel to Uoleva Island, but also to spot several small islands on the horizon as well. To the west side of the point, there is a slight mound: this was an ancient burial site for the chiefs of the Mata'uvave line. These leaders were sent to Ha'apai in the 1700s to establish political control there.

The best way to reach Hulu'i Paongo Point is to bike. Bikers need only head straight south down the main road from Pangai through Hihifo, past the hospital, past the last village area, and through the bush, until, finally, the dirt path ends at the beach. From the middle of Pangai, it will take about twenty to thirty minutes to bike to this spot.

HISTORICAL SIGHTS

Lifuka contains a number of locales integral to Tonga's history. Some of these sights have only recently been identified. They are not maintained, however, and, due to the hot weather and rainy, humid conditions, there is little left to see there. (Although they do, of course, retain their important historical significance.) Recently, the tourism office began to post informational signs and maps at some of the sights, thus making visits there more meaningful. Visitors should be aware that the sights are not well-maintained, so they should not go to them expecting to be able to see a lot.

Familiar Sounds

Here in Ha'apai, the noises of Tonga have become familiar. We sleep in later than we once did, having already become sensitized to the ever-crowing roosters, oft-grunting pigs, and frequently-fighting dogs. Around 6:00 am or so, the neighbors' kids spill out of their house, yelling, crying, singing, banging on random pieces of metal that they may find lying around. For a while, we used to yell, "Quiet!" through the *louvre* windows; now we just roll over and fall back asleep. On our slow journey back into sleep, we catch the sound of our *sima vai* gushing out water just outside the bedroom window. (Everyone in our housing compound uses our *sima vai* for drinking water, because it's the cleanest.) Well, either that, or the roaming pigs have once again broken into the water pipe.

On Sunday mornings, we hear church bells chime quietly in the distance, as the deep, rhythmic, resonating sound of the wooden drums of the Church of Tonga start to sound, calling people to the morning church services. Soon after the sounds of the chimes and drums, we hear the church choirs and congregations strike up, all singing a cappella. Some tunes are the familiar ones of English church songs, but with all of the accompanying words sung in Tongan. As the services continue, the ministers shout their sermons to the congregations.

On other mornings, we are treated to totally different morning musical selections. Instead of hearing hymns, we hear the neighbors' radio blaring traditional Tongan songs, old American songs, Christmas music...sometimes, they will mix it all with odd songs, like rap or "The Macarena." They will also blast the news, which is broadcast mostly in Tongan. (There are about ten minutes of news in English per day.) And so our day begins.

During the day, walking through town, we often hear kids yelling "Nio, Nio!" (This is my husband [Brett]'s, local Tongan name.) Many of the local kids know him from school. Once in a while, someone will yell out my name. Usually, we have no idea who all of these people calling to us *are*. They simply know us because we're the foreigners in town. Sometimes, we will still hear the Tongans yelling out, "*Palangi!*" When this happens, Brett will respond, "Tongan, Tongan!" The kids also yell, "Bye!" as we walk by, without understanding that it is not proper in English to say "bye" to people who are just passing by on the street. When the kids do this, we'll usually respond by saying something in Tongan. *(Continued on next page)*

Velata Fortress

Velata Fortress saw the last battle in Ha'apai on the way to the ultimate unification of the islands of Tonga. Taufa'ahau first laid siege to the Velata Fortress in 1820, but it did not fall until 1826. In attacking Ha'apai, Taufa'ahau had two goals: to unite all of the Tongan Islands, and to spread Christianity throughout the nation. In order to accomplish this, Taufa'ahau wiped out the people's traditional religious practices.

Once he had won the battle at Velata and Ha'apai had fallen under his control, Taufa'ahau went on to conquer Vava'u and, later, Tongatapu. At this point, Taufa'ahau united all of Tonga under his rule; he then became the first king of Tonga. While nothing remains of the old Velata Fortress, it is still possible to visit this place and see the area where this mighty structure once stood. In addition, a sign maps out the area where the fortress once stood. Looking around, it's still possible to see some of the sunken trenches which once surrounded the fort. *The Velata Fortress is located off of a bush road just east of Hihifo.*

Since we walk down the middle of the roads, we can hear cars approaching from afar. When this happens, we move to one side of the road. We also notice the sound of the plane landing once or twice each day. If the DVD store near our house is open, it always blares loud music. The store does this in order to make sure people that know that they are open. In fact, at any local event, the music always plays at the loudest level possible.

During the afternoons and evenings, things quiet down considerably. In our house, there will be the sound of Brett playing his guitar; he's learned many new songs since we moved here. In fact, the oldest of the neighbor boys is now learning to play guitar as well. During the afternoon, we will often have lots of kids and dogs running through our house; in that case, there is a lot of noise again. Sometimes, we'll shut the door to keep them all out, and then play music or movies on the computer.

Even then, small noises create the sound texture of the inside of our house, as the little *moko*, geckos—which live inside, on our ceiling and walls—make little chirping noises, almost like birds. I also love the sound of the waves breaking on the beach onto all of the loose shells and coral pieces there. This creates a kind of swishing noise, as the waves pull the shells back and forth, back and forth, back and forth. From our beach, we also hear the *Pulapaki*—the only ferry boat, which now brings all of the supplies to Ha'apai. It arrives twice each week. We hear the engines of the boat as it pulls into the wharf. Later, in the evenings, we hear a steady, low voice calling, "*Ma...ma...ma.*" This person is beckoning their pigs to come and eat. Every Tongan calls their pigs this way, and every pig knows its individual owner's voice, coming only to that sound. When the pig arrives, it gets to eat the coconuts which its owner has cut open for its dinner.

At night, things quiet down considerably. The sound of waves crashing on the beach dominates the soundscape. Now, anytime anyone tries to approach the property, we hear all of the dogs bark like crazy outside of the window. In fact, the barking travels along in a straight line, passed from dog to dog to dog, up and down the street. Some nights, we hear the men at the local *kava* club, just a few hundred yards from our house, as they laugh, sing, and make merry. Once in a while, they play guitars. On other nights, we can hear one of the church choirs practicing, singing in such perfect unison I almost swear it's the radio. Though I can never quite distinguish the song they're singing, it doesn't matter. It is always beautiful.

- Kate Asleson

Olovehi Tombs

These tombs, thought to date back to the sixteenth century, once served as the burial grounds for the ancestors of noble *Tuita*, the estate holders of Hihifo village. In addition to the nobles themselves, the girl servants of some of the noblewomen also lie buried here. It is believed that these servants were buried alive with their mistresses in order to accompany them into the afterlife. Around the outside of the burial area, tall terraces are visible alongside the grounds. A posted sign explains the history and significance of the site. *The Olovehi Tombs are located in Hihifo village, just off of one of the main roads.*

Shirley Baker Cemetery

Another significant burial ground lies on the northern outskirts of Pangai: the Shirley Baker cemetery. Shirley Baker was an English missionary who lived in Ha'apai in the 1800s. Baker exerted significant influence upon Taufa'ahau, the man would (later) be the first king of Tonga. In fact, Baker accomplished many things during his time in the Friendly Islands. He engineered the spread of Christianity through Tonga through his influence upon Taufa'ahau, and he later became Taufa'ahau's political advisor when Taufa'ahau rose to be the first king of Tonga. (See page 20 for more information about Baker.) This cemetery is also home to European traders and missionaries who lived in Ha'apai in the eighteenth and nineteenth centuries. The cemetery is a European-style cemetery with tombstones; it also has a monument to Shirley Baker. Across the road from Shirley Baker cemetery, there is a Tongan cemetery—it contains lots of fake flowers and quilts. What's more, sand and coral are mounded up into a pile on top of the graves. *Located on the main road on the north side of Pangai.*

Port au Prince Massacre Beach

In 1806, the English privateer ship, *Port au Prince*, anchored just off of Lifuka. The local Tongans decided to seize the ship in order to obtain the curious metal cannons and guns onboard. They burned the ship at anchor, killing most of the fifty-two crew members onboard. Fifteen year-old English cabin boy William Mariner was one of the few spared. Chief Finau 'Ulukalala took a great liking to the boy, eventually adopting him as a son. Mariner learned a great deal about the native Tongan culture and language, and he accompanied Finau on many of his expeditions to unite Tonga. Mariner later wrote a book detailing life in native Tonga before the country was united; this excellent account of early Tonga can be found in the Friendly Islands bookstores. *The beach is located on the west side of Lifuka, down a dirt path just past the airport before the land bridge.*

Diving or snorkeling near this beach, it is possible to glimpse what is believed to be the original anchor from the *Port au Prince*, just offshore. This site was discovered in 2009, by Fins 'n Flukes Dive Shop.

LIFUKA SECRET SPOTS

As small as the Lifuka Island is, there are, nonetheless, a few hidden spots. Some of these sights have been named by ex-pats living in the area. Thus, asking a Tongan how to reach any of these sights (Poseidon's Gate, for instance) may yield nothing but a blank stare in reply.

Poseidon's Gate

This rocky beach area, on the wild (*liku*) east side of Lifuka, features unique plant-covered rock formations. In fact, by climbing up on top of the rocks, it is easy to obtain a great vantage point over the surrounding sea and land. There is also a step-like rock and coral formation in the water. At low tide, adventurous travelers can venture out to the edge of the formation and watch waves break over the rocks beside them. It is truly a surreal and wonderful experience. Although this beach is not for swimming, the natural beauty of the landscape is so incredible that visitors will barely even notice. The best way to reach the beach is to bike. *Located on the east side of Lifuka, just south of the power plant, down a long bush road. When the bush road comes to a fork, keep going to the left.*

Airport Beach

There is a hidden beach in Koulo near the airport. It is a nice sandy beach; it also has some beautiful reefs, which provide the perfect setting for snorkeling. The beach offers a great vantage point on the several-times-daily takeoffs and landings of the island's miniature runway. In order to get to the beach, travelers should walk west down the runway, then turn and walk north.

Snorkeling Monster's Alley

Named for all of the large fish that live there, Monster's Alley is actually a big valley between two reefs. The site can be reached either on foot or by bike. In order to get there, visitors should take the main road from Pangai which heads toward the airport. They will then stop at the old refueling tanks, where there will be a clearing of grass and a beach. Monster's Alley itself is located around the old refueling pipes sticking out of the water. This area is a great place to snorkel, and it's right on Lifuka Island. Out in the water, a long reef follows the shoreline, stretching all the way from the refueling pipes to the wharf in Pangai. Snorkelers can simply jump in and follow the reef.

Old Rock Quarry

There is an old rock quarry on the east side of Lifuka, just north of Billy's Resort. The quarry features an unusual sight: long rectangular shapes carved right out of the stone at the beach. Low tide is the best time of day to view the quarry, since the sea water covers these dugout shapes at high tide.

Haʻapai

Foa Sights

Nukunamo Island

This island is located just north of Foa, across a deep, narrow channel. It is the King's Island. The royal family owns land throughout Tonga, and Nukunamo Island is one of their properties. However, this island is actually up for lease at the moment, so the ownership of the island could change in the near future. Should the new owner decide to develop it, the island itself could be changing very soon.

For the time being, however, there are no villages or buildings on this small island. Nukunamo Island can be reached in one of two ways. It is possible to rent a kayak and paddle across the channel to Nukunamo. Another way to reach the island is by hiring a boat. Beware: the currents in the channel can be strong, so it is definitely not safe to swim across the channel to the island.

Lotofoa Methodist Church

This old church has a beautiful traditional rounded roof. Furthermore, it has a unique curved ceiling inside, thus making it a good example of traditional Tongan architecture. The church is easily visible from the main road, which goes through Foa.

FOA SECRET SPOT

Ancient Rock Carvings

At the northern tip of Foa, just around the bay from Matafonua in the east, there are ancient petroglyph images carved into two slabs of rock on the beach. Currently, the carvings lie buried under the sand due to a cyclone that hit in 2010. But with the next storm and the shifting shoreline, they may reappear. While it is unfortunate that the petroglyphs are not now visible, their burial may actually be for the better, because it will keep the carvings preserved from the elements.

In fact, these petroglyphs were discovered surprisingly recently. In 2008 a huge storm system caused rapid coastal erosion which, in turn, uncovered the rocks. The fifty or so etchings in the rocks depict everything, from humans, to fish, to turtles, to dogs, to other more exotic-looking (yet less readily-identifiable) shapes. These types of drawings are rare in Tonga and may prove a link between Tonga and other Polynesian countries located further to the east.

Because the carvings have been slowly eroding with exposure to waves and the elements, they are difficult to see in the daylight. Therefore, it is best to visit them at dusk or in the evening. The strong beam of a flashlight cutting through the dark will hit the rocks and cause the images to "pop" out from the wall. Unfortunately, no steps are currently being taken to preserve these ancient rock carvings. It is likely that they will soon disappear, taking with them their silent history. *No signs or markings indicate where the carvings are. To find them, inquire at Matafonua Lodge. It is also possible to simply walk along the beach to find the petroglyphs.*

Shopping

Fanga i-he-si Market

Fanga i-he-si Market, the only market in Ha'apai, is located south of the main wharf, on the ocean road in Pangai near the tourism office. The products available there depend largely upon the season. In the summer, it is possible to find all kinds of fruit there; in the winter, there are vegetables. Regardless of what type of produce they are selling, the sellers will always lay it out on wood tables, in piles. Shoppers usually find root crops, such as yam, taro, bananas, and papayas. Typically, shoppers must purchase fruits or vegetables by the pile, but it may be possible to buy produce individually. Vegetables are not available in the summer months, from November through May, and fruit tends to be less available during the winter months, from June through October.

There is also a handicraft store in the market, Hasata Handicraft, which sells shell and bone jewelry, wall hangings, mats, *tapa*, wood carvings, and shells. It is best to visit the market in the early mornings when there is the most variety and choice. It is ideal to visit on a Saturday morning. On Saturdays, many Tongans from other villages come in to buy and sell products. Furthermore, Saturday morning market is more of a social event than anything else. That day, there is also a flea market in one area of the market, where vendors sell clothes, kitchen supplies, and other random items. Some Saturdays, there are even choirs singing, bands playing, or students performing a play.

Across from the market, huge banyan trees stand tall, shading a group of stone tables and benches. This is a great area for lounging. Locals will also sometimes sell fish out of coolers at these tables, out of vehicles near the market, or inside of a small shack across from the market, near the water. The market provides a social gathering place for locals to meet, share stories, and catch up on the latest gossip from across the island. *Hours weekdays 8 am – 4:00 pm, Saturday 6 am – 10:00am.*

Hasata Handicraft

This local handicraft store has recently been expanding; it now has locations in the market, at the airport, and at the owner's own personal Pangai residence. The owner, Mafi, is a carver by trade, and his wife works in the market. He carves intricate bone pendants for necklaces; he also creates decorative wood carvings. Hasata Handicraft also sells shell necklaces and earrings, woven bracelets, wall hangings, and *tapa* mats. *Hours at the market: weekdays 8 am – 4:00pm, Saturday 6 am – 10:00 am. Hours at the airport: when there are planes landing or taking off. Hours at the owners' residence vary: if the shop is open, just yell for the shopkeeper.*

Friendly Islands Bookstore

This is part of the chain bookstore located throughout Tonga. The Ha'apai branch is much smaller than the main store in Tongatapu. However, the Ha'apai store does sell paper, pens, tape, fabric, postcards, and other small trinkets. There are also a few books available for purchase, including Tongan/English dictionaries and volumes

Ha'apai

concerning Tonga and its history. *Located next to Fins 'n Flukes on the main road in Pangai, Hours 9 am – 4 pm.*

Local Stores

There are many local stores on Lifuka and Foa, in all of the villages. Tongan-run stores are located both in the main town and in the residential areas. There are five Chinese-run stores in Pangai; they are all located along the main road, and in the large three-story building by the wharf. These larger stores have aisles displaying a wide variety of products, including noodles, flour, sugar, frozen chicken, eggs, canned goods, candy, soda, cigarettes, and kitchen and cleaning supplies. All of the local stores accept cash only.

Eating

Buying Food

There are a few options for buying food in Ha'apai; most of these options are located in Pangai. It is important to note that grocery selection will be limited, depending upon the season and recent ferry shipments. The Fanga i-he-si Market is definitely the best option, in terms of buying fresh fruit and vegetables.

Falekoloa, or local stores, will carry a variety of basic food supplies which travelers can buy in order to do their own cooking. The small pink *falekoloa* on the main road, across from Fins 'n Flukes, also sells ice cream cones. These are a great treat on hot days. The pink store also sells egg sandwiches and samosas to-go at lunchtime. The larger walk-in Chinese *falekoloa* will have more items available.

Bakeries

There are two bakeries in Ha'apai, both of which are located on Lifuka: one is located in Hihifo, the other on the eastern side of Pangai. The title of "bakery," however, may be slightly misleading, as these shops sell only butter and loaves of uncut white bread. The bakery in Hihifo—which sits next to Lindsay's Guesthouse—becomes a local hangout spot on Sundays. In order to reach the other bakery, which is found near the bush on the eastern side of Pangai, visitors will walk past the local low-security prison, with its open gates, and the large hollowed-out banyan tree, which serves as a pigpen. The ideal time to buy bread is on Sunday afternoons, when it is fresh out of the oven. However, those who don't make it to the bakeries on Sunday should not fret. The shops also distribute the bread that they bake to local stores to sell during the week. *Hours are Sunday usually 3 pm – 6 pm.*

Buying Fresh Fish

Since Ha'apai is surrounded by water, it's easy to imagine that there is an abundance of fresh seafood there. However, this is not always the case. In fact, buying fresh fish can prove quite tricky. Anyone who is interested in buying fresh fish should listen for the sound of a whistle being blown constantly. They should then follow this noise, which will lead them to a truck selling fish out of a cooler. In fact, the fish trucks are similar to ice cream trucks, playing songs for kids to run out and buy ice cream.

Sometimes, the fish trucks drive slowly through town; other times, they might be stationed near the market. These trucks sell the fish by the kilo. Once they have procured the fresh fish, visitors can cook the fish themselves, if their guesthouse has kitchen facilities available for guest use; bake the fish over a beach bonfire; or ask their guesthouse if the staff might be able prepare the fish for them.

RESTAURANTS

Ha'apai does not offer many options for dining out. Locals generally don't eat at restaurants and, since there are not as many tourists in this area as there are on the other islands, there is no need for many restaurants. Locals tend to eat at cheaper barbeque places or take-away places. Every once in a while, a new cheap restaurant or take-away stand opens its doors in Ha'apai.

Mariner's Café This serves as the meeting hub for travelers in Ha'apai; it's a great place to swap advice and travel stories. Mariner's Café offers breakfast, lunch, and dinner, serving western-style food, such as burgers, pasta, and pizza. The prices are slightly higher than at local establishments, but they are worth paying for the social atmosphere. The restaurant is owned by two ex-pats, Craig and Magda. At night, it is the only bar in town. Mariner's Café also has Internet service, dartboards, satellite TV, and karaoke.

The entire restaurant is located on a patio under a roof offering open-air breezes with a quaint white picket fence bordering the establishment. There is wireless Internet available (it costs TOP$3 for 30 minutes). There is also a computer with an Internet connection. *Located under Fifita's Guesthouse, just off the main street in Pangai. Cost: breakfast/lunch TOP$5 – $10, dinner TOP$10 – $25. Hours: Monday – Saturday 9 am – late (depends on customers), and Sunday 6 pm – 9 pm. Hours can vary during off-season. Phone: 60374, marinerstonga@yahoo.co.uk*

Talahiva's Barbeque A local spot, Talahiva is a modest restaurant located just behind the gas station in Pangai. Talahiva's Barbeque serves large plates of fried chicken, barbeque, curry, and fish and chips, all at cheap prices, for both lunch and dinner. This eatery just opened in 2009, as an addition to an existing meat shop. The décor feels quite homey; in fact, the dining area even features a sink where diners can wash their hands after eating. *Located behind the gas station down the dirt path in Pangai. Cost: TOP$5 - $8 per plate. Hours: Monday – Thursday 12 pm – 9 pm, Friday 12 pm – through Saturday 9 pm (all night Friday). Closed Sundays. Phone: 60818*

Matafonua Lodge This resort on Foa features an attached restaurant, which is open to the public for lunch. It is also open by reservation for dinner. The restaurant offers excellent western-style food and a bar; at times, the Lodge even has visiting chefs prepare the menu. Diners at Matafonua Lodge can eat sitting on a covered patio terrace, enjoying stunning views of both the ocean and of the channel between Foa and Nukunamo. *Located on Foa at Matafonua Lodge. Average cost: TOP$12 – $30 per plate. Hours: Every day 8 am– 9:30 am breakfast, 12 pm – 3 pm lunch, dinner by reservation. Phone: 69766, www.matafonua.com*

Nightlife

Mariner's Café Not only does Mariner's Café house the only bar on the island which is reliably open, this bar also offers the largest variety of drinks on the island, including wine, imported liquor, and bottled New Zealand and Australian beer. Mariner's Café is the only place on Lifuka offering wine. Travelers may want to try

Ha'apai

the Mariner's specialty drink, rum punch. Mariner's Café has a dart board, Internet, satellite TV, and karaoke. *Drinks start at TOP$6. Hours: Monday – Sunday 8 am – 2 pm, 4 pm – close (depends on customers).*

Evaloni's Bar This place is more of a local hangout spot and, as such, it does not keep regular hours. The bar, connected to Evaloni's Guesthouse, features an outdoor covered seating area, a pool table, and a music system for entertainment. However, unlike Mariner's Café, Evaloni's Bar does not have an actual bar with a bartender. Instead, patrons go into the kitchen and buy beer from the guesthouse owners when it is available. *Located at Evaloni's Guesthouse, near the churches in Pangai. Beer costs around TOP$4. Hours are irregular, depending on customers.*

Buying Alcohol

In addition to selling alcohol to consume on-premises, Mariner's Café also vends alcohol to take away and consume off-premises. Sometimes the Tongan or Chinese stores sell liquor or beer but since liquor licenses are difficult to obtain, stores often end up closing down that part of their business. Currently, there is a new local store selling beer for take-away, across from the gas station on the main road in Pangai. The guesthouses are generally the best source of information about whether any local stores are selling alcohol at any given time.

Accommodation

LIFUKA

There are many guesthouses located in Pangai, all of which feature very similar amenities and pricing. These establishments all offer both private and shared rooms, as well as kitchen facilities. All of the owners are very friendly, and the guesthouses give travelers the feeling of being included in the local culture. There is also one resort, Billy's, on Lifuka, though it is not a high-end resort. Billy's, a mid-range accommodation, offers private *fales* along the beach.

Fifita's Guesthouse Centrally located in Pangai, this guesthouse is situated right above Mariner's Café. Amenities include hot water in the shared bathroom, free use of the kitchen, and a balcony area for dining. Fifita's Guesthouse offers three types of rooms: single and double rooms with shared bathrooms, and en-suite rooms. *TOP$30/Single, TOP$50/Double, TOP$65/Double ensuite. Phone: 60213, fifitaguesthouse@yahoo.com*

Evaloni's Guesthouse Like Fifita's, Evaloni's is centrally located near the churches in Pangai. Evaloni's Guesthouse offers seven rooms. The guesthouse also boasts many sitting areas, a veranda, and a bar serving beer. Evaloni's has bicycle rentals available for TOP$15/day, as well as airport transfers for TOP$7. Guests may use the kitchen for TOP$2, or they can have the owners cook meals for them. The upstairs rooms feature the nicest decorations and offer more ocean breeze. *TOP$20/Single, shared bathroom, TOP$45-75/Double ensuite, prepared meals TOP$15-20. Phone: 60029.*

Langilangi Guesthouse (also known as Fonogava'inga) This friendly guesthouse offers a delicious taste of the local culture of the islands. Located on the east side of town, near the bush, Langilangi Guesthouse sits only a five minute walk from the center of town. The guesthouse has five rooms available, all with shared bathrooms. The owners can cook delicious lobster dinners upon request for TOP$30/person, or any other meals that the guests desire, also upon request. *TOP$15/Single per person, TOP$25/Double per person, kitchen use TOP$2/day, airport transfers TOP$5. Phone: 60038, vimahi@kalianet.to*

Lindsay's Guesthouse This guesthouse, located in Hihifo, just south of Pangai, is attached to the local bakery. The price of the stay includes free airport transfers, breakfast, and guests also enjoy free use of the kitchen facilities. Lindsay's Guesthouse has Internet available, as well as bicycle rentals for TOP$15/day. The owners offer boat tours to Uiha and Uoleva islands, as well as rides to Foa. *TOP$30/Single, TOP$45/Double, shared bathroom, TOP$60/Double ensuite, TOP$65/Family room, Phone: 60107, finauwalter@gmail.com*

Billy's Resort Anyone who wants to stay on the beach should choose Billy's Resort, as it is the only beach resort on Lifuka. Billy's Resort sits on an old banana plantation on the secluded east side of the island, located about fifteen minutes outside of Pangai, through the bush. The resort has four *fales* available, each with electricity and a separate bathroom building. Guests can use the resort bicycles for free, and breakfast is included. Billy's Resort also has kitchen and barbeque available for guest use, along with a nice covered patio seating area. *Fales TOP$45 - 75, kitchen/bbq use TOP$5/day. Phone 60336.*

Mele Tonga Guesthouse The only guesthouse in Koulo, the northern village of Lifuka, Mele Tonga Guesthouse is located about fifteen minutes from Pangai. The accommodations there feel a bit more like a homestay. There is a separate house with four bedrooms for guests, along with a bathroom, living room, and kitchen. The kitchen is available for guest use for TOP$3/day. Mele Tonga Guesthouse is located on the beach, and it offers free rides into Pangai. Do note that this guesthouse looks to be in need of renovation. *TOP$20/Single, TOP$30/Double, TOP$40/Family, prepared meals TOP$12 – 20. Phone: 879-1686, ilaisaaneanalose@gmail.com.*

FOA

The only accommodations on Foa are two resorts. Both resorts are more upscale, and they are located at the northern tip of Foa, on one of the best beaches in Tonga. These places offer guests more amenities than the local guesthouses, and they cater specifically to tourists.

Sandy Beach Resort Those seeking an upscale resort will love Sandy Beach Resort, the only high-end accommodation in Ha'apai. Sandy Beach Resort boasts a beautiful location right along one of the best stretches of beach in Ha'apai. This resort, built and owned by German ex-pats, offers twelve beach-front bungalows. Com-

Cyclone Wilma

In January 2011, Cyclone Wilma came through Tonga, striking Ha'apai the hardest, as a Category 3 storm. Wilma hit during high tide and a full moon, so the waves were at their highest and most destructive. In the end, the storm destroyed dozens of homes, damaged buildings, and killed crops, ultimately doing an estimated TOP$5.5 million worth of damage. Uiha was hit hardest, as all of the low-lying areas flooded. Matafonua Resort, on Foa, also sustained a great deal of damage, as four of its bungalow *fales* were washed out to sea. The resort, however, remained open for business, and they quickly rebuilt the bungalows.

The Lulunga island group, to the south, also experienced damages due to Cyclone Wilma. Fortunately, though, no one on those islands was hurt or killed by the storm. The local Tonga Red Cross responded immediately, setting up tents as temporary shelters. What's more, the government's National Emergency Fund allocated TOP$1 million in funds for the basic necessities and relief needed.

Ha'apai

plete with ceiling fans, hot solar showers, fridges, and private balconies. Other amenities include an on-site dive base, wireless Internet, horseback riding, cultural shows, and day trips to other islands. Furthermore, guests enjoy free use of kayaks, snorkel gear, bicycles, as well as a complimentary shuttle bus to Pangai for sightseeing. The on-site restaurant/bar offers breakfast and dinner. *Double bungalow TOP$195/person (€80 Euro/person), breakfast TOP$37 (€15 Euro), 3-course dinner TOP$94 (€38 Euro), Phone: 60600, sandybch@kalianet.to, www.sandybeachresort.de*

Matafonua Lodge This mid-range resort, recently under new management, is, like Sandy Beach Resort, located right at the northern tip of Foa Island. Matafonua Lodge offers ten Tongan-inspired bungalows, which feature private balconies and gorgeous ocean views. There is a shared bathroom with a hot solar shower. There is a dive base next door at Sandy Beach Resort, and wireless Internet is also available there. Guests can enjoy activities like Tongan feasts, cultural shows, bicycle and kayak rentals, and horseback riding. The on-site restaurant/bar features an open veranda, as well as ocean views between the islands. Although this resort was hit by Cyclone Wilma in January 2011, it was rebuilt quickly and the resort is currently open for business as usual. *Bungalow for 2 adults TOP$175/night, additional person TOP$36/night, children TOP$18/night, Phone: 69766, info@matafonua.com, www.matafonua.com*

Uoleva

This island, located just south of Lifuka, is completely uninhabited, save the owners of the three rustic accommodations there. Uoleva is ringed by pristine sandy beaches, and the entire island is fringed by reefs. The perfect island escape, Uoleva is marred by neither roads, nor stores, nor crowds. (The island is, however, beginning to become more of a hot spot during the tourist season.) There is neither electricity nor running water on the island (except for a generator at Serenity Beaches resort and a few water towers to get running water in sinks, toilets and cold water showers at the resorts). However, in exchange for the rustic amenities, travelers to Uoleva enjoy quiet, peaceful, starry nights, and they will often find that they have huge stretches of beach entirely to themselves. On Uoleva, travelers can gather around a campfire at night with tourists from around the world, exchanging travel stories and enjoying this hidden gem of an island.

Uoleva is also ringed by incredible untouched reefs, which are filled with different kinds of hard and soft corals and colorful fish. These make ideal spots for snorkeling and diving. During the winter, humpback whales like to stay around Uoleva, so the island is also a superb whale-watching spot. This is a favorite location in Tonga for its unspoiled beauty, beaches and reefs.

GETTING THERE

Travelers can arrange for a boat ride to Uoleva through their Uoleva accommodations; sometimes, the resort will even send someone to meet the visitors at the airport. Another way to get to Uolvea is by taking a local boat. However, travelers should remember that this option puts them at the mercy of the boat's timetable. Visitors can also arrange for a ride with Fins 'n Flukes dive shop (TOP$25/person one way, two person minimum), or they can rent a kayak and paddle over to Uoleva themselves.

For extremely budget-conscious travelers, there is one more option: it is possible to walk from the southern tip of Lifuka across a reef in order to reach Uoleva. However, this is more dangerous than it was in years past. A few years ago, following a large earthquake, the reef sank, so the water over the reef now reaches depths of approximately four feet. There is also a strong current coming through this channel; several locals have been swept off of the reef out into the open sea, resulting in at least one death. Walking across the reef takes about thirty minutes; upon reaching land on Uoleva, it takes another half an hour of walking to reach the first resort on the beach. Anyone who decides to walk across the reef to Uoleva needs to check the tide charts (www.tide-forecast.com), since the reef should only be crossed at low tide.

ACTIVITIES

Though Uolvea is a tiny island, it offers plenty of sandy beach for swimming and sunbathing. Unlike other beaches in Tonga, there is no need to worry about covering up or dressing as the locals do, as there are no villages there. Swimsuits, shorts, and tank tops are all perfectly acceptable. In fact, guests have even been known to skinny-dip at night at the resorts on Uoleva!

Snorkeling

With all of the pristine reefs in Uoleva's crystal clear waters, it would be a shame to miss out on an opportunity to snorkel there. To do this, it is best to either rent snorkel gear from one of the local dive shops, or to borrow snorkel gear from the resorts on Uoleva. In order to ensure that the gear is in working order, it is highly recommended that visitors rent gear from the dive shop. Heading out from Serenity Beaches, there are reefs right off of the beach near the resort with interesting coral shelves.

Those walking from Captain Cook's Hideaway should take a left at the beach; from there, it is easy to see the reefs, which lie just out from the sandy beach between this resort and Serenity Beaches. There are coral reefs dotted all along this area, featuring some large brain coral. From Taina's Resort, the reef is located around the point to the right, at the spot where there are visible waves breaking around the coral reef, about five minutes down the beach. From this spot, there is a long line of reef heading into the ocean, housing a lot of fan coral. All of these reefs have amazing marine life and coral. Those who have adequate time to do so should check out a few different reefs on Uoleva; each one is different and beautiful in its own way.

West Is Best!

The safest place to swim off of Uoleva is off of the west coast of the island. The east side has a stronger current and bigger waves, both of which make swimming more dangerous and difficult.

Fishing

Fishing enthusiasts should head to the great reefs near Uoleva. Interested parties should ask Fins 'n Flukes in Pangai about fishing trips; they can coordinate a fishing excursion in conjunction with a trip to Uoleva. Alternately, travelers can ask at Serenity Beaches about fishing trips around the Island of Uiha.

Kayaking

Kayaking offers a great way to see Uoleva from a different viewpoint. Serenity Beaches provides free sit-on kayaks for guest use. Kayaks are also available for rental from Fins 'n Flukes in Pangai.

Another exciting water sport in which to partake on Uoleva is kite-surfing; there are some perfect spots to do it near the island. Unfortunately, no outfitter in Ha'apai currently offers gear rental for this sport, so anyone who wants to kite-surf there must bring their own gear.

SECRET SPOTS

Pigeon Mounds

The ancient pigeon mounds of Uoleva were once used by Tongan chiefs and nobles to snare pigeons. At that time, their meat was a rare delicacy. In fact, like other species in Tonga, the pigeons most likely disappeared from overhunting.

Those travelers who do decide to venture inland to see the pigeon mounds, which are simply piles of earth reinforced with stone, should note that there may be a lot of mosquitoes near the mounds. Furthermore, the pigeon mounds are not maintained; accordingly, there will not be any directions or signs to point the way there. In order to visit the mounds, adventurers should ask at Taina's Resort for a guide; there is a large pigeon mound located directly to the north of the resort. They can also ask at Serenity Beaches about the pigeon mounds. There is a pigeon mound located to the south of the resort which is nearby, and it is fairly easy to find independently.

ACCOMMODATIONS

It is important to remember that this island is not set up for inhabitants—there is no electricity or running water. The three accommodations on the island are rustic. Two are budget accommodations, while one is mid-range, offering more guest services and conveniences. All of the resorts use candles or lanterns for lighting at night. In addition, each accommodation has a water tower to feed water pressure to the toilets, showers, and sinks. Since the two budget accommodations' water towers are hand-pumped, they may occasionally run out of water pressure. Serenity Beaches has a generator; the generator runs electricity to a fridge, a washing machine, and the water pump.

Serenity Beaches Travelers searching for a perfect island escape at a mid-range resort will love Serenity Beaches. Opened in 2009 by a friendly American ex-pat and a Tongan, the resort features teak wood bungalows on the beach: three large bungalows with lofts, and two smaller one-room bungalows. All of the houses have shades on every side which open up, allowing for gentle breezes and gorgeous ocean views. The property, which sits at the narrow southern tip of the island, stretches all the way from the east side to west side of the island, and it features nice wooded trails.

A large, open-air main building houses the kitchen and dining/lounging area. There are also small huts filled with hammocks and pillows for lounging in. The resort has free kayaks available for guest use, and the owners can cook meals upon request. They can prepare either Western-style or Tongan meals, as they import vegetables and other foods from the main island. Guests can also request lobster dinners, depending on availability. Massage treatments are also available. *Bungalows TOP$180/small, TOP$260/large, prepared meals TOP$20-40, or all three meals TOP$75/person per day. Phone: 13010 or 873-4934, info@serenitybeaches.com, www.serenitybeaches.com*

Taiana's Resort Travelers can experience a low-key, laid-back beach bum island getaway at Taiana's, a resort which caters to backpackers and budget travelers. This property, located on the west side of the island, is also the farthest north of all of the accommodations on Uoleva. The resort features little huts along the beach, each with its own hammock. The huts, Tongan-made *fales*, contain mattresses on the ground. The resort also has a rustic common bathroom and shower area, as well as a kitchen, which is available for guest use. Alternately, the owners can cook Tongan meals for guests upon request. The owners, Kalafi and Taiana, are very hospitable and friendly. Camping is also available at this resort. *Fales TOP$28/Single, TOP$35/Double, TOP$20/Tents, prepared meals TOP$7-15. Phone: 883-1722 or 60612*

Captain Cook's Hideaway Resort This resort, situated just above a sandy beach, offers budget accommodations in the form of wooden bungalows with beds. Like Taiana's Resort, Captain Cook's has a rustic common bathroom area, and a kitchen available for guest use. The owners can also cook Tongan meals upon request. Camping is also available. (This resort does not come as highly-recommended as the other two resorts available on Uoleva.) *Bungalows from TOP$25/person per night. Phone: 60014 or 879-1144*

Volcanic Rumblings in Ha'apai

In March 2009, an underwater volcano exploded near the volcanic islands of Hunga Ha'apai and Hunga Tonga, to the south of the Ha'apai island group. The explosion came as a surprise, as there had been absolutely no volcanic activity in this area for over twenty years prior. The huge explosion shot ash, smoke, and steam thousands of feet into the sky. In fact, the explosion was so huge that people on the islands of Ha'apai, and even Tongatapu, saw it. The explosion created a new island! The incident quickly gained international attention, showing up in news around the world. Because the nearby islands are uninhabited, no one was injured by the explosion, and it posed no threat. Shortly after the explosion, a series of small earthquakes occurred.

Outer Islands - North

Anyone afforded the opportunity to visit the outer islands of Ha'apai is highly encouraged to do so—it will be an unforgettable experience. The outer islands boast spectacular, isolated beaches, immense reef systems ripe for exploration, and a real glimpse into traditional Tongan culture and village life. In order to reach all of the islands listed below, it is necessary to take a boat.

LUAHOKO

This tiny dot of an island lies slightly to the northwest of Lifuka. The island is not only completely uninhabited, it is also tiny: it takes about twenty-five minutes to walk around the entire island! Luahoko makes for a wonderful day trip from Lifuka or Foa, and it offers fantastic snorkeling and diving. There is a reef located just off-shore, where adventurers can dive and snorkel. Visitors can also enjoy Luahoko by swimming to shore and exploring the island itself. The south side of the island is dominated by a sandy beach, while the rest of the shoreline consists of dramatic rocky ledges. Because this island attracts many sea birds—which is in fact uncommon in this area—Luahoko is a bird-watcher's paradise. Luahoko is renowned for its population of sea snakes. However, no one should not let this deter them for swimming or snorkeling around Luahoko, as sea snakes generally avoid humans.

KAUVAI

Kauvai is often called Ha'ano, after the largest village on the island. A visit to Kauvai offers insights into outer island living, traditional villages, and local Tongan culture, all without having to leave the main island group of Ha'apai. The island features well-kept villages, dotted with neat gardens and fences. Kauvai lies to the north of Foa, though the small island of Nukunamo sits between them. Kauvai has four small villages: Ha'ano, Muitoa, Pukotala, and Fakakakai. The only guesthouse on the island, however, is located in Ha'ano. Fakakakai is the main village and it's where most of the visiting boats will dock.

Getting There

The easiest way to get to Kauvai is to take a local boat from the wharf in Faleloa on Foa. To learn when the boats are departing for Kauvai, it is best to inquire at a guesthouse. In addition, the guesthouses can assist in making other travel arrangements to the island, if necessary. Typically, local boats head to Kauvai almost every day, except on Sundays. The boats usually come into Foa in the early morning, and return to Kauvai in the afternoon. Each passenger should give the boat skipper money for gas, around TOP$10. Although the ride time depends slightly on the weather, the boat journey should take approximately one hour.

Those who would rather not depend upon the timing of the local boats can also arrange their own transportation to the island through Fins 'n Flukes on Lifuka.

Activities

This small island is the perfect place to come visit in order to become completely immersed in Tongan culture and daily life. In fact, the locals may even invite visitors to village happenings, church services, *kava* circles, classes at the local school, or sports events. Tourists can also swim at the wharf with the local kids—in full clothing, of course. Another wonderful activity is to wander the trails between villages, exploring every corner of this beautiful island.

Mushroom-Rock Beach

This gorgeous beach, located near an old abandoned resort, lies southeast of Ha'ano, just off of the trail between Ha'ano and Pukotala villages. Adventurers will know that they are near the beach once they see a clearing and the old resort from the trail. The old resort consists of a main building and two smaller wood buildings. The sandy beach nearby has a unique mushroom-shaped rock just offshore. Because Mushroom-Rock Beach sits between villages, it is acceptable to wear a swimsuit there. However, visitors should be mindful of their surroundings, covering up if any locals do appear. There is also an amazing reef just offshore; it's located just to the right of the mushroom-shaped rock. In fact, it is so close that travelers can swim right out to it.

Port au Prince Cannon

An old cannon from the famous ship, *Port au Prince*, sits on land just outside of Ha'ano village, near a water tower. Although for a time it was believed that all four surviving cannons were in Nuku'alofa at the British High Commission (the Tongans gave the cannons to the British as gifts), this single cannon remains in Ha'apai, in this little village.

Accommodations

There is a church-run guesthouse located in Ha'ano village. It has several basic rooms available, all with shared bathrooms. The guesthouse collects donations for the church; it is generally best to leave a donation comparable to the amount that it would cost to stay at other guesthouses in Ha'apai. This usually amounts to approximately TOP$20/person.

In order to find the guesthouse, visitors need only to ask for directions when they arrive at the dock from Foa. It is also possible to reach the guesthouse by walking straight inland, past a rugby field, and toward the churches. The Tourism Office can also call the guesthouse in advance; that way they can send someone to meet the arriving boat.

OFOLONGA

The island of Ofolonga, to the northwest of Lifuka, is famous for an amazing underwater coral archway, one of only a few such archways in the entire South Pacific. It is also the biggest coral archway in the region, at twenty meters wide and fifteen meters high. Ofolonga also offers one of the most mystifying dive sights in the region. Underneath the island, there is a series of massive underwater caves. One of these caves, known as Hot Springs Cave, sometimes spouts hot water. This cave can be reached through one of the dive shops or by arranging a private yacht.

Outer Islands - South

UIHA

Uiha, a very traditional island, has two villages: Uiha and Felemea. Since few foreign visitors make it to Uiha, visitors tend to elicit attention from locals there.

Uiha is well-known throughout Tonga for its fishing and its reefs. The large, long reef, located to the south of the island, supplies a large quantity of fish for the island, as well as for export to the rest of Tonga.

Getting There

There are two ways to reach Uiha: by arranging a ride with a local dive shop, or by taking one of the local boats leaving Pangai. The local boats usually go to Uiha in the afternoon or evening, and return to Pangai in the morning.

Sights

Wesleyan Church

There is a very unique-looking church on Uiha Island. Upon studying the building, it is impossible not to think of European fairy tales, due to the church's prominent spires and cannons. These cannons at the church were actually confiscated by the Tongans from an early exploring ship.

Ancient Rock Site

On the northern end of the island, there is an old rock formation in an "L"-shape. This mystery rock is something of a puzzle because this type of rock is not native to Tonga. Most believe that the ancient Tongans obtained the rock by voyaging far away, to other island nations.

Reefs for Fishing

Uiha is known for its abundant reefs and fish. In fact, the island supplies fish to many of the islands of Tonga. Limu Reef, a very long reef just south of Uiha, is the place where much of the fishing occurs. Anyone who would like to go fishing can ask either the staff at their guesthouse or local Tongans whether there are any fishing trips planned during their visit. If there are trips planned, visitors can ask to tag along. Those who do join a local fishing excursion should make sure to compensate their companions for fuel costs.

Accommodations

Esi 'o Ma'afu This traditional Tongan resort, located in Felemea, offers basic Tongan *fales* for those on a budget. The resort is run by a friendly family, who is happy to provide meals, which will, most likely, involve lots of local fish and seafood. Staying at Esi 'o Ma'afu can be a unique experience, providing travelers with a unique and privileged glimpse into traditional life in this small fishing village. *Fales TOP$20 - $25. Phone: 60438 or 60605, or book through the Tonga Visitors Bureau.*

TATAFA

Adventurous travelers can reach this small, uninhabited island by walking across the reef from Uiha at low tide. However, they should ask locals for advice on how and when it is best to cross. Travelers can also reach the island by hitching a ride with a local boat, arranging transportation with a dive shop, or kayaking across the channel. There is nothing on the island, which makes it a nice, relaxing spot to spend a day, or even to camp overnight, due to its incredible isolation and splendid beach.

FOTUHA'A

Fotuha'a is a small island located to the southwest of Lifuka, closer to the volcanic islands of Kao and Tofua. Fotuha'a is unique in that it is much higher than the other flat coral islands, and it has rocky cliffs on every side. In order to reach the island, local boats pull up next to the rocky cliffs and use ladders to unload passengers and cargo. When either the ocean or the weather does not cooperate, it is nearly impossible to land safely on the island.

Lulunga Group

GETTING THERE

The only way to reach the islands in the Lulunga group—Ha'afeva, Tungua, Kotu, Matamaka, and O'ua—is by boat. There are two ways to get to the Lulunga group: on the ferry heading north from Nuku'alofa, and on the ferry heading south from Pangai. Alternately, visitors arriving in Tonga by yacht can stop in the island group on their own. It is also possible to hire a local boat from Pangai. However, this practice is less common, and it would probably be more expensive than taking a ferry.

Those who choose to take the ferry should prepared to either spend one day in the Lulunga island group before catching the next ferry coming south; or to spend one week in the area until the following ferry travels through the area. It is good to keep in mind, however, that it is possible to become stranded here for an even longer period of time than one week, if any kind of bad weather occurs.

> The ferry runs once a week, making a stop in Ha'afeva on the way north to Pangai; it then stops again the next day on the way back south to Nuku'alofa.

Depending upon the size of the ferry, the ship might be able to dock at the wharf. If the ferry is too big, however, it will anchor out at sea between Ha'afeva and Tungua, where small village boats will come out to meet it. People on the ferry then throw boxes and cargo onto the small boats to take to shore; passengers jump from the lower level of the ferry onto the small village boats. All of this chaos at sea makes for quite the spectacle, but the locals are very skilled at completing this routine, and nothing winds up thrown overboard into the ocean. Ferry passengers who transfer to a small village boat to get to Ha'afeva or Tungua should give the boat skipper TOP$5-10 for fuel costs. If the ferry docks at the wharf, travelers either have to catch a ride with one of the very few vehicles on Ha'afeva, or walk to the other side of the island. This is where the village is, on the dirt road through the bush.

HA'AFEVA

Ha'afeva is the main island in the small Lulunga island group of Ha'apai. The island, located approximately twenty-five miles south of Lifuka, is not easy to reach. However, those who have more time in their schedule, and who want to see real village life in Ha'apai, should make the effort to get there. There are only local stores on the island; nothing caters to tourists. Both the island and the village itself are gorgeous, from the sandy beaches, to the close-up views of the volcanic islands, to the picket-fenced yards lining the few gravel streets. Because the island is so small and closely-knit, it is quite common and easy for outsiders to receive the opportunity to become involved in village events there. For instance, travelers may be able to sit at *kava* circles, try their hand at weaving, lend a helping hand at the local school, or attend church events. Since Ha'afeva is the main hub for the Lulunga island group, the island does have a small medical facility and nurse on staff. For anyone planning a longer trip to the volcanic islands of Tofua and Kao, Ha'afeva is a great jumping-off point.

Accommodation

There is a local family who will open up a room in their home as a guestroom for travelers. The easiest way to find this family is to ask about a guesthouse when arriving at the wharf. Since there is only one guesthouse on the island, almost any local can give directions there. Another option would be to inquire at the Tourism Office to see if they could possibly make arrangements with the guesthouse in advance. The local guesthouse may be willing to cook for guests. Alternately, visitors can buy food and ask to use the family kitchen. There are no restaurants on the island.

It's a Rock! It's a Shoal! It's...Jack-in-the-Box Island!

On the south side of the Ha'apai island group lies the famous Jack-in-the-Box Island, or *Fonua Fo'ou*, meaning new land. Throughout history, this island has doubled as an underwater shoal and an above-ground island, making periodic appearances throughout history. It has been underwater for the last hundred years or so. The island was first discovered in 1865, by the crew of *HMS Falcon*. (Upon sighting the island, this crew simply concluded that they had been out at sea for far, far too long!)

Nomuka Group

TELEKIVAVA'U

Villa Mamana

This tiny, private island, located thirty-seven miles south of Pangai, plays host to the most exclusive private resort in Tonga, Villa Mamana. Those who choose to stay at this resort can actually rent out the entire complex, complete with a chef and housekeeping staff; the maximum guest capacity of the resort is four guests. The rate for this all-inclusive resort includes all meals, drinks, excursions, boat transfers, and even satellite phone use! Interestingly, few guests have stayed at this high-end resort at this time, due to its remote location and high price tag. *Resort: USD$1,475 /night (TOP$2,785) for up to four people. Phone: 866-vm-tonga or +872 761 616 028, mamana@les-raisting.de, www.villamamana.com*

NOMUKA

Because Nomuka is known to be a dusty, dirty island and, for some reason, the island's inhabitants have a reputation for unfriendliness, Nomuka does not tend to be a popular tourist destination. The island does, however, house one of the larger villages in the southern Ha'apai islands, so there is a ferry which travels from Nuku'alofa to Nomuka.

The island itself has a large brackish lake at its center. The early European explorers, such as Abel Tasman and the famous Captain Cook, visited this island quite frequently; they favored Nomuka because there were fresh drinking water sources there. They could also trade and stockpile food and other provisions. While there are no guesthouses on the island, it may be possible to find a public hall in which to stay, a willing Tongan host family, or a nice camping spot.

MANGO

Mango may be one of the most isolated outer islands; it's also one of the most inviting to visit. The Tongans who live there don't receive many visitors, and their only means of communication with the outside world is a radio-link telephone which, often, doesn't work. Thus, anyone who stops on Mango can expect to be greeted by friendly locals, who may well offer them a local fruit drink, a tour of the school, or perhaps even a tour around the entire immaculate island. Because they may be one of the first white people that the children have ever seen, Caucasians should not be surprised if the island children want to touch their skin (kids want to see if white skin feels different from their own skin).

Outer Islands – West

TOFUA & KAO

Tofua and Kao are two volcanic islands, both located about twenty-five miles, or seventy kilometers, west of Lifuka.

One of the last unexplored, mysterious frontiers, Tofua is the larger of the two volcanic islands. In fact, the volcano is still quite active, periodically bellowing huge quantities of smoke into the air. Dense tropical rainforest covers sixty percent of the island.

Tofua was once a very large cone-shaped volcano; however, when it erupted long ago, the entire top of the island blew off into the air, strewing ash throughout the islands. A large freshwater lake sits in the middle of the island, and there is an active

Ha'apai

volcanic cone to one side of the crater. Adrenalin junkies can climb up to the edge of the crater and look down at the glowing lava inside, if they dare. Making matters even more interesting, it is rumored that the lake holds a large, mysterious creature. Once, a man who was snorkeling along the surface of the lake saw a very large shadow pass beneath him.

Up until the 1980s, Tofua was inhabited, and it had one village with a school. The national government decided to evacuate the village when volcanic activity started to become more and more frequent there. Though the island is now officially uninhabited, residents from nearby islands in the Lulunga group do venture over to Tofua several times each year in order to cultivate *kava* and other crops there. More recently, it has been alleged that a number of escaped convicts made it to Tofua. They are rumored to be living on the northwest side of the island.

Kao, the cone-shaped volcano, is dormant. The island is incredibly steep on all sides, with the trail to the summit seemingly heading straight up through the trees. Though Kao has never been inhabited, people have camped there, and locals make occasional trips to the island.

Getting There

Those adventurous enough to attempt a trip to Tofua or Kao need to invest a good deal of thought into planning the trip, allowing ample time for travel, as well as for possible delays. The best season to travel to these islands is the winter, when the yachts are there, and there are not as many storms or rainy days. However, it can be tricky to find transportation to these islands. The best chances are from the Lulunga group on the islands of Ha'afeva, Tungua or Kotu, where locals depart to Tofua and Kao to harvest their crops there. It is also possible to inquire in Pangai at the tourism office, but may not have much luck with local boats (although you can always hire a few of them out).

The local dive shop, Fins 'n Flukes, can also provide transfers to and from Tofua, as well as arrange for a local guide to lead travelers around the island. It is definitely best to have a local Tongan guide on these volcanic islands. The islands have no marked trails, so it is very easy to get lost there. A guide can also help find water sources, as well as food.

An alternate way to get to the volcanic islands is to ask around and find out if there are any yachts heading to Tofua or Kao. Those travelers departing from the

---

The Year Of Living Deliberately

In 2008-2009, Swiss champion snowboarder Xavier Rosset decided to go alone to Tofua, where he would live off of the land for ten months in an experiment to discover life without money, time, or social constraints. All he brought with him was a machete and basic camping gear; he survived solely on fruit and seafood. Rosset did take a satellite phone with him, which he used to make recordings and update a blog about life on a volcanic island. To read more about his adventures, travelers can check out his blog at www.xavierrosset.ch.

Lulunga island group to head to the volcanic islands will start their journey in Ha'afeva, where the ferry harbors. From there, travelers can ask about any local boats going to Tofua or Kao, as local Tongans often go to these volcanic islands to maintain their crops there. If there are no local boats heading from Ha'afeva to Tofua or Koa, there may also be boats heading there from the islands of Kotu and Tungua, since many of the men's groups and youth groups have land on these islands.

Fins 'n Flukes offers packages to the volcanic islands upon request and with enough notice—a three-day minimum stay is suggested. The shop can also arrange for a local guide to lead travelers in to the volcano and back out again. Suggested itineraries, packing lists, and full expedition information are available from Fins 'n Flukes. This is a serious expedition; as such, it requires careful planning. *Phone: 73-13261 or 73-13549, email info@finsnflukes.com, www.finsnflukes.com/islandtransfers*

Finding a boat heading out to the islands is not the only difficult step of the journey. Once the boat gets close to Tofua or Kao, it may well have to anchor farther out than usual, depending upon weather conditions and the size of the boat. The islands have no safe landing beaches or harbors; instead, the ocean surrounding these islands is full of jagged volcanic rocks. Travelers may well have to swim from the boat in to land, carefully avoiding the surf on the rocks. Otherwise, they might take a smaller lifeboat from the boat to the shore. In either case, it's a true adventure.

Accommodations

There are no accommodations on Tofua or Kao, so travelers will need to bring camping supplies or stay off-shore on a yacht. Furthermore, anyone heading to the volcanic islands will need to bring a blanket, cooking gear, matches, a machete, a medical kit, and food or fishing gear. It is generally prudent to bring along a healthy supply of water, although it is possible to get rainwater from the water tank at the old school, as well as from green coconuts.

Ha'apai

Below: The beaches of Ha'apai.

Above: Ha'amonga 'a Maui coral archway (Tongatapu). Below: The Free Church of Tonga in Tongatapu. You may see the King of Tonga in attendance here.

Above: Sunset on Nomuka Island (Ha'apai).
Below: The entrance to Swallows Cave (Vava'u).

Above: Kietahi Beach (Vava'u).
Below: The view from Mt. Talua (Vava'u).

Above: Maui's Archway (Liangahuo a Maui) in 'Eua.
Below: Resorts along the Western beach of Tongatapu

Below: A Tongan feast, more food than the crowd could ever eat piled high on the table.

Vava'u

Introduction

Invariably, whenever anyone tells a Tongan that they are going to Vava'u, have been to Vava'u, or want to go to Vava'u, the Tongan will respond by saying, "*fakaofaofa*," meaning "beautiful." Vava'u's hilly terrain marks a sharp contrast to the mostly-flat Tongatapu and Ha'apai island groups. Furthermore, the island's hills, along with its close proximity to neighboring islands, provide Vava'u with a rare commodity: extremely calm, well-protected waters year-round.

Vava'u boasts some of the most protected waters in the world; this makes it a favorite place for yachts from all the world over. Add in the magnificent clear blue ocean and amazingly secluded beaches, and it is easy to understand why the population of Vava'u swells during the winter season.

The name, "Vava'u," can be pronounced three different ways, but there is really only one correct way to say it. It's "va-VA-ooh." The most common mispronunciation is "Va-Vowel" or, occasionally, "va-va-OOH." Though Tongans almost never correct anyone who says the name incorrectly, they certainly appreciate all efforts to say it properly.

HISTORY

When Captain Cook first journeyed to the islands of Tonga, he did not visit Vava'u. At the time, the Tongans told him there was no safe place to harbor there, thus steering him away from one of the most protected harbors in the South Pacific. The people of Vava'u are very proud of their differences from Tongatapu; this tradition stretches back many, many years. When William Mariner wrote his history of the Tongan Islands, he tells how the King of Tonga came to Vava'u to "conquer the island group." To his great surprise, the king was greeted peacefully by the people of Vava'u, who offered him a deal. According to the proposed agreement, the people of Vava'u would recognize him as king, as long as he promised never to come back to the island. The King rejected the deal, and a very bloody battle ensued, which ended when the King eventually conquered the island.

Even today, although the people of Vava'u will often tolerate the things which are decided on the main island of Tongatapu, the people of Vava'u prefer to do things their own way. That is, the people of Vava'u are not only far removed geographically, but also politically, from Tongatapu. For example, in 2006 when Tongatapu was exploding with protests over education, the people of Vava'u were holding a parade to celebrate their schools and teachers.

More so than any of the other islands, Vava'u has felt a large impact from tourism, which has affected the history and development of the island. Visitors come to visit to see the island's beauty, and many then choose to stay and live on Vava'u, because they enjoy the Vava'u lifestyle so much. By law, *palangis*, or non-Tongans, are limited in what they can do in Tonga. For instance, the law allows non-Tongans to run businesses only in fields in which Tongans do not possess the requisite practical expertise to run that kind of business. This generally means that *palangi* operate most of the tourist businesses on the island. There are, however, also a few expatriates who work in fields like architecture and computer technology. However, foreigners often find that running a business in Tonga can be risky. Most *palangi* business owners will note that they must "tread lightly," so that they won't upset the wrong person and get their business license revoked.

Up In Flames

In 2008, two fires had a significant impact on Vava'u. The first fire, which took place in November, destroyed a large portion of the Paradise Motel, including its bar and restaurant. Eventually, the debris was removed, but someone decided to use some of the debris to fill in potholes on the road leading to Mt. Talau. Unfortunately, because the debris was filled with nails and rough metal, this patchwork repair led to a number of flat tires on the road, thereby forcing many of the residents to park their cars below their homes and walk home, in order to avoid getting yet another flat tire on the faultily-repaired roadway.

The second fire, which happened just one month later, destroyed a large portion of the downtown Neiafu business district. The first started with some young children, who were trying to burn away a beehive near a property on the edge of town. However, the small fire quickly spun out of control, destroying several restaurants, a bookstore, a travel agency, a liquor store, and some other businesses. While most of the businesses have now relocated, some others never reopened. Although much of the debris was removed, the land, which sits along the waterfront, remains vacant to this day.

In 2010, a guesthouse on the main road caught fire and burned down. The guesthouse was reportedly having financial problems, but the cause of the fire was ultimately ruled to be accidental. And in May 2011, yet another fire gutted the Mermaid Bar and Restaurant, arguably the most popular nightspot in Vava'u. The cause of the fire was not determined.

Vava'u

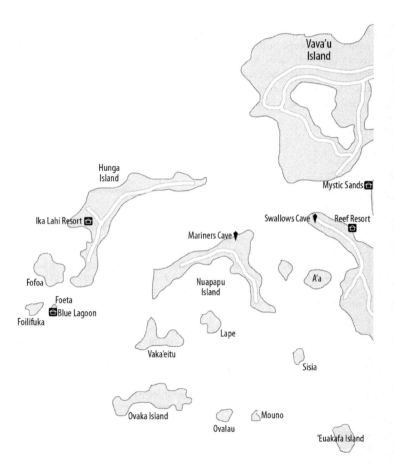

Utula'aina Point

✈ Airport

Leimatu'a

Mataika

🏖 Kietahi Beach

Mototo Cliffs

'Ene'io Botanical Gardens ■

🏖'Ene'io Beach

Mt. Talau National Park

Neiafu

Koloa Island

🏨 Tongan Beach Resort

🍴 Ovava Restaurant

🏨 Twin View Motel

Faloa

Oloua Island

Mafana Island

Umuna

Ofu Island

Kenutu

'Eno Beach 🏖

Kapa Island

Tapana

Taunga Island

Vava'u

MYTHS

As in most Polynesian cultures, and for that matter, the rest of Tonga, myths abound throughout Vava'u.

One legend tells that the island of Lotuma used to be the top part of Mt. Talau. Looking at Mt. Talau, one of the highest places in all of Vava'u, the island's flat top, not to mention its location proximate to Lotuma, certainly make the story plausible. According to the legend, evil spirits from Samoa came to Vava'u to steal the top of Mt. Talau. However, they only made it a short distance when they saw a bright light, which they thought was the rising sun. Fearful, the spirits fled, dropping the mountain top into the ocean, forming the present-day island of Lotuma. The bright light, however, was not the rising sun; it was in fact a Tongan woman exposing her buttocks, "mooning" the evil spirits, reflecting the light toward them and frightening them away.

Another story—one that has some modern day evidence to support it—involves the island of 'Euakafa. According to legend, an enemy of the Tongan King had se-

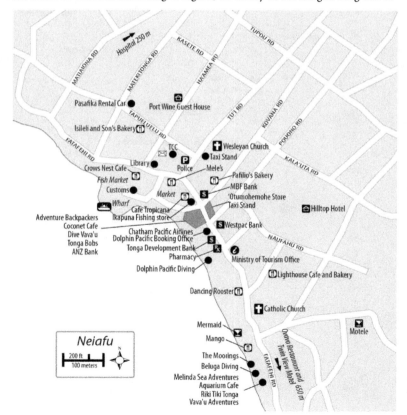

duced the King's wife, then tattooed her with his special mark in order to show the King what he had done. When the King saw the tattoo, he took his wife to the island of 'Euakafa, where she was beaten and buried. Today, walking along the beach of this beautiful tropical island, it is still possible to see where the gravestone was cut from the rocks. Those who hike to the top of the island can even see the remains of a grave there.

ORIENTATION

The heart of Vava'u is the hillside town of Neiafu. Since Neiafu is the only place in the island chain with a business district, almost all trips to Vava'u start there. Those who arrive by boat will dock at the wharf just below town. From the wharf, it's just a short walk to the market and up to the main road where restaurants, bars, and stores are located. However, some of the best places to eat and drink are rather difficult to find, and there is little signage indicating their location. Furthermore, Tongans don't generally give directions using common words like "left" and "right." Instead, they usually say that something is "that way," pointing in the general direction of the place about which they have been asked.

> The name "Vava'u" refers not just to one specific Tongan island, but rather to a group of islands within the Tongan nation. Officially, it's the "Vava'u Island Chain," a group of forty islands located nearly two hundred miles north of Tonga's main island, Tongatapu.

Those who arrive by plane will come into the airport, located near a small village about a fifteen-minute cab ride from Neiafu. Along the way, they will ride through the villages of Leimatu'a and Mataika. Though Leimatu'a is the second largest village in Vava'u, as well as the closest village to the airport, there are no accommodations or restaurants there. Along the road into Neiafu, there is one common yet notable sight: the roadside is dotted with wooden tables, tables covered with locally-grown fruits and vegetables. Here is how the tables work: if there is no one at the table, there are usually prices written on the items. Shoppers should simply take what they want, leaving the money on the table. Of course, it goes without saying that if there is already money there, that money should be left on the table.

Businesses change hands all the time in Neiafu. Many of the businesses geared to tourists, as well as most of the restaurants, are owned by *palangi*, not Tongans. Those interested in buying fresh produce and local handicrafts should head to the market, which is open six days a week. However, plan to arrive early at the market, because Tongans will head home once they have made enough money for the day. Another important note to keep in mind is the fact that the selection varies greatly with the season. If pineapples are in-season, they taste absolutely incredible. Vava'u pineapples possess a distinctive sweet taste; many claim that these pineapples are among the best-tasting in the world. Tongan pineapples are smaller than other varieties and they have a soft, edible core in the center. Although pineapples do grow on the other islands, most Tongan pineapples come from Vava'u, because of its hotter climate.

Vava'u

GETTING THERE

Arrival

Passengers arriving by plane will come in on a domestic flight, so it will not be necessary for them to clear customs. Anyone transferring to a flight to Vava'u directly from an inbound international flight should remember to exchange currency at the international airport on Tongatapu (there is no currency exchange or ATM at either the domestic airport on Tongatapu, or at Vava'u Airport). However, despite this fact, it is necessary to have Tongan currency immediately upon arrival on Vava'u, simply in order to get anywhere from the airport.

Anyone who made their booking in advance can ask their hotel to arrange to send someone to meet them at the airport. Some larger accommodations have their own transport; others may simply send a taxi or a family friend in order to pick up the guests and drive them into town. There may be other, unsolicited taxis meeting the flight at the airport, but not always. In addition, it is not uncommon for strangers to approach travelers and ask them if they would like a ride to town. It is perfectly safe to say yes, but it is important to find out how much the driver will charge for the ride before getting in the car. Some Tongans will happily drive travelers into town for free if they are heading that direction anyway, while other Tongans may be looking to make a few extra dollars. If a Tongan has offered to take someone to town for free, the traveler should not embarrass the local by trying to force money on them. Instead, they can just place TOP$10-15 on the seat next to the driver as they are getting out of the car. The driver will probably just ignore it until the passenger is out of sight, but the gesture will be appreciated.

Chathams Pacific office is located in the small shopping center next to the Tonga Development Bank, across the street from Westpac Bank. *Phone: 71280, www.chathamspacific.com.*

As mentioned earlier in this book, visitors should never get into a cab in Tonga without first agreeing with the driver upon the price in advance. The ride from the airport into Neiafu should cost around TOP$20; however, that price can vary depending upon circumstance. Another piece of cab etiquette to be aware of is that, often, the driver will cram other people into the vehicle along with the original passengers that he has picked up, even after he has agreed to take the first customers into town. Often, the other people that the driver picks up are friends or family members, and it would be considered rude for the driver not to take them along as well. He may also pick up other paying passengers en route to town. While it is possible that female taxi cab drivers exist on Vava'u, it would be very rare to have a female taxi driver anywhere on Vava'u.

Another way to reach Vava'u is by boat: either aboard a ferry, or on a private yacht. Those arriving on a ferry will come into the harbor, which is located right in town. Many of the accommodations listed in this section are within a short, easy walk of the harbor, at least for those who do not have a large amount of luggage. Finding a taxi at the dock can be a challenge, as most of the passengers arriving by ferry are met by family members, and not many tourists arrive in Vava'u this way. However, there is a taxi stand located rather near the wharf. Readers should see the taxi information later in this chapter for details. Ferry service has been quite unreliable in past years. The Japanese government, however, just donated a new ferry to Tonga, which will hopefully provide regular service to Vava'u once each week.

Those arriving in Vava'u by yacht should note that, if this island is their first arrival point in Tonga, they will need to clear customs and immigration. The customs wharf is located on the northern end of Neiafu Harbor. Customs operates only on weekdays, from 8:30 am- 4:30 pm, with a one-hour lunch break from 12:30 pm - 1:30 pm. Those who arrive during lunch hour or after-hours must make arrangements in advance of their arrival, as well as pay an extra fee.

The Immigration Office is located on the second floor of the Tonga Development Bank building in the main business district. *Customs phone: 70053 or 70928, VHF 16, Immigration phone: 71142*

The ferry office is located at the wharf, near the area where the ferry arrives. It is usually only open on days when the boat is scheduled to arrive on the island. The sign which indicates the projected arrival time is notoriously inaccurate. Those waiting for the arriving ferry can only listen for the horn which signals the ship's arrival. Fortunately, missing the boat is never a worry since the ferry sits at the dock

> About once a month, the ferry continues on to the Niua island group. Anyone who travels to the Niuas (pg 209) by ferry may have to wait one month or more in order to get back to the main island.

for hours, unloading its cargo and then reloading again before departing. One important note: travelers should make sure, before getting on the boat, that the boat is heading to the island to which they want to go. Generally, the ferry runs once each week. However, the ships are plagued by delays, so a twelve-hour trip can easily become a twenty-four hour adventure.

Sailors can download a free island guide from www.vavau.to. This guide, written by the owners of Tropicana Café, does tend to favor their establishment, but it also contains a lot of useful information. A more extensive guide, the "Sailingbird Guide to Tonga," is available in shops around Neiafu for about TOP$90.

Yacht Crews

When yachts arrive in Vava'u, the boat owners will often stay several months. Therefore, the owners typically "drop off" those people who have sailed with them on the island on which they land. When, a few months later, it comes time for the yacht to depart again, the owners will often be looking for new people to help crew their boat to the next destination. Anyone who agrees to work on a boat will usually get a free ride wherever that ship is going—to Australia, New Zealand, Fiji, even Hawaii.

While the yacht owners typically prefer to take people who have sailing experience, they are often more interested in traveling with people whom they like. Anyone who is interested in hitching a yacht ride to another South Pacific nation should post signs around town and express their interest to boat owners.

Vava'u

GETTING AROUND

While there are plenty of taxi cabs in Vava'u, it is by no means always easy to get a ride. There are two taxi stands in downtown Neiafu and often it is possible to get a taxi at either location. One stand is located next to the Vava'u Trading Center (Phone: 70-136), the other next to 'Otumohemohe, the large green store in the center of town (Phone: 70-240). Roadrunner also provides reliable service; this cab is run by a Tongan named Seimisi. (Phone: 12094 or 883-45 86). If anyone calls Seimisi and he tells them that he will pick them up, he will actually come—this is a bit of a rarity for island taxis. However, Seimisi lives outside of downtown, and he is not always available. Seimisi also has a VHF radio; he can be contacted on Channel 16.

Almost every village has its own bus, which functions primarily to take children into Neiafu for school. The bus also doubles as a way for village people to travel into town, since many Tongans don't have cars. Each bus primarily runs from one village into Neiafu and back. There is no bus which runs everywhere on the main island of Vava'u.

Buses do not operate on a regular schedule. In fact, if there is no school, the buses may not run at all. Or if the students get dismissed early, the bus may head back to the village early. That said, buses usually go into town in the morning and head back to the village in the afternoon. For the larger areas, the bus may make several trips between the village and the city each day.

Buses generally depart and arrive in the area near the post office, and they will pick up passengers anywhere and drop them wherever they ask to stop. Those who are outside of the downtown area who see a bus heading in the direction of town should flag the bus down; it will take them to town. In terms of the fare, the passenger should simply ask the driver how much to pay. If the driver says that there is no charge, it is best to pay a few *pa'anga* for each passenger.

Suto, or hitchhiking, is generally very safe, especially during the day. In fact, the biggest risk involved with hitchhiking probably arises from the safety of the vehicle itself. Tongans drive cars well beyond the time when the average westerner would have sent the vehicles to the scrap yard. Walkers will note that, interestingly, even if they don't flag down a car, Tongans will often stop and ask them if they want a ride nonetheless. One word of warning: Tongan drivers do not always head directly to their destination and are notorious for making stops along the way to pick up extra people, drop off other people, or stop for other (mysterious) reasons known only to the drivers themselves. Eventually, hitchhikers get to where they want to go, but this won't always happen immediately.

There are no car rental facilities at the airport. All those planning to rent cars need to get a ride to town in order to pick up their rental vehicle. Pasifika Rental (70-781 or 75-12628) and Avis (70-873) are both located in Neiafu. There are two factors which car renters should keep in mind. First of all, the price of fuel in Tonga is incredibly high. In addition, every person—traveler and local alike—who rents a car on Tonga is required to obtain a Tongan driver's license from the police station. The station is open from 8:30 am - 4.30 pm Monday and Tuesday, and from 8:30 am - 12:30 pm Wednesday through Friday.

Many visitors may find that renting a car is unnecessary, and that it is cheaper to take a taxi or to book a trip to see the island. In and around Neiafu, it is easy to walk to most of the interesting sights. Another thing to keep in mind about renting a car is the fact that, though all of the main roads are paved, potholes are plentiful everywhere. The bush roads are usually privately-owned, so travel on them happens at the driver's own risk.

Those who do rent a car can park pretty much anywhere. There are no parking meters or paid parking lots on Vava'u. Anyone who plans on driving on Vava'u should know that sometimes a car will stop in the middle of the road because the driver wants to talk to a passerby. This interaction will completely block the road. Tongans are very friendly, and they would consider it very rude to drive past a person whom they know without stopping to say hello.

BANKING

Vava'u has three commercial banks: Westpac, ANZ, MBF, plus the government owned Tonga Development Bank. All four banks have locations in the Neiafu business district and are open from 9 am – 4 pm on weekdays. Westpac and ANZ also have limited banking services available on Saturday. Both Westpac and ANZ have ATMs.

The three commercial banks should all be able to exchange Australian, New Zealand, and American dollars, as well as Euros. However, besides the types of currency listed above, it can be hit-or-miss: the Tongan banks do not accept currency from all countries.

In addition to the banks, there are several money transfer services in town, including Western Union. Because the other, smaller firms tend to come and go, they are not listed here. *Western Union Phone: 70-888*

Using a credit card on Vava'u can be a challenge. Nearly all of the businesses there are cash-based. While some of the businesses that cater to tourists do accept credit cards, almost all of them charge an additional 5% fee for the use of a credit card. This occurs because the banks charge the merchants 4% for each credit card transaction, and so the merchant then charges an additional 1% for the "hassle" of accepting the cards. Because of this, it often proves much cheaper to just exchange currency than to try to use credit cards.

> Americans who do their banking with Bank of America can withdraw money from Westpac ATMs without paying a transaction fee.

COMMUNICATIONS

Both of Tonga's telecommunication providers, TCC and Digicel, have offices in Vava'u. The TCC office is located just up the hill from the harbor. These offices sell cell phones, as well as provide phone booths, from which customers can make international phone calls from a landline. Digicel has its office just one block away from TCC on the main street. It shares space with a hardware store. Digicel also sells mobile phones.

Next door to TCC sits the post office and some other government offices. While mailing a package or a postcard from the post office is usually successful, receiving a package on Vava'u can be a challenge. In the past, some packages have arrived a year late while some never arrived at all. Thus, it is generally a good idea to have important packages sent to the main post office in Nuku'alofa, rather than to the branch office in Vava'u.

There are just two Internet providers in Vava'u: TCC and Digicel. TCC dominates the market. One thing to note is the fact that, if the Internet is not working at one location, it is most likely out all over the entire island. This occurs because all Internet connections come into Vava'u via satellite, so if there is a problem at the station, there is be no Internet anywhere. Connection speeds are incredibly slow, even slower than those on the main island. However, for those who simply want to check their e-mail or browse the Internet, this should not present a problem.

There are numerous Internet cafés in Vava'u, with prices ranging from free to TOP$10 per hour. In some cafés, ten or more computers share a very slow connection. In others, there are so many viruses on the computers that it is impossible and unsafe to do anything. Virus protection is not common in many of the Internet cafés.

The Aquarium Café gives customers one of the best deals on the island. The café offers free Internet access to customers, as well as free Wi-Fi for those with their own laptop. The connection is fast, at least by Vava'u standards, and the café also sends its Internet signal over the harbor, so boat owners can access the Wi-Fi as well.

Other reliable Internet cafés are Tropicana, which runs the Vavau.to Internet portal. Coconet, located on the water below Tonga Bob's Bar, is a bit harder to find, yet it is usually reliable.

TOURISM & BOOKING OFFICES

Although there is a small official Ministry of Tourism office on Vava'u, generally the many booking offices located in Neiafu can provide better, more useful information. The Langafonua Women's Handicraft Association, located next to the Ministry of Tourism, has a small gift shop, which offers local handicrafts similar to those available at the market. The Association sells crafts made by local Vava'u women. These include hand-woven items, such as mats, placemats, and wooden carvings. The shop also offers many items made from *tapa* for purchase. See page 52 for information about *tapa*.

Before using a booking office, it may be helpful to note that each booking office typically receives a flat 10% fee from the activity operator. Bookings can also be very political with an office having an exclusive agreement with a particular operator. That means, like most things in Tonga, it pays to shop around and see what is available. While the price for a certain activity may be the same at all booking offices, the selection of activities available varies.

Despite the backroom politics, the booking offices are usually a good source of information. In fact, most of them also provide information about the free activities in Vava'u, as well as information about special or seasonal events. Reputable, reliable booking offices are located at Tropicana, Adventure Backpackers, Dolphin Pacific Diving, and The Aquarium Café.

IMMIGRATION

Tourist visas can be extended at the Immigration Office, located on the second floor of Tonga Development Bank near the end of downtown Neiafu, across the street from Westpac Bank.

Those planning to extend their stay should bear in mind that it is usually easier to get a visa extension there than it is on Tongatapu.

MEDICAL & EMERGENCY SERVICES

Getting medical service in Vava'u can be a challenge. The Vava'u Pharmacy, located next to the Tonga Development Bank, can help visitors with many medical problems; in the past, there has sometimes been a doctor at this location. For more serious problems, it is best to head to the Prince Ngu Hospital on Mt. Talau. However, the quality of the care offered there is not on par with that of many other developing countries. On the other hand, at various different times of year, there are visiting medical students from the United Kingdom practicing in Vava'u as part of their training. In a medical emergency, it is best to just ask to be taken to the hospital. One item to note: sheets and food are generally not provided to those who stay overnight in the hospital, so it is expected that patients provide these items on their own. *The police station is located next to TCC and the post office. For emergency assistance, call the police at 922, the hospital at 933. Other emergency assistance is available at 911.*

Activities

SWIMMING WITH WHALES

There are nearly twenty companies in Vava'u that are licensed to offer whale-swimming trips. Unfortunately, most of these businesses have the license simply as a way to make money, but they do not possess any real experience around, or understanding of, whales. In fact, one of the main reasons why tourists visit Vava'u is to have the once-in-a-lifetime opportunity to swim with whales. Thus, it is recommended that no one short-change a potentially incredible experience by signing up with a sub-par operator who lacks the expertise to lead a trip, the desire to educate visitors about the whales, or both. That being said, with this much competition, it is easy to find a cheaper trip than the ones offered by the two companies listed here. However, those cheaper options might ultimately leave travelers disappointed at the end of the day.

It typically costs about TOP$150 to swim with the whales. An important item to note is the fact that there is no guarantee, on any given trip, that participants will actually get to swim with the whales. Although thousands of whales cruise through the warm waters of Tonga, the animals don't tend to follow a schedule. This makes whale-swimming trips hit-or-miss. Keeping that in mind, for the best experience, travelers should consider booking three days of whale-swimming excursions. While this will not guarantee an actual encounter, it certainly increases the odds of getting to swim with the whales. Although having a waterproof camera for this activity is a plus, trip participants should make sure that they do not spend all of their time in the water taking pictures. After all, the pure sensory experience of just *being* in the water with the whales is incredible in and of itself.

Swimming with Whales

How do you describe the experience of being just feet away from one of the largest mammals on the planet? How do you describe the experience of watching a baby whale calf play under the watchful eye of its mother? And how do you possibly describe the feeling of being pushed by gentle turbulence as a giant humpback softly swings its tail, creating a mini-wave around you?

Words simply fail. Swimming with whales is one of those rare and beautiful things in life which simply must be experienced firsthand in order to fully understand it. After a day of swimming with whales, something very few people ever get a chance to do, I feel truly humbled by these gentle giants, at a loss to find the appropriate adjectives to describe my experience.

I spent the fateful day with Dolphin Pacific Diving. The day started out slowly; I started to wonder if we would actually encounter any whales at all. After all, it was late in the season, and many of the whales who had been in the islands all winter had left. Though I had been close to whales before, this was the first time that I had actually planned to *swim* with them.

During our (early) lunch break, one of the guys on the boat suddenly asked, "is that a whale?" Though I didn't see it at first, it was indeed a whale. We quickly made our way toward the whale and, as we approached, we saw a baby calf jump completely out of the water, spinning as it landed back in the water. That sight would prove to be the perfect beginning to an amazing experience. Once we had gotten (carefully, quietly) into the water, we swam out. At first, the water was too dark to see anything, but then I noticed (what I first thought was) a reef on the ocean bottom. However, as we got closer, I realized that I was looking down at a giant humpback whale directly below me. This was NOT the baby whale we had seen jump out of the water; it was the mother, taking a rest. And she wasn't on the ocean floor. She was floating!

Because the whales swam away, the first stop was short. On the next stop, however, the whales were in a playful mood, especially the baby who seemed almost to be chasing us. At one point, I felt like he was putting on a show just for the five of us in the water. "Mama" kept her eye on us, and on her baby. As I looked her straight in the eye, I wondered what I must look like to her.

On the last stop of the day, we spent perhaps forty-five minutes in the water, just watching the whales play. All day, I had been shooting photos, rapid-fire, awed. But at that last spot, I just shut off my camera and floated, watching these two incredible beings just go about their lives below me. It was peaceful, tranquil—the creatures seemed to exert a calm upon us that was like nothing that I had ever before experienced.

- Steve Hunsicker

There are a number of rules for swimming with the whales. Only four people (plus a guide) can be in the water with the whales at one time. Furthermore, everyone in the water is required to stay a certain distance from the whales. However, if the whales should swim up to the people—which they frequently do—the swimmers are not required to back away from the animals. Finally, all of the swimmers need to stay on the same side of the whale (that way, the animal will not feel trapped or surrounded).

Reputable whale-swimming trips are offered by the following companies:

Dive Vava'u This company, located on the waterfront just below Tonga Bob's Bar, offers quality whale-swimming trips. *Phone: 70492, www.divevavau.com.*

Dolphin Pacific Diving Dolphin Pacific Diving, another reputable company, is also located on the waterfront, situated just below the Tonga Development Bank. This shop also has a store and booking office located next to the Tonga Development Bank on Neiafu's main street. *Phone: 70292, www.dolphinpacificdiving.com.*

DIVING AND SNORKELING

The islands of Vava'u are literally surrounded by great snorkel spots. Brightly colored fish and coral abound in the warm Pacific waters there. However, anyone who wishes to snorkel in Vava'u will need to remember to bring their own mask and snorkel. While some of the charter boats offer gear for guests to borrow, it can be quite difficult to find decent gear on-island. A snorkel with a valve on the top is recommended so the snorkel will not fill with water upon diving down to the ocean floor to have a closer look at all of the plants and creatures down there.

Snorkeling, diving, PADI instruction, and scuba gear rental are all available at **Dive Vava'u** and **Dolphin Pacific Diving**, as well as two other dive shops in Neiafu:

Riki Tiki Tonga This outfitter, located at The Aquarium Café, offers diving and snorkeling trips in a small boat, with a maximum capacity of four people per trip. *www.rikitikitonga.com*

Beluga Diving Another reputable dive operator, Beluga Diving, is located on the waterfront, between Aquarium Café and Mango's Restaurant. *Phone: 70-327, www.belugadivingvavau.com*

CAMPING AND HIKING

Vava'u doesn't have any official campsites, but that doesn't mean that there is no camping there. In fact, remains of campfires dot many of the beaches, as well as the uninhabited islands. While most locations are on private land, the old adage, "take only pictures, leave only footprints" serves as a handy rule of thumb at many locations throughout Tonga. Provided that campers behave themselves and do not leave a mess, most Tongans will happily let them camp anywhere.

Tongans don't really use camping gear; they usually just sleep on a mat. Therefore, those who plan to camp on Vava'u should either bring their own gear or check with Friendly Islands Kayak Company for gear purchase or rental.

Vava'u

Mt. Talau

The "must-do" hike of Vava'u is the climb to the top of Mt. Talau. As the highest point on the main island, the summit offers stunning vistas, both of the main island and of several of the outer islands. In order to climb Talau, it is best to start the climb in Neiafu and then just continue walking up the road. When hikers see the sign that says "Mt. Talau National Park," they should look for the trail, then follow that trail to the top of the mountain. There is a cell phone tower near the peak, but hikers should not stop there. Instead, they should take the trail to the other side of the top, which provides great views of the islands of Lotuma and 'Otea. The hike can be strenuous, so it is important to stop and rest periodically, especially when tired. It will take approximately forty-five minutes to one hour to walk from central Neiafu to the top of the mountain.

BOATING

Not only are boats plentiful in Vava'u, they also provide the only way to reach the outer islands. Boats are available for rental by the day, the week, or even the month. A great way to see the sights around Vava'u, including Mariner's Cave and Swallows Cave (see below), is to charter a boat for the day.

The cost to rent a boat depends upon the size of the boat, the size of the crew, and, of course, the length of the trip. Prices are usually negotiable, since there is a lot of competition, and all of these boats are owned by *palangi*, non-Tongans. Prices range from TOP$350 for a day trip to more than TOP$3,000/night.

Riki Tiki Tonga In addition to offering dive trips, this outfitter, located at The Aquarium Café, offers a twenty-six foot Folk Boat for charter. *www.rikitikitonga.com*

Manu-o-ku Sailing Charters This company offers a thirty-seven foot Searunner Trimaran, available for both day and overnight charters. The captain, who is from Hawaii, has years of experience in the Tongan waters, and he can help those without prior sailing experience learn to sail. *Phone: 73-13305, www.manuoku.com*

Cyber The Hilltop Hotel owns one of the largest, most modern catamarans in Vava'u. The boat comes with a full crew, and it can be booked for day, sunset, and overnight cruises. *Phone: 70209, www.hilltophotelvavau.com/sailing_aboard_cyber.html*

The Moorings Since this outfitter has eight different sizes of boats, The Moorings easily claims the title of largest charter boat operator in Tonga. Because they are also the most expensive charter boat operator, they cater to an upscale crowd. Reservations are handled in New Zealand. *Phone: +64 (9) 378-7900, www.tongasailing.com*

Melinda Sea Adventures This company offers a fifty-two foot cutter, available for day and overnight charters. The boat, *Jocara*, often races in the weekly Vava'u yacht race, and the owners will sometimes take passengers on the race around the harbor. *Phone: 70975, www.sailtonga.com*

BEACHES

Vava'u has some fabulous beaches; none of these beaches, however, are located in the immediate Neiafu area. In town, the local children (and occasional adults) compensate for the lack of beach by jumping off of the dock into the harbor.

While all of the outer island resorts have beaches, here are four options on the main island:

Kietahi Beach may be one of the best beaches in Vava'u, but it's also one of the hardest to find. It is generally easiest to reach this beach by taxi, since the driver will know how to get there. However, that does not always mean that he will drive all the way down to the beach, because the road is extremely rough. Those who do take a taxi should make sure to arrange a time to be picked up again, as there is no regular taxi service to the beach. In fact, there are no services of any kind at Keitahi Beach: no restaurant, no bathrooms and, certainly, no lifeguards. However, anyone who visits this beach during the week will likely have the whole place to themselves.

'Ene'io Beach is located a little farther down the road which leads to Kietahi Beach. Unlike Kietahi Beach, 'Ene'io Beach has a restaurant, as well as a telephone, from which it is possible to call a taxi for transportation. Generally, visitors to 'Ene'io Beach will not be asked to pay to use the beach. If they want to use the bathroom, however, it's good practice to order some food or drinks from the restaurant.

Tonga Beach Resort has a nice tropical setting, and the resort will allow tourists to use the beach in front of the resort, as long as the guests buy a drink or a food item during the course of their visit. Those who do not purchase anything should expect to be charged a fee for beach access. Those who wish to take a taxi to the beach should be sure to book the cab themselves, as the resort will mark up the price for those who call and inquire about transportation. However, the beach is very nice and well-maintained. Anyone who might feel that they are being gouged can simply walk away. Again, most visitors can enjoy a wonderful beach for the price of a drink.

'Eno Beach, located about fifteen minutes from Neiafu by taxi, may be small, but it is a comfortable place to relax. In fact, it often serves as the site for the Tongan feasts which are conducted especially for visitors. On the downside, following a feast on the beach, flies tend to congregate there, feasting on the remaining food.

ADVENTURE SPORTS

Caves

There are a number of caves in Vava'u, but the two most famous caves are only accessible by boat. Those who hire their own boat shouldn't have any trouble locating Swallows Cave, though finding Mariner's Cave may prove more of a challenge.

Mariner's Cave

Mariner's Cave is probably the most famous of all of the caves in the entire Vava'u chain. The cave can be entered only by swimming down under water, traveling through an underwater passage, and then emerging from the water inside of the cave. This can be daunting, but once a swimmer has committed to going into the cave, there is really no going back, because it is impossible to surface for air until emerging inside the cave. Generally, wearing a mask and flippers makes the swim much easier.

It is only necessary to dive down about six or eight feet in order to reach the tunnel entrance. Swimming into the cave, it's quite dark, so it can be difficult to tell when it is time to surface. Most people will swim a lot farther into the cave than needed. However, those who don't swim far enough will bang their head on the way up.

The inside of the cave is amazing. The most unexpected thing is the change in pressure. As the waves come in, everyone's ears pop as the pressure inside the cave changes, and the cave fills with mist from the waves crashing outside.

Getting out of the cave is much easier than getting in. It is easy to see the bright blue water illuminated by the sun when swimming out; this takes the guesswork out of knowing where to surface.

Swallows Cave

Not far from Mariner's Cave sits another cave, Swallows Cave. This cave is so large that small boats can fit inside of it. On maps, Swallows Cave is located on the island of Kapa. However, anyone who asks a Tongan about Kapa will hear that Kapa is a small village, not an island. Tongans will instead say that the island is near the village of 'Otea, or they may even claim that the island doesn't have a name, or that the island's name is 'Otea.

Swallows Cave has two entrances: one at water level, and one about fifty feet below the surface of the water. This lower entrance allows light to illuminate the ocean floor below. The cliffs along the cave walls make popular spots from which to jump into the water, and the water is certainly deep enough to allow for safe diving. There is usually an abundance of sea life near the cave entrance, including many varieties of fish. There is also an underwater passage near the bottom of the cave; it is large enough for divers to leave the cave and enter the ocean. This passage, however, lies too deep for snorkeling.

The Creature from the Blue Lagoon

According to legend, the ancient Governor of Vava'u ordered that the family of a chief be massacred. However, another young chief had fallen in love with the chief's daughter who was about to be executed. The young chief hid the girl inside Mariner's Cave. He planned to keep her there until he could find a way to transport her to safety in Fiji. The young man brought the girl mats and food so she could survive inside the cave. The girl, of course, soon fell in love with her savior. Finally, the young chief arranged to receive an invitation to go on a trip to Fiji.

Before he left in the large canoe for Fiji, the others asked the young man if he wanted to take a Tongan wife along on the trip. He answered no, but he added that he might try to find one along the way. As the canoe approached Mariner's Cave, the young chief dove into the water, swam into Mariner's Café, and retrieved the young girl. When he emerged from the sea with this beautiful woman, the others in the canoe thought she must be a goddess from the water. Then, they thought the girl must be an appartition, the ghost of a woman whom they had all believed dead. The canoe safely arrived in Fiji, and they all lived there for two years, until the tyrannical governor of Vava'u died. At that time, it was safe for everyone to return to Tonga.

FISHING

The Ikapuna Fishing Store, located on the main street of Neiafu, offers both plentiful information on fishing and a full line of fishing supplies. This store is run by a couple, a Tongan woman and an American man, Paul Mead. Paul has been fishing for two decades in Vava'u, and he has a small boat available for charter. He is a colorful character, and he will even offer charters on Sunday when nearly everything else on the island is closed. (He evades the Sunday restrictions by taking his Sunday charters out into the open ocean, away from the island and the locals.) *Phone: 70-698, ikapuna@kalianetvav.to*

For big game fishing at a big price, contact Steve Campbell, proud record-holder of most of the Tongan game fishing records. Steve, a New Zealander, and his partner own the Ika Lahi fishing lodge, as well as two fishing boats. A full-day charter costs NZ$1550. Though the deposit is charged in New Zealand currency, it is possible to pay the balance in either New Zealand dollars or *pa'anga. Phone: 70611, www.tongafishing.com*

KAYAKS

There are two ways to get around Vava'u on kayaks: the old fashioned way, and the high-speed way. Friendly Island Kayak Company offers tours around the Vava'u Islands, as well as around the other Tongan island groups. Participants on these trips have the opportunity to camp, snorkel, and attend a Tongan feast. The Flying Coconut Jet Kayak, on the other hand, offers a fast way to travel, using a jet engine to propel the kayak over the smooth protected waters surrounding Vava'u.

Friendly Island Kayak Company Day trips start at TOP$270; multiple day packages run into the thousands, depending upon length of the trip and the activity options. *Phone: 70173, www.fikco.com.*

Flying Coconut Jet Kayak Tours Currently, these tours exist exclusively in New Zealand and Tonga. *Tours cost TOP$200 per person. Phone: 874-6247, www.jetkayaktours.com.*

KARTS

Vava'u Adventures This outfitter offers two hour tours of Vava'u on four-wheel all-terrain vehicles known as "karts." On these tours, adventurous travelers hurtle down the main roads out to some of the remote villages, along bush roads, and down overgrown trails. The result? Visitors see some of the most spectacular sights Vava'u has to offer. *TOP$200 for a single kart, and TOP$300 for a double kart. Both types include a guide. Phone: 874-6249, www.vavauadventures.com*

CULTURAL ACTIVITIES

Tongans love to eat, and they have regular feasts. Anyone who happens to walk by a feast-in-progress should not be surprised to hear someone call out, "*Ha'u kai!*" This phrase means, simply, "Come eat." Those invited to participate in a feast should accept the invitation. In fact, saying no would be viewed as extremely rude. There is always plenty of food at a Tongan feast and, when the first group of people is finished eating, more people sit down and eat the leftovers.

Travelers who are not lucky enough to discover a feast on their own can choose to attend one of the traditional feasts which are put on for tourists. While these feasts are not exactly the same as true traditional Tongan feasts, these events offer a chance to sample authentic Tongan foods and enjoy some traditional Tongan entertainment. Those interested in attending a feast can check at the booking offices around town to find out about any of the feasts scheduled during their visit. In addition, Mango Restaurant will occasionally hold feasts during tourist season.

For men—sorry, no ladies allowed—there are always plenty of chances to take part in an authentic Tongan *kava* circle. At the *kava* circles, men gather around at different locations every night to drink *kava*, tell jokes, sing songs, and play music. Upon seeing a *kava* circle, it is perfectly acceptable for adult men to enter and join in the drinking. However, all of those who choose to participate should contribute TOP$5 toward the cost of the *kava*, around the time when the Tongans take up the collection. This money will help pay for the cost of *kava*. Alternately, sometimes, the event is actually a fundraiser to raise money for a community cause or for an educational scholarship. Anyone who leaves before the money is collected should ask the person in charge what amount to give, and they should give their money to that person. They should never just hand a donation to a random person in the circle; that man will probably think it is simply a gift for him, as opposed to a contribution to defray the cost of the *kava*.

Two *kava* circles meet with reliable frequency: one at the police station, another at the hall across from the Catholic church, which sits along the route from town to The Aquarium Café. In traditional *kava* circles, the men sit Indian-style on the floor. At the kava circle near the Catholic church, however, the men use tables and chairs. While this type of set-up is a bit more comfortable for the participants, it is very unusual.

While women travelers cannot participate in the *kava* circles, they can become

Helping Out

As mentioned elsewhere in this book, Tongans survive on the generosity of others. In that respect, the people of Vava'u are no different than the people of any other island group. Fundraising happens all year long. In Vava'u, there are a number of ways to assist the locals, in addition to contributing to the traditional Tongan fundraisers mentioned on page 86.

Every Saturday, the local library, which is located in front of the post office, offers the chance for people to read to Tongan children. The children will come and listen to volunteer (Anglophones) read English language books to them. Anyone who would like to read to the children should drop by the library and ask how to volunteer.

In addition, the Vava'u Environmental Protection Association, a new organization, focuses on cleaning up the islands and protecting their natural assets. Those who want to help should check out the organization's website for a list of the upcoming activities that they have planned: *www.vavauenvironment.org*.

involved in the local culture by making handicrafts or weaving *tapa*. In order to do this, they can simply ask one of the vendors at the market. The vendor will probably let them help. Those seeking something more structured should inquire at one of the booking offices in order to see if they can arrange a structured craft-making activity for them.

Anyone who finds themselves in Vava'u on a Sunday should not miss the chance to attend a Tongan church service, regardless of their own personal religious beliefs. The music is amazing, and Tongans love to sing. In the smaller churches, families may even invite the visitors to dine with them afterwards. As with the feasts, it is rude to turn down an invitation, and the experience will, assuredly, be amazing.

The 'Ene'io Botanical Gardens

Located near the village of Tu'anekivale, near 'Ene'io Beach, these gardens showcase a wide variety of native Tongan plants and flowers; the garden also offers cultural activities. The Polynesian Cultural Tour, which includes a tour of the garden; along with various demonstrations, including one demonstration detailing how tapa is made, one illustrating the method for making vanilla essence, and one showing the process of making coconut milk. This costs TOP$180 per person. Lunch is included. Alternately, there is also a one-hour guided tour of the garden only. This tour costs TOP$40 per person, while the Tongan feast and dance costs TOP$35 per person.

The nearby beach is open to the public, and there is a restaurant and bar just down from the gardens, on the beach. *Phone: 71048, www.vavaueneiobeach.com*

Yacht Race

Every Friday afternoon during the winter tourism season, yachts from all over the world race around the Port of Refuge. Often, visitors can tag along for the ride. On the day of the race, the boat captains start gathering around 4 pm to register for the race. Anyone who is around during the registration and is interested in crewing, should just ask the boat captains if they have extra room on the boat. Depending on the boat, guests might have to actually help sail the yacht or they might just get to sit back and enjoy the ride. After the race, everyone gets together for the prize presentation and drinks. For many years, the registration and prize presentation was done at Mermaids. However, a fire in May 2011 destroyed the bar. The staff at the Aquarium Café should be able to provide current information on the Yacht race.

SECRET SPOTS

Fungamatoto

The Cliffs at Fungamatoto certainly merit a visit. The name, Fungamoto, is derived from the Tongan word for blood, because the moon rise is visible from this spot, and it tends to have a reddish tint.

From the road, it is only a short hike through the woods to the top of the cliffs, where a nice meadow offers an excellent view of the ocean below. Fortunately, the climb from the cliff top down to the water below is not as treacherous as it might appear from the cliff's edge. However, it is still important to wear good shoes and exercise caution in order to avoid slipping. At the bottom of the cliff sit small crystalline pools: a perfect spot to soak and swim in the cool waters of the Pacific. This is only possible at low tide; at high tide, it would be deadly.

Often, when passengers tell a taxi driver that they want to go to Fungamoto, the driver will just drop them off at the 'Ene'io Botanical Garden, which is located just past the trail to Fungamatoto.

Utula'aina Point

Utula'aina Point is a really nice camping spot on the northern side of Vava'u, near the village of Holonga. Although some taxi drivers take passengers right to the point itself, others simply drop passengers off once the road begins to get rough.

Campers and early risers should make a special effort to be at Utula'aina Point for sunrise: this is a spectacular place to watch the sun come up, illuminating the cliffs and beach below.

From the cliff, it is possible to hike down to the beach below. However, it is important to use caution on this trail, as the hike back up the hill is extremely strenuous, especially for those carrying backpacks.

Kenutu

Most of the islands in the Vava'u island group are uninhabited. Some of these islands are very small—sometimes, the "islands" are just giant rocks with a few trees on them. Other islands are so low-lying that they are visible only at low tide. However, there are also some large uninhabited islands. The island of Kenutu, for instance, is one such island. It's located about a forty-five minute boat ride from the main island.

Regardless of how visitors arrive—whether by water taxi or in their own boat—there is no dock on Kenutu, so it is necessary to anchor a few feet offshore, then wade in to the beach.

From the beach, it is possible to climb through the bush to a popular campsite. Pine needles blanket this area, which sits on top of a tree-covered cliff, offering majestic views of the water below.

Shopping

There are plenty of grocery stores in Neiafu but, after visiting several of them, it is easy to believe that all of the "different" stores sell the exact same products. At any given time, all of the stores will stock the same flavor of jelly, the same brand of pasta, the same boxed milk, even the same kind of frozen meat! This phenomenon occurs because everything arrives on Vava'u by boat and, while some stores get supplies from different places, most of them get some (or all) of their inventory from the boat. As in the rest of Tonga, prices on many staple products are fixed and the amount of markups are limited, both by law and by culture. Many Tongans would find it offensive to make too much profit on an item.

In-season fruits and vegetables are available at the market, on the waterfront near the wharf. Items there are sold in piles, and the posted price is the cost for the whole pile. However, larger items, like melons, are an exception; they are usually priced individually.

In addition to produce, the market also features a large number of arts and crafts, most of which were made by Vava'u locals. There are also several arts and crafts stores in the main business district. Generally, it is best to pay the marked price for an item. Often, however, the seller needs money and will voluntarily, without solicitation, lower their price so that they can sell the product and use the proceeds to pay for school or church obligations.

Ark Gallery It would certainly be an understatement to say that the Ark Gallery is a fairly unusual store. The gallery is operated by an American artist who sells her paintings in handmade *tapa* cloth frames. The Ark Gallery is located on a houseboat; to get there, shoppers will need to either take a boat or make their way by car or taxi to 'Ono Beach and then call the gallery owner and ask her to pick them up in a dinghy, a task she is always happy to perform. Some of the art is also available for sale at Tropicana Café. *Phone: 75-12673, arkgallerytonga@yahoo.com*

Eating

Restaurants in Vava'u seem to come and go as often as the tide. Most, but not all, of the restaurants are owned by *palangi*. Many of these foreigners arrived on Vava'u by yacht, fell in love with the island, and decided to open a business there. Unfortunately, too many people have had the same idea, so there are too many restaurants to support the tourist population and the few locals who like to dine out. (Most Tongans do not eat at restaurants, because they are too expensive for most of them to afford.)

Running a restaurant can be a tough business. Depending on the type of license the restaurant holds, it may not be open for dinner, it may be closed on Sundays, or it may not sell alcohol. Because of the high turnover rate, the very-seasonal business, and the different kinds of restaurant licenses, there is a chance that one of our restaurant recommendations may no longer be in business, or it may be closed for the off-season. (Tourist season runs from June through October.)

In addition, all of the restaurants are at the mercy of the local farmers and the foreign boats for their ingredients. So if there are no tomatoes at the local market, it is unlikely that diners will find any at a restaurant either. All produce is either grown locally or shipped to Vava'u; almost all other kinds of food come in by boat. When the boat isn't running, it is not uncommon to find that a restaurant has run out of many of the items on its menu.

However, that doesn't mean that the restaurants are not worth exploring. Vava'u has a variety of eating establishments catering to all palates and budgets.

RESTAURANTS

The Aquarium Café This lively locale serves breakfast, lunch, and dinner, seven days a week, in a waterfront setting. The open air café boasts both free Internet access and a helpful staff. The Aquarium is a good place to meet other travelers and catch up on the latest happenings in the area. *TOP$15-$25, Phone: 75-70493, AquariumCaféVa-vau.com.*

The Crow's Nest A delightful café serving breakfast and lunch, the Crow's Nest makes all of their bread, desserts, and yogurt from scratch. During tourist season, The Crow's Nest offers a full-course Indian dinner one night each week, by reservation only. No alcohol is served at this restaurant. *TOP$10-$15, Phone: 75-74450.*

Tropicana Due to its location, right near the main intersection in town, Tropicana may be the first restaurant which visitors see after arriving in Vava'u. The restaurant serves breakfast and lunch and, because they are a fully licensed café, they can also serve alcohol. Tropicana also operates the Vava'u web portal, vavau.to; and they make bookings for many of the tourist activities in the area. *TOP$10-$20, Phone: 71-322.*

The Dancing Rooster It only takes one bite of the superb food to realize that this restaurant is owned and operated by a Swiss chef. This lunch and dinner establishment is certainly worth a splurge, even for the most budget-conscious traveler. The Dancing Rooster features homemade pastas, local lobster, and steaks. *TOP$20-$40, Phone: 70-886.*

Mango's This spot, a full-service bar and restaurant, is the place where the King likes to dine when he is visiting Vava'u. Thus, if the King is visiting the area, Mango's will set aside an area for his Majesty, just in case he decides to stop in for a meal. The restaurant, which features local seafood, is open for lunch and dinner. It sits in a peaceful waterfront location, and it would be a great place to eat, if not for the extremely uncomfortable chairs, which make diners want to leave before dessert even arrives. *TOP$15-30, Phone: 70-664*

This Provincial Life

As I think back on my Peace Corps service, I think that shopping at the Vava'u Market will be the one thing I will miss the most. Lettuce, carrots, potatoes, squash, pumpkin, tomatoes, cucumbers, zucchini, green beans, cabbage, peppers, avocado, watermelon, pineapple, papaya, bananas, mangoes, oranges, star fruit, limes, and passion fruit are all available there…but never all at once. Ultimately, I have come to accept the harsh truth that there is only a mere three-month period during which I can make a salad consisting of both tomatoes and peppers.

Another thing that the market has given me is a newfound appreciation for eating foods that are in-season, now that I recognize how fresh fruits and vegetables are supposed to taste in their natural state. In addition, I have keenly noted the financial benefit of buying in-season fruits and vegetables. Throughout November and December, it is possible to buy up to five pineapples for TOP$4 (about US$2). If I had wanted to buy a pineapple before or after pineapple season, however, the cost could jump to TOP$10 for one pineapple, and it would be nowhere near as delicious.

The fair majority of people who sell their goods at the market come from my village. So, when I go to market, everyone knows my name, and they ask with genuine interest how I am and what I am doing. Many times I have to force people to take my money for their goods, and I almost always leave with a complimentary watermelon, head of cabbage, or zucchini, along with all of my other purchases.

Shopping here, I've realized the striking contrast between shopping at a big grocery store and the shopping which I've grown accustomed to over the past two years at the local market.

- Sarah LaRosa

The Ovava One of the area's newest restaurants, The Ovava could be called a phoenix risen from the ashes. The owner used to manage Bounty Bar, before it was destroyed by a fire in December 2008. The Ovava has an extensive wine list, along with one of the largest menus in Vava'u. However, it lies a bit of a walk from town, and it does not always keep regular hours. Therefore, it's always a good idea to call ahead in order to ensure that the restaurant is open before heading out. *TOP$15-40, Phone: 70-700*

SELF-CATERING AND TAKE-AWAY

There are a number of grocery stores in Neiafu, so it is easy to procure provisions for self-catering. However, like the restaurants, the stores will run out of certain items while awaiting the arrival of the next boat. And, as with the restaurants, if shoppers try two stores and can't find an item, it is likely that that particular item is not available at any of the other stores either. For the most part, the stores carry fairly basic supplies. The market features fresh, locally-grown produce and eggs. In order to get the best food at the market, it is wise to arrive early, since most vendors actually leave once they feel that have sold enough items for that day. In addition, because most Tongans head to the market on Saturday, the Saturday market has the best and broadest selection. Tongans start shopping shortly after sunrise. The market opens early, but people often keep selling items until as late as 5 pm.

Fresh fish is also available at the fish market, located just past the customs warehouse on the main wharf. In addition, fishermen will occasionally sell fish directly off of their boats. Anyone who sees a Tongan sitting by the water with a cooler should ask him if he has any fish for sale—they might well be handsomely rewarded for their query.

Just adjacent to the market, there is a small mall filled with take-away restaurants. These places, almost all of which are Tongan-owned, feature local plate lunches of fried fish, root crops, and sandwiches. Among these restaurants is **Mele's**; this place serves delicious sandwiches on homemade buns, as well as ice cream.

There are several Tongan bakeries in Vava'u: **Lighthouse Café and Bakery**, near the Catholic church; **Pafilio's**, behind MBF bank; and **Isileli and Sons Bakery**, near the Pasifika rental car lot. Prices do not vary because the price of white bread is fixed by the government, and most of the bakeries only sell items made with white flour. Those craving items made with wheat flour should head to the **Crow's Nest Bakery** (pg 204).

Nightlife & Entertainment

Like all other businesses in Tonga, the bars in Vava'u are legally required to shut down at midnight on Saturday night, and they cannot reopen until midnight on Sunday. What's more, all of the bars keep rather irregular hours in the off-season, so it is not uncommon to show up at a bar and find the place closed. The bars that serve food generally open around lunchtime, then stay open until well into the evening. If it's an "off" night, a bar may close early.

Drink prices do not vary much between bars; local beers start at around TOP$5 most places, and wine and mixed drinks generally start around TOP$7. However, when the boat has not arrived and supplies are running low, bars will either mark up the prices of the drinks they do have, or they will simply offer a vastly-dwindled selection. Almost all of the wine in Vava'u is boxed wine; bottled wines are usually very expensive.

Tonga Bob's Bar This bar, located near the center of town, escaped damage from the destructive fires of December 2008. In fact, Tonga Bob's was even renovated in 2009, adding an outdoor patio and bar. On Wednesday nights during tourist season, Tonga Bob's hosts a *fakaleiti* show. This show, one of the highlights of the week, draws a large crowd. On Thursdays, many people head to the bar for the always entertaining pub quiz, where contestants play for free drinks and other prizes. Tonga Bob's also offers kite-boarding. Anyone who is interested in kite-boarding should ask the staff if they will take them out on the water. *Phone: 59220*

Motele Although "motele" is the Tongan word for a motel, anyone who says the word "motele" on Vava'u is assumed to be referring to the after-hours club located in the Old Harbor. Because Motele is very much the "after-hours" club, the best time to go there is after midnight on a Friday night. Motele stays open until the sun comes up, and the club features a lot of young drunk Tongans. There is a cover charge most nights, with the money collected at the door going to help a local organization or school. Inside, there is never a line at the bar, since most people had plenty to drink before arriving, and so instead spend their time dancing and flirting.

Though Motele has a reputation for being unsavory, or even unsafe, the crowd is generally quite well-behaved. The club is still very much a locals' scene and travelers should be prepared to be among the few non-Tongans there. While Motele has no phone number or website, any local can explain how to get there. Once that person finishes explaining to the visitors why they don't want to go there, they will gladly give them directions.

Accommodation

There are plenty of places to stay in the Vava'u island group. However, what Vava'u does not offer is a big, traditional resort. While the Warick Hotel group has announced plans to build the Kingdom's first real resort in Vava'u, this project has been plagued by innumerable delays, and no one knows when the resort will finally open its doors for business.

Many, but not all, of the accommodations are owned by non-Tongans. Many places will not have air-conditioning or televisions, and almost all will charge extra for airport transfers. Most places will have hot showers. The variety of accommodations ranges from backpacker-style shared rooms to small full-service resorts. Those arriving during tourist season (June through October) would be wise to book ahead. During the off-season, it should be simple to find a place to stay, though some places will close for several months during this time of the year.

The authors of this guidebook are happy to recommend the places listed below. While there are a number of accommodations available in Vava'u, these places really stand out from the crowd.

NEIAFU/MAIN ISLAND

Adventure Backpackers Located in the center of town, offering views of the harbor from its balcony, Adventure Backpackers is sitting pretty, boasting the best location in town. The staff also does bookings, and they can provide tips on most of the activities in the Vava'u island chain. Accommodations include shared rooms and bathrooms, as well as private rooms. *Shared dorm rooms start at TOP$30 while private rooms start at TOP$89. Phone: 70955, www.visitvavau.com/vv/backpackers.*

Twin View Motel and Backpackers This Tongan-owned and operated facility has a very friendly staff, and it is located just outside of Neiafu on the top of a hill, offering great views of both the old and new harbors. The spacious hotel rooms feature kitchens, living areas, and one or two bedrooms. Twin View also has backpacker accommodations, which were built in 2008; these feature both shared and private rooms. *Shared dorm rooms start at TOP$40 while private rooms start at TOP$100, Phone: 70-597, www.twinview.to.*

The Port Wine Guest House This small, four-bedroom accommodation sits just a short walk from the main business district, on a quiet side street. Guests can use a shared kitchen, shower, and toilet facilities. *Price is TOP$40/ person, camping on the property costs TOP$20. Phone: 70479, portwine_guesthouse@yahoo.com, www.tongaholiday.com/?page_id=208.*

The Hilltop Hotel Overlooking both Neiafu and the old harbor, this place offers unparalleled views. The Hilltop Hotel has air-conditioned rooms and hot showers. Though the road to the hotel is in bad condition, the facility certainly merits the ride through the potholes to get there. The co-owned restaurants are no longer in business. *Rooms start at TOP$130. Phone: 70209, www.hilltophotelvavau.com.*

Mystic Sands Although this resort is located (slightly less conveniently) outside of town, the drive is worth the trouble. Mystic Sands sits right on the water, in a tranquil setting near a small Tongan village. *Rooms start at TOP$220 per night. Phone: 75-84027, www.mysticsands.net*

OUTER ISLAND RESORTS

There are a number of accommodations located on the outer islands of Vava'u, and it seems like a new one opens or an old one closes or changes hands almost every year. Although the three outer island resorts listed below are not suitable for budget travelers, they do come highly recommended.

Ika Lahi With a name that literally translates to mean "lots of fish," this fishing lodge earns its name, as it is the spot where many people participate in big game fishing. Co-owner Steve Campbell holds most of the Tongan big game fishing records, and fishing charters are a big reason to stay at Ika Lahi. The other co-owner, Caroline Hudson, is a renowned chef. In fact, each year, during the off-season, she travels to a different country in order to learn how to cook in the style of that country. Although it is not necessary to book a room at Ika Lahi in order to eat at the hotel's restaurant, advanced reservations are definitely a must. *The resort will often quote prices in New Zealand dollars, with rates starting at NZ$250 (TOP$360). Phone: 70611, www.tongafishing.com.*

The Reef Resort Although The Reef Resort is located just a short boat ride from the main island, it does provide an unparalleled opportunity to experience outer island life firsthand. Reef is located on Kapa Island; the resort shares that island with three local villages. Though the Tongans who live on Kapa have no electricity, Reef has its own generators and, thus, it can provide air-conditioned facilities and an on-site restaurant. *Prices start at TOP$360/night off-season, and TOP$480/ night during the season. Phone: 75-59276, www.reefresortvavau.com.*

Blue Lagoon While Blue Lagoon is a long boat ride (TOP$145/person) away from the main island, this resort boasts a beautiful setting on its own private island. The resort is powered by windmills and solar energy, and it is a great place for those who want to get away from everything. There is a restaurant on-site, and most guests will want to take advantage of the meal plan, since there are no other options nearby. *Room rates start at TOP$295/person, with a TOP$145/person transfer fee to get to the resort. Phone: 867-1300, www.bluelagoontonga.com.*

A Tongan Success Story

Most Tongan-owned businesses are very informal and often family-run. In this environment, basic business concepts, such as record-keeping, are unfamiliar and many business owners opt to contribute profits back into their communities rather than reinvest in their business. There are, however, a few exceptions.

One of the most successful business owners in Vava'u is Pafilio Tangitau. Pafilio owns the largest bakery in Vava'u, two trade stores, and the land and buildings which house many tourist businesses, including The Aquarium Café and Mango's.

Like many Tongans, Pafilio started out as a farmer. Beginning in 1954, he farmed exclusively for two years, before branching out into fishing. He continued to manage both businesses until 1978 when he began to scale back his farming operation in order to concentrate largely upon fishing, which proved more profitable. In 1985, he bought two forty-foot fishing boats which helped earn him enough money to secure a loan to build a tourism complex at a cost of 1.4 million *pa'anga*. At that time, he also founded a trade store and opened a bakery.

Over the years, he took out seventeen loans from the Tonga Development Bank, totaling $780,000. By 2006, Pafilio had repaid all of his loans and today he is able to run and expand his business without borrowing any money whatsoever.

When asked why he was successful in an area where so many other Tongans had failed, Pafilio said: "In order to run a successful business, you have to follow your plans. And I believe you can achieve anything in this world, but you have to follow business rules. If you are playing football, you must exercise and follow the coach's rules to become a good player. And if you want to run a business, you must follow business rules, depending on the industry you're in, to become successful. I believe that if this is done, you will become successful and achieve good results. Otherwise, don't try it, as it will just be a waste of time."

Pafilio has now handed the day-to-day operations of his businesses over to his children, but he still impresses upon them the importance of following the business plan. He has also been featured in a video produced by the Tongan Development Bank in order to encourage other Tongans and show them how they, too, can be successful in business.

Niua Islands

Introduction

Any travelers who make it to either one of the Niua Islands should consider themselves extremely lucky, as very few tourists make it there, because the islands are so much more difficult to access than any other part of Tonga. These islands exude a mysterious beauty, and they are unknown to much of the world, existing in near-complete isolation. Located about three hundred miles north of Tongatapu, Niuatoputapu and Niuafo'ou are the northernmost islands of Tonga. In fact, the islands are actually closer to the country of Samoa than they are to the rest of Tonga. This extreme isolation has helped foster a proud, independent culture, a culture which mixes influences from both the rest of Tonga and from neighboring Samoa. The local Tongans in the Niuas speak much faster than do their counterparts in the rest of the country, and they even speak with their own dialect. It is important to note that very little English is spoken on the islands, and it is generally advisable to bring along some food supplies, because the food selection in the Niuas themselves is quite limited (locals survive mostly on agriculture and fishing). Those who do have the means and time to make this journey will be rewarded with rich cultural experiences and dramatic scenery.

HISTORY

Because the islands of Niuatoputapu and Niuafo'ou are so distant and isolated from the rest of Tonga, the countries of Samoa and Futuna have had a significant influence on both the culture and language of these islands. In fact, these islands are even isolated from each other, as they are located over one hundred miles apart. There is also another small island, Tafahi, close to Niuatoputapu. Due to the extreme isolation of the Niuas, the islanders had no known contact with outside Western explorers until 1616 when Dutch explorers first anchored off the shores of Niuatoputapu.

Surprised upon seeing these ships, some of the local Tongans came out in dugout canoes, and they started attacking the intruders with clubs. The frightened Dutch explorers responded by firing cannons and muskets at the islanders. However, both parties eventually came to an agreement and traded some supplies. One of the

Dutch explorers, Jacob Le Maire, compiled a list of about thirty words from this encounter, thereby making Tongan the earliest known recorded South Pacific Island language. The Niuas had little interaction with Westerners following this first encounter.

MYTHS

There is an ancient legend in Niuatoputapu about a fish god. Once upon a time, there were two sons of the traditional line of rulers on the island: Moimoi, the elder son, and Seketo'a, the younger son. According to cultural tradition, the older son could order the younger son around, demanding that he execute their father's orders. However, their father, the king, loved the younger son more. The older son, Moimoi, grew jealous and yearned to kill Seketo'a. One day, the brothers began to quarrel, and Seketo'a threatened to go drown himself in the sea and become a fish, leaving Moimoi to run errands for their father. Seketo'a would then watch the island from the sea, allowing only the family to call upon him in a time of need.

Even today, there is still a tradition in which the chiefs of this island go throw kava roots into the ocean. The roots then attract sucker fish, who in turn attract bigger fish, and who finally attract one or more sharks. One of the sharks is Seketo'a, and he can help them with whatever the chiefs need.

TRANSPORTATION

It is very difficult to travel to and from the Niua Islands. Those who plan to include a trip to one or both of these islands must plan extra time for delays and travel.

Flights head to each of these islands about once a week. The flights to and from Niuatoputapu occur on Wednesdays; the flights to Niuafo'ou are less regular. This is due to the fact that Niuafo'ou has very strong winds, and the airstrip is exposed to the elements. This makes landings sometimes impossible. In these instances, the plane has to return to Tongatapu and try again another day. Both flights have a stopover in either Ha'apai or Vava'u.

The Niua Islands are accessible by boat. The ferry usually runs about once a month, although the schedule is irregular and weather-dependent. The trip takes at least twenty hours, making the journey there a true ocean voyage. Several cruise ships also pass by the Niua Islands. However, since there is no large wharf or safe anchorage there, the ships do not stop on the small islands, but press on instead to Vava'u and Tongatapu. It is also possible to travel to Niuatoputapu by private yacht, though Niuafo'ou has no harbor or anchorage.

On these islands, there are no taxis or buses, and there are only a handful of vehicles. The best ways of getting around are by hitching rides with locals, by hiking, or by borrowing a bike from an islander.

Traveling to the far Niuas

The *Olovaha*, a seven hundred-seven ton, forty-nine-and-a-half meter inter-island ferry, finally came chugging into the wharf in Pangai, Ha'apai, tilting to one side operating on one of two engines. This would explain why I'd waited all day long as the operators of the wharf kept changing the arrival and subsequent departure times of the ship. It was a decidedly Tongan way to spend the day, hanging around the wharf from 4 am on, until we finally left for the north twelve hours later. At least we were on the water, moving in the right direction. Our destination? The Islands of Niuatoputapu and Niuafo'ou, the two northernmost islands of the Tongan island chain. This was a trip which only occurred every six weeks or so, to take supplies and personnel to those isolated chunks of rock lying well off-the-beaten-path to…almost anywhere.

The second engine had supposedly been fixed back at the wharf, but we still limped along on just one of them, traveling at a speed of about four to five knots. I slept on deck in a corner near the wheelhouse, sheltered from the driving rain. We arrived at the intermediate island of Vava'u the next morning. As we pushed off for the Niuas, I noticed that the passenger list had grown. This was indeed a service trip. The Minister of Justice was onboard; he would be on the bench for cases which would be tried on both of the islands once the boat docked at their wharf. There were workers headed out to fix the beacon at the airport on Niuatoputapu, the hopes of restarting weekly flights to the islands pinned to their overalls. Others onboard were heading to the islands to check and replace defunct batteries for the solar power units there. A dentist would be checking teeth. Four high school teachers would be starting their work, albeit a couple of months late. Three or four prisoners would be starting their terms there…I guess the Niuas are the Tongan version of the *gulag*, to some minds. And we were there, heading up to the Niuas to speak with local teachers about English-teaching activities and school funding.

After another night sleeping on the deck, Niuatoputapu appeared on the horizon, looking like a cowboy hat sitting in the water, its lowlands surrounding a high volcanic ridge running down the middle. The entire town was out on the wharf as we arrived. Whenever the boat comes in on Niuatoputapu, everyone drops whatever they're doing to go out and meet it. In fact, the day that the boat arrives is actually a declared island-wide holiday. Getting off of the ferry, stretching our rubbery sea legs, we waded through the crowd to another boat, a small Tongan craft which had pulled up alongside the wharf.

We then got into the small boat, before heading across the channel to Tafahi. We were traveling to Tafahi because no one from the Ministry of Education had seen the school for at least five years.

Tafahi is a classic volcanic cone, rising straight out of the water to perhaps a one thousand foot summit. They grow a lot of *kava*—Tonga's best—on those slopes. Furthermore, it is said that, on a clear day, you can see Samoa from the top of the island. As we approached the coast of the island, I was just thinking that there must be a safe approach around the next corner when the skipper made a hard right and headed straight for the reef. I braced for impact. In an instant, we had waves breaking on either side of the boat and behind us, as we shot through a sidewalk-wide gap in the reef and pushed straight onto a white sand beach. That skipper knows his island. We walked along the narrow beach and into the bush. I remember thinking, "So, where's the town? Is there a flat space *anywhere* big enough for houses?" *(Continued on next page.)*

Niua Islands

We rounded a bend in the trail, coming to a huge flight of stairs which disappeared above us into thick foliage. It was like something straight out of *King Kong* or *Temple of Doom*. About three hundred feet of elevation later, we left the stairs and walked into the village, which looked as though it had been carved out of the mountainside eons ago. There was no flat space, not even enough for a flip-flop—we walked over basalt lumps, and watched our knees carefully. The houses were perched on platforms of rock that jutted out from the mountainside. The plants seemed stunted and coarse. We were told that the village consisted of five families; the school had a population of nine.

Hardly anyone goes to Tafahi—there's little reason. I was stoked to get the chance. We had a brief meeting with the school's sole teacher, Makalasi inspected the school, and we returned to the boat. Back on Niuatoputapu, we joined the party atmosphere, and we later met with the teachers there. We then hopped back on the *Olovaha* for the overnight voyage to Niuafo'ou.

The captain must have made the trip a longer-than-needed one, because we arrived just as it was light enough to see. Once there, I understood why. The wharf on Niuafo'ou looks like a sidewalk jutting out into the sea. There are old lava flows on either side of the wharf, with no room to pull up alongside it. Thus, the arriving ship has to land with its nose to the end of the thing, controlled, somewhat, by an anchor off of the stern and a tie that runs from the bow to hawsers on either side of the boat, out in the surrounding lava. A tricky maneuver to say the least. We finally made it on the third try, the first two having taken the bow of the ship within feet of the angry rocks protruding from the water. And this was on a really calm day! It's hard to imagine the attempt succeeding on one of the (relatively common) choppy, high-swell days.

We tied up to the wharf, as the landing-barge type bow was lowered onto the cement. A forklift rolled out. It was promptly knocked into the sea, as a small swell swung the ship *just* enough to pivot the landing ramp into the forklift. Though nobody was hurt, it was immediately apparent that this was going to be a long day. The crew and the villagers, who had spent all night at the wharf, worked to unload the ship by hand, fire-brigade style, as Makalasi and I caught a ride to the towns in the high center of the island.

As we bumped along the narrow, rocky road, I thought I saw one of the famous incubator birds which live only on this island. In fact, Niuafo'ou very much reminded me of the Big Island of Hawaii, with recent lava flows covering all sides of the island, interspersed with patches of dense foliage. We reached the first town, checked out the school, and then quickly looked for a ride back to the wharf, as we were somewhat nervous about the boat leaving without us, an event which would mean a six-week stay on this island. It turned out that we need not have worried. We made it back to the dock, had our meeting with the teachers under a tree near the wharf, got back on the boat, and proceeded to wait another three hours, as the crew struggled to raise the drowned forklift. Mission (eventually) accomplished, we struck out once more, this time for an overnight passage back to Vava'u.

- Phil Curtis

PREPARATION

Those who plan to visit the Niua Islands need to keep several key points in mind. First of all, it is highly recommended that all travelers bring some food supplies—such as bread, fresh produce, and canned meat. The only foods available on the Niuas are food from a few local stores, various locally-

> Since English is not very prevalent on these remote islands, it is a good idea to brush up on some basic Tongan phrases before arriving.

grown root crops and fruits, and whatever fish have been freshly-caught that day. However, these supplies run out between shipments and during periods of bad weather. It is also vital to bring local currency to the islands. While it is sometimes possible to exchange money or traveler's checks at the Treasury Office, this office has been known to run out of cash at times. Credit cards are not accepted anywhere on these islands.

Another point of note: the inhabitants of the Niua Islands live in small, conservative villages and it's important to respect their culture and way of life. Be sure to dress conservatively in these islands, more so than anywhere else in all of Tonga. Travelers should not wear any skin-baring small tank tops, short shorts, or swimsuits. In exchange for obeying these cultural norms, those who visit will gain a truly unique cultural adventure which very few people can boast.

COMMUNICATIONS

There is cell phone and Internet service now available in the Niua Islands, although it is not reliable. There are also land lines and a post office.

Niuafo'ou

Niuafo'ou remains one of the most isolated islands in the world; a trip is for only the extremely adventurous. In fact, it is sometimes called "Tin Can Island," since mail and supplies were dropped off at sea and picked up by strong local swimmers because there was no wharf or harbor to dock the boat. There still isn't one. Niuafo'ou truly has been cut off from the rest of the world throughout much of its history.

The island has had a turbulent history of volcanic eruptions. In the past one hundred fifty years, there have been ten major recorded volcanic eruptions. One eruption occurred in the 1940s and was so large and potentially dangerous, that the national government moved the entire population of Niuafo'ou to 'Eua for their own safety. Some of these people stayed and became permanent residents of 'Eua, while others moved back to Niuafo'ou once it was thought safe again. While there have been no major recorded volcanic activity since the eruptions of the 1940s, the volcano is still classified as active.

The population of this island, about six hundred-fifty people, is spread out, amongst several small villages. Because lava fields cover the west side of the island, all of the villages on the island are located on the northern and eastern sides of the island. The main village, Esia, is located near the airport.

The island is a doughnut-shaped collapsed volcano with a large crater lake in the center. This lake, *Vai Lahi*, has several small islands inside of it. The southern and western sides of the island are covered by barren lava fields left by previous volcanic explosions.

Because Niuafo'ou is surrounded steep cliffs and rough seas, it has no wharf, safe anchorage, or beaches. Instead of swimming in the ocean, the locals swim in the large lake. For travel to and from the island, boats throw out ropes, and they are then pulled up to a cement block to unload.

ACTIVITIES

Hiking & Bird-Sighting

There are scenic hikes around *Vai Lahi*. The trail, a loop around the lake, goes through the small string of villages. It takes approximately six hours to hike all the way around the lake. On the southern and western sides of the island, there are old lava flows and, between the small villages of Mata'aho and Mu'a, there is a great

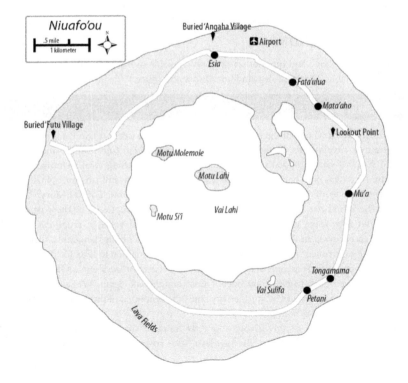

lookout point, offering excellent views of the lakes and islands of Niuafo'ou's interior. Another beautiful hike begins in the village of Petani and ends at the sulfuric lake *Vai Sulifa*.

While hiking, keep a lookout for the mysterious Niuafo'ou megapode bird. This large bird, the only megapode bird left in all Polynesia, is now teetering near the brink of extinction. Locals have long hunted this large bird and scavenged the large eggs—about one-fifth the size of an adult bird—that it leaves buried in the warm volcanic soil to incubate. The chicks emerge fully feathered and ready to fend for themselves. Although the birds are supposedly protected, locals still hunt the birds and eggs, and roaming pigs dig up the incubating eggs. However, both the small human population, and the extreme isolation of Niuafo'ou have helped to preserve this species. These birds are most commonly spotted in the center of the island near the lake.

Camping

Those who bring their own camping gear may be able to camp in the center of the island near the lake, or even on one of the small islands in the lake.

ACCOMMODATIONS

Because so few outsiders make it out to visit Niuafo'ou, the island is not set up for tourism and no accommodations are available on the island. However, it is always possible to stay in a church hall, or to find a place to camp. There are many good campsites around the large lake. In addition, although there is no official lodging on Niuafo'ou, the locals warmly welcome all travelers. Locals may even extend invitations to visitors, asking them to stay with their family during their stay on Niuafo'ou.

The Tale of Tin Can Island

Niuafo'ou is most famous for its tin can mail. This system began in 1882, when an Australian trader, William Travers, was living on the island. He arranged with the Tongan post office to use kerosene cans or biscuit tins as a way to waterproof mail for transport to and from the island. For years, this was the only means of communication with the outside world on Niuafo'ou. In the early days, locals would swim about a mile out to sea, where passing boats would drop off the tin can mail. In 1931, however, a shark took one of the swimmers, so the islanders began to use outrigger canoes instead. The tin can mail was decorated in colorful original stamps. Along with tin can mail, attempts were also made to get mail to the island by shooting it off in rockets, but oftentimes the mail ended up in flames. In the mid-1930s, the tin can mail service was much publicized, and cruise ships would pass by the island so that passengers could drop off tin can mail. When Niuafo'ou Airport was built in 1983, the mail became less popular, although some forms of plastic containers carrying mail were still used. The Niuafo'ou stamps are now very popular with collectors.

Niuatoputapu

Niuatoputapu is surrounded by beautiful white sandy beaches, and its offshore reefs offer excellent snorkeling. The tiny island has a population of around 1,400 residents, spread over three villages. The island does not have much to offer in terms of entertainment, restaurants, or tourism services. Instead, Niuatoputapu is more of place to experience genuine cultural activities and to enjoy the solitude of a peaceful Pacific paradise.

Although Hihifo is the capital of this island, it is still a very small village. There are a few small stores there, and the only bank, the Tonga Development Bank, is in this village. Hihifo also houses a police station, several schools, the post office, and a bakery.

ACTIVITIES

Hiking

There is a great hike along the central ridge of the island, just inland from the main town of Hihifo. Because this ridge is one of the higher points in Tonga, reaching, at points, a height of over one hundred fifty meters, the trail provides fantastic views of

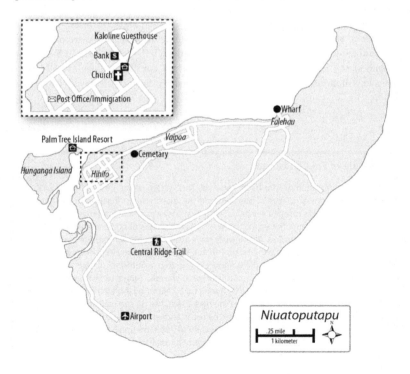

the volcanic cone island of Tafahi. Another hiking option is to walk between the villages, since the dirt road makes a loop around the island.

Water Activities

For beach and water activities, it is important to wear full clothing, not skin-baring swimsuits. This island is very conservative, and the locals will be extremely offended by bikinis, skin-baring tank tops, or short shorts.

The pristine reefs are Niuatoputapu are perfect for snorkeling. One great spot is in the protected lagoon between Hunganga Island and the main Island of Niuatoputapu. Some of the best white sandy beaches are also located in this area, and the scenery is striking. Several more great spots for swimming are located south of Hihifo.

The waters around the island also house some great dive sights. However, those interested in diving will need to bring their own equipment, since there are no dive shops on the island. To reach the dive sights, ask to tag along on local fishing trips. This can be easily arranged, provided that the divers help to pay for gas.

Just west of the village of Hihifo, there is a long freshwater spring, *Vai ko Niutoua*, or Niutoua Spring. Adventurers can swim there in the crystal-clear waters to cool off. This sight is a must-see for all those who visit the island.

On a Clear Day...

Tafahi is a volcanic cone island, located just offshore from Niuatoputapu. There is one very small village on this steep island. Although the island is not easy to access, those who do make it to Tafahi on a local boat can hike up to the top of the island. From that point, on a clear day, they might even spot the neighboring nation of Samoa.

ACCOMMODATION

As on Niuafo'ou, there are no real tourist accommodations on Niuatoputapu. There used to be a small resort there, but it was recently destroyed in the tsunami waves of 2009. There is one small guesthouse but, with very few travelers visiting the island, it

---

Earthquake!

In September 2009, there was a major earthquake just north of Tonga near Samoa. The earthquake produced a tsunami wave, which devastated Samoa, and even reached parts of Tonga. Because Niuatoputapu lies much closer to Samoa than does the rest of Tonga, it was hit by the tsunami waves. There was very little warning, and in the sparsely populated villages, seven people died. Many Tongans fled to higher ground, as the wave destroyed houses, public buildings, and the airport runway. The waves also destroyed The Palm Tree Island Resort on the uninhabited island of Hunganga, just offshore. Furthermore, the entire island was cut off from outside communication, and the water supplies in the rainwater tanks filled with salt water. The Tongan government sent out their navy boat with supplies, and some foreign aid and assistance came in to the Niua islands. In 2011, there will be construction on eighty-five new houses for Niuatoputapu residents on higher ground. Furthermore, the airport is now operating again.

may or may not be operating at this time. It is generally best to inquire at the Tonga Visitors Bureau for assistance in arranging accommodations on Niuatoputapu, whether with the guesthouse or with a Tongan family. Similar to Niuafoʻou, everyone who arrives on the island is warmly welcomed by the locals. Visitors may even be invited to stay with a family or to stay at the local school or church hall. It is also possible to bring camping gear and find a spot to pitch a tent.

Kaloline Guesthouse The only official lodging available on the island, this guest-house is located in the main village of Hihifo. Because this guesthouse is actually inside of a family home, those who stay there will have the distinct feeling of being part of the larger island community. The kitchen facilities are available for guest use; alternately, it is possible to book meals in advance. *Accommodations TOP$20 - $25: book through the Tonga Visitors Bureau, or just show up at the guesthouse. Phone: 85021*

Language Reference

In the Tongan language, all words must end in a vowel. There are only seventeen characters in the language, as opposed to the twenty-six of the English language. Because many words have multiple meanings, context is incredibly important. Some words have been Tongan-ized from English by adding a vowel sound at the end of the word. This genre of words includes such words as *telefoni* (telephone) or *pasi* (bus). Those who wish to explore more in-depth studies on the Tongan language are encouraged to check out Eric Shumway's book *Intensive Course in Tongan*.

PRONUNCIATION

Letter	Pronounced like...
a	s<u>aw</u>
e	h<u>ay</u>
i	s<u>ee</u>k
o	s<u>o</u>
u	s<u>ou</u>p
ai	sk<u>y</u>
ng	so<u>ng</u>
p	a soft "p"
t	a soft "t"

COMMON RESPONSES

Yes	Io
No	Ikai
No thank you	Ikai malo pe
I don't know	He'ilo
Maybe	Mahalope

GREETINGS

Hi/Hello	Malo e lelei

This phrase literally means "thank you for the goodness"

Hello(formal)	Male 'etau lava
Goodbye	Nofo a

When the speaker is leaving and the person they are speaking to is staying

Goodbye	Alu a

When the speaker is staying and the person they are speaking to is leaving

See you later	Toki sio

This is a common saying when a person is leaving

How are you?	Fefe hake?
And you?	Fefe koe?
Fine thank you.	Sai pe malo
Okay	Sai sai pe
Bad	Kovi
Terrific	Totoatu
Thank you for working	Malo e ngaue
Thank you for sweeping	Malo e tafi
Thank you for coming	Malo e ha'u
Where are you going?	Alu ki fe?

This question is used as a common greeting in passing.

To there (pointing)	I he

The answer does not have to be specific if the question is asked in passing.

Just staying here.	Nofo pe
What is your name?	Ko hai ho hingoa?
My name is …	Ko hoku hingoa ko…

EXPRESSIONS

Thank you.	Malo
Thank you very much.	Malo aupito
Please	Kataki
Sorry	Fakamolemole
Excuse me	Tulou
Really?	Mo'oni?
Stop it!	Tuku ia!

Wow!   'Oiaue
This expression (pronounced oh-ee-ow-ooh-ay) can be used to express disbelief, surprise or amazement.

LANGUAGE ISSUES

Help me.	Tokoni mai
I don't understand.	Ikai mahino
Do you speak English?	Oku ke lea faka palangi?
Please speak slowly.	Kataki lea mamalie

SHOPPING

How much?	Oku fiha?
Tongan dollar	Pa'anga
Cents	Senite
Give me	Omai
What is that?	Ko e ha e?
Buy	Fakatau
Expensive	Mamafa
Cheap	Ma'ama'a
Little/small	Si'isi'i pe
Big/large	Lahi
Do you have …?	Oku i ai …?
None	Hala
Finished/already	Osi
Bottle	Hina
Is it ripe?	Oku momoho?

DIRECTIONS/TRAVEL

Where is …?	Ko fe …?
Where is the toilet?	Ko fe e falemalolo?
Boat	Vaka
Airplane	Vakapuna

This word literally means "flying boat."

Vehicle/car	Me'alelei

This word literally means "thing that runs."

Bus	Pasi

To drive	Faka'uli
Road/street	Hala
Bicycle	Pasikola
Walking	Aka aka maka

This expression (which means "kicking stones") is used as a funny colloquial expression for "walking."

Stop here	Tuku 'i heni
Turn	Afe
Straight	Hangatunu
Left	Hema
Right	Matu'a
Far away	Mama'o
North	Tokelau
South	Tonga
East	Hahake
West	Hihifo
How much is it to go to …?	Oku fiha alu ki …?
Town	Kolo
Bathroom	Falemalolo
Women	Fefine
Men	Tangata
Shower	Falekaukau
Store	Falekoloa
Restaurant	Falekai
Bank	Pangiki
Hospital	Falemahaki

This word literally means "house of sickness."

Church	Falelotu
School	Faleako
Wharf	Uafi
Ocean	Tahi
Beach	Mata tahi
Bush land/farm land	Uta
Island	Motu

TIME

Do you have the time?	Oku i ai uasi?
When?	Fakaku?
Today	Aho'ni
Yesterday	Aniefi
Tomorrow	Apongipongi
Morning	Pongipongi'ni
Evening	Efiafi
Right now	Taimi'ni
Begin/start	Kamata
Later	Anenai
All the time	Taimi kotoa
Finished/done	'Osi

DAYS OF THE WEEK

Monday	Monite
Tuesday	Tusite
Wednesday	Pulelulu
Thursday	Tua'pulelulu
Friday	Faleite
Saturday	Tokonaki
Sunday	Sabate

FOOD/DRINK

Eat	Kai
Drink	Inu
Food	Me'akai
Pray	Lotu

Anyone who eats a meal with any Tongans should wait to begin eating until after Tongans pray.

Underground oven	Umu
Full	Fiu
Thirsty	Fie'inu
Hungry	Fie'kai'ia
I already ate	Osi kai

Thank you for cooking	Malo fiamatokoni
Eat until you die	Kai ke mate

This is a favorite local expression as Tongans like to eat large portions.

Delicious	Ifo

This word can also be used as a verb meaning good; "the beach was ifo."

Smells good	Namu lelei
I don't eat meat	Oku ikai ke ou kai kiki
Cold	Momoko
Hot	Vela
Pineapple	Faina
Papaya	Lesi
Banana	Siaena
Breadfruit	Mei
Vegetables	Vesitipolo
Spinach-like vegetable	Lu

This refers to a type of vegetable similar to spinach; the leaves are used to hold meat cooked in the umu, or underground oven.

Bread	Ma
Egg	Fo'i moa
Fried dough	Keke
Meat	Kiki
Mutton	Sipi
Chicken	Moa
Fish	Ika
Lobster	Uo
Crab	Paka
Shellfish	Fingota
Octopus	Feke
Turtle	Fonu
Shark	'Anga
Cow	Pulu
Horse	Hoosi
Pig	Puaka
Dog	Kuli
Beer	Pea

Water	Vai
Bottled water	Hina vai
Local juice	'Otai
Milk	Hu'akau

WEATHER

Sunny	La'a
Hot	Afu
Very hot	Afu aupito

The word "aupito" can be used to add "very" to any description.

Rain	Uha
Windy	Hivili
Cold	Momoko
Tsunami	Peau kula

This word literally means "red wave."

Cyclone	Cyclone (in English)

DESCRIPTIONS

Foreigner	Palangi
Girl	Ta'ahine
Boy	Tomasi'i
Ne	He/she

There is one word for both sexes; this explains why Tongans often get "he" and "she" confused when speaking English.

Priest/pastor	Faifakau
Shopkeeper	Faifakatau
Teacher	Faiako
To like	Sai'ia
To dislike	Ikai sai'ia
To hate	Fehia
Beautiful	Faka ofo'ofa
Handsome/pretty	Talavo
Ugly	Palaku
Smart	Poto
Naughty/outgoing	Pau'u

Lazy	Fakapikopiko
Smile	Malimali
Funny	Faka'ole
Bad	Kovi
Sad	Faka'ofa
A pain/tiresome	Fakahela
Dirty	'Uli
Sick	Puke
Sleep	Mohe
Sing	Hiva
Dance	Ta'ulunga
Swim/wade/shower	Kaukau
Fishing	Tautai

NUMBERS

One	Taha
Two	Ua
Three	Tolu
Four	Fa
Five	Nima
Six	Ono
Seven	Fitu
Eight	Valu
Nine	Hiva
Ten	Hungafulu
Eleven	Taha taha
Twelve	Taha ua

Continue on to "taha tolu," and so on for higher numbers.

CPSIA information can be obtained at www.ICGtesting.com
Printed in the USA
LVOW04s2026100815

449561LV00023B/595/P